PEOPLE GET SCREWED ALL THE TIME

PEOPLE GET SCREWED ALL THE TIME

Protecting Yourself From Scams, Fraud, Identity Theft, Fine Print, and More

ROBERT MASSI

Collins
An Imprint of HarperCollins*Publishers*

This book is for the victims: Those of you who have been wronged by the system, by people you trusted, or by people you had no control over. This book is a voice for you and the beginning of a movement. Follow along because we have only just begun.

PEOPLE GET SCREWED ALL THE TIME. Copyright © 2007 by Robert Massi. All rights reserved. Printed in the United States of America. No part of this book may be used or reproduced in any manner whatsoever without written permission except in the case of brief quotations embodied in critical articles and reviews. For information, address HarperCollins Publishers, 10 East 53rd Street, New York, NY 10022.

HarperCollins books may be purchased for educational, business, or sales promotional use. For information, please write: Special Markets Department, HarperCollins Publishers, 10 East 53rd Street, New York, NY 10022.

FIRST EDITION

Designed by Lovedog Studio

Printed on acid-free paper

Library of Congress Cataloging-in-Publication Data is available upon request.

ISBN: 978–0–06–1145872

06 07 08 09 10 ❖/RRD   10 9 8 7 6 5 4 3 2 1

CONTENTS

Part III

MONEY, FINANCES, AND DEBT: HOW TO STEER CLEAR OF MAJOR FINANCIAL HASSLES

Part IV

YOUR HOME: HOW TO LIVE IN YOUR HOUSE WITHOUT RUINING YOUR FUTURE

Part V

CARS: HOW TO KEEP ON THE GO WITHOUT ENDING UP IN DEBT, IN JAIL, OR WORSE

Part VI

WORK AND BUSINESS RELATIONSHIPS: HOW TO MAKE A LIVING WITHOUT RUNNING INTO LEGAL NIGHTMARES

INTRODUCTION

YOU MAKE A QUICK STOP AT AN ATM TO WITHDRAW SOME POCKET CASH. You are shocked to discover that your request is declined. How could that be? Just this morning, you had nearly $3,000 in your checking account. Hours later, your balance is inexplicably in the negative.

Your sister signs a forty-eight-month lease agreement on a great car. She's sad to turn it in when the lease expires—but she's absolutely outraged when the dealer hands her an additional bill for $7,000 from the leasing company. It seems she was charged an additional 25 cents for every mile over the yearly allowance, but no one at the dealership had mentioned anything about a yearly mileage allowance.

Your brother and his wife are getting divorced. What starts out as an amicable split turns ugly when she manages to have him evicted from the condo they had lived in—and he had purchased.

Your parents have retired to a gated community, where their harmless decorating scheme and confusion over the fine print of their purchase agreement has resulted in outrageous homeowners' association fines that have snowballed to the point where their retirement savings are dangerously close to being wiped out and they are in jeopardy of losing their home.

You hear it every day: stories of good people, innocent people, who suddenly, without warning, find bad things happening to them, and then the system they expect will protect them reaches out to hurt them. The system is a tool, and tools are only as good as the people who wield them. Even competent professionals make mistakes, and too often, the people in the system are neither competent nor professional. The legal system is a bureaucracy, and bureaucracies are inflexible. They move slowly. They're impersonal and overtaxed. The victims all say, "You never think it will happen to you." And the rest of us, viewing from afar, think, "How terrible—good thing that didn't happen to me."

The truth is that anyone's life can be transformed, his or her destiny changed forever, by poor judgment, inadequate preparation, a lack of caution, an absence of information or of simple common sense. Ordinary people really do get screwed all the time.

As an attorney for the past twenty-five years, I've listened to the most incredible tales of frustration and woe. The damage done to innocent people who run afoul of the system can be irreversible, because the average person on the street does not have the financial means to either fix the problem or challenge the monster that created it in the first place.

When I listen to these people tell me their stories, it's with an empathy born of personal experience. I know how they feel, because I came dangerously close to being just another victim of the system myself. I know what it takes to protect oneself from indifferent bureaucrats and impersonal and inflexible rulings, because I had to overcome these very obstacles in my fight to practice law.

After I graduated from law school in Texas in 1976, I moved to Las Vegas to clerk for a judge and to study for, and take, the Nevada bar exam. I was young and idealistic, and ready to put my knowledge of the law to practical use. Not sure where I would begin my law career, in 1977 I returned to Texas, where I had gone to law school, to take the bar exam. Having grown up in Pittsburgh, I also took the bar exam in Pennsylvania. I also took the bar in Nevada, where I was living at the time. I got the results from Nevada first—I had failed the bar. Then I learned that I had failed the bar in Pennsylvania, too. When I asked about the results from the bar in Texas, I was told that, since I was no longer a resident of that state, the exam was nullified. At first, I didn't feel too bad. Plenty of successful lawyers need more than one attempt to pass state bar exams. So I took the Nevada exam again in 1978 ... and again in 1979. Each time I failed I felt a little more embarrassed. Despite my tenacity, I began to question my future in my chosen career, and my self-confidence became shaky.

This could have been the end of the story right there. Many people would have moved on, written off thousands of hours of study and effort and tens of thousands of dollars worth of education. Luckily for me, I had the support of people who believed in me, and in my talents, and encouraged me to look for a reason for these failures. The turning point for me came one night over dinner with an old friend from law school. "It doesn't make sense," he was saying. "I've seen you coach people through these same exams. You know this material cold. I can't understand why you haven't been able to pass." And then he suggested something radical. What if my failure on these tests wasn't a lack of knowledge but a lack of ability in taking the test itself? He urged me to contact a doctor in California who specialized in the diagnosis and treatment of learning disabilities.

Today, the diagnosis and treatment of dyslexia is common. But for me, as an adult in the early 1980s, to learn that there was a reason for my poor test results was a major enlightenment. Years of embarrassment lifted away as I began to understand my inability to perform on multiple-choice exams. I remained in California with my wife and infant son and worked with professionals to master strategies that allowed me to cope with my dyslexia.

In 1980 I returned to Las Vegas and petitioned the State Bar Association for a special accommodation in retaking the exam. When they said no, I prepared a petition to the State Supreme Court, arguing that I was being discriminated against. I became the first person to plead before the Nevada Supreme Court that my learning disability was just that—a disability, as real as any other legally recognized impediment. I argued that people in my situation required special accommodations when taking the exam. My argument was successful. The Supreme Court ruled that I could take the test using a proctor, who would mark the multiple-choice answers as verbally dictated by me.

On my fifth try, in 1980, I passed the Nevada bar exam.

My four years of struggle taught me a valuable lesson. I knew firsthand how easy it could be to fall through the cracks, to be left behind, and to be stymied by the system. I also knew how fortunate I had been. I had a working knowledge of the system that was screwing me. I had emotional support. I had access to people who could help me navigate through a maze of petitions and appeals. At the same time, I realized there were many, many people who did not have this insight, who were intimidated by the complexities of our legal system.

Maybe because I had to fight so hard to begin my career, I've always felt that it's up to those of us who have been blessed with an understanding of the legal system—and the financial wherewithal to challenge the Goliaths in these cases—to speak for those who do not have the means or the emotional strength to do it themselves. The public has yet to fully recognize the extent to which people are getting screwed. In my opinion, it's an epidemic. This book will sound the alarm.

It has long been a personal calling to stand up for the proverbial underdogs. In my legal work I have championed the little guys—from kids with special learning needs, wronged by their school systems, to elderly citizens exploited by their caregivers at home or in nursing homes. In my office, in the courtroom, and on both local and national television and radio, I have tried for decades to educate the masses on how the system works and how it could work so much better. *People Get Screwed All the Time* will take this cause to a new level. I believe with all my heart that if all of us increase our awareness of the problems, and are willing to work to be heard, change can and will happen. I am also looking to those in positions of power—those at the top of the heap, from the bench, to legislators, to bar associations, to us as lawyers—to effect changes that will right these wrongs in the system.

I strongly believe that we as experts have a responsibility to help those in more disadvantaged positions by fixing what's broken.

Everyone can learn to safeguard the most vital spheres in our lives—family and relationships, work, finance, and the home. To that end, I have distilled my knowledge and expertise—and my years of listening to horror stories—into clear lessons that you or anyone can apply in your life, lessons that will help protect you in ways the system can't. By the time clients show up at my door or call my office, it is most often too late. They are in situations over their heads, and serious—sometimes irreparable—damage has been done to their families, relationships, livelihoods, or reputations. With this book, you will have an advantage that, tragically, none of those people had.

The stories you will read are all true. Some of these people have been my clients; others have had their stories made public. In all cases, the locations, names, and identifying characteristics have been changed. But the facts remain the facts, and the situations dramatized in this book have happened to real people—people just like you.

The stories within will undoubtedly tug at your emotions. Specifically, they will make you angry—and they should. I hope, though, they will also make you think, and make you take the small steps in your life today that might avert a major catastrophe for you and your family down the road. Here at last is a book that will give hope to those finding themselves ground down by the wheels of justice and on the verge of despair. My legal education was hard won, as were the lessons gained from my twenty years representing people screwed by the system. My hope is that your education will begin not in the school of hard knocks, but here.

Part I

IDENTITY

How to Make Sure You Don't Get Caught in Somebody Else's Mess

You can use simple preventive measures to guard your personal information. If you are a victim of mistaken or stolen identity and find yourself inadvertently caught in the system, there are damage-controlling steps you must take.

When your name and personal information are wrongfully appropriated, extracting yourself from the aftermath can be a bad dream that never ends. The digital age is here, and there's no turning back. You cannot be too careful about protecting your personal information. All the information anybody would ever need to know about us has already been reduced to a binary sequence of ones and zeros. Computers are getting more powerful: faster, smaller, cheaper, and easier to use. Cell phones leave records that are easily tracked. Personal digital assistants (PDAs), such as Palm Pilots, BlackBerries, and Treos, hold a wealth of personal information. Legitimate private companies are already mining some of these data, looking for ways to capture and redistribute them. The damage that thieves or others can do, once they come into the possession of your personal information, is unfathomable.

Yet, many people who have lost personal information take only the most minimal steps to protect themselves. They may replace credit cards and their driver's license, but otherwise, they often simply assume that everything will just "turn out all right." Sadly, in many cases, they couldn't be more wrong. The following stories will highlight what you can do to safeguard your identity as well the steps you can take to clear your name, should you become a victim of identity theft or mistaken identity.

Chapter 1

STOLEN PURSE, STOLEN IDENTITY

JANET M. WAS TWENTY-FIVE YEARS OLD, THE DAUGHTER OF A SUCCESSFUL Las Vegas businessman. She was pretty, with fine wavy brown hair that fell to her shoulders. Her parents were no longer together, but she had been brought up in a stable home by good churchgoing people. She gave birth at twenty to a boy, Bobby, but separated from her husband four years later, moving with her son into a large house with five other people, including a couple upstairs who fought a lot. But the place was affordable, and there was room for the two of them when Bobby wasn't with his father. The future looked bright. Janet had a job as a bartender at a casino, for which she had to go through the trouble of obtaining a sheriff's card (required of all casino workers), certifying that she had no criminal record. It was worth the hassle; she liked her boss, and she was making decent money. Things were good until one night in November 2002. While Bobby was staying with his father, she went to a local pub with her friend David, in what she thought was a safe neighborhood, not far from the shopping malls and the multiplexes. When they came out of the bar, shortly after midnight, they saw that one of the car windows had been broken. Shards of shattered glass sparkled on the pavement. Janet had left her purse in the car, and now it was missing.

She called to cancel her credit cards as soon as she got home, wary of the hassle that was to come, resigned to standing in lines at the Department of Motor Vehicles (DMV) to replace her driver's license, filling out forms to replace her Social Security card, her health insurance card, her sheriff's card. The next morning, when she called the police department to report the theft, she was erroneously told that she couldn't do so until David reported the break-in. She went to the DMV and reported the theft of her license and cards. She figured that was pretty much the end of it.

Six months later, the couple upstairs were at it again, screaming at each other. This time somebody called the police, who arrived shortly to settle the disturbance, afterward taking down the names of potential witnesses, including Janet's. Cops were in and out of the house. One went to the squad car to enter names into the computer. Janet went back to what she was doing. Soon, an officer knocked on her door. She assumed he had some follow-up questions.

Instead, he informed her that she was a wanted fugitive and that the computer had been showing warrants for her arrest for credit card fraud, coming from St. George, Utah, about a hundred miles northeast of Las Vegas.

"What?" she said.

It took her a moment to get over the shock. Obviously, there was some sort of mix-up, some kind of mistake. She was completely cooperative. The police seemed to understand and didn't arrest her. Instead, they gave her the phone number of the prosecutor's office in St. George and told her she could take care of it herself.

"My purse was stolen last November," she told the prosecutor. "Whoever took it is running up those charges, not me. I've lived in Las Vegas my entire life." The St. George prosecutor was polite and seemed nice. Janet understood that St. George was a conservative Mormon town where things had to be done by the book. She agreed to send her fingerprints, as well as proof of residency and employment, and had them in the mail within the week. She figured she'd hear from the prosecutor that everything had been straightened out.

Days passed, then weeks.

She called the lawyer's office several times, trying to get an answer, trying to put the matter to rest. Finally, his secretary told Janet, "We received your packet, but you should know that the prosecutor is not on your side. He's not going to help you. You need to get a lawyer and come down here and fight this."

Not on her side? Wasn't the legal system supposed to protect the innocent?

She found it unbelievable.

She was fortunate in that her father was in a position to help her hire a competent lawyer, who soon discovered that a woman had opened a post office box in Janet's name in St. George. The criminal had used Janet's I.D. to have cell phones and credit cards sent to that post office box. The lawyer also discovered that the woman had used the identities of several other people to order cell phones and credit cards and other items in their names as well. Janet couldn't understand—if her own lawyer could discover these things, why couldn't the prosecutor in St. George see that she was a victim of identity theft—and not even the only victim?

On the advice of her attorney, Janet got a voice-analysis stress test, went to a handwriting specialist, and had her photograph taken for a photo lineup, but it all took time. Meanwhile, she lived in fear of being arrested at any moment. She had to leave her job as a bartender because she didn't have an up-to-date sheriff's work card and couldn't get one until the matter was resolved. She didn't want to get her boss in trouble, a man who'd been good to her and kept her on longer than he probably should have. She was afraid of driving for fear of getting pulled over for something simple, like a broken taillight, and then the warrants would pop up on the computer and trouble would undoubtedly start. It meant she couldn't drive Bobby around or take him to school. Soon, she saw him only when her ex brought him over to her house. She spent time taking care of her mother, who had diabetes, or riding her bike, or going to church, where she prayed for the ordeal to end. Some nights she had insomnia. Some mornings she couldn't get out of bed. Some days she'd console herself with too much food. At other times she just wasn't hungry; her stomach was tied in knots. She spent as much time with her son as she could, unable to explain to him how their normal life had been stolen by a woman who was still committing crimes in Mommy's name.

As time passed she learned that the woman who'd stolen her identity had a male accomplice, a man who'd once worked at a car dealership until he quit and took with him paperwork that included his clients' phone numbers, addresses, and vital information. He'd passed this information to his girlfriend, the woman who'd stolen Janet's identity, as well as the personal information of four other victims. She learned that the two suspects were "tweekers," who liked to get high on Ecstasy.

Janet's heart soared the day the prosecutor's office in St. George called to say that the male accomplice had been arrested and that he was willing to testify that she wasn't the one committing the crimes. Her heart fell a few days later, when she learned he'd been released and skipped town.

She continued to keep a low profile while she waited for something good to happen. One day she rode her bicycle to the park, where a photographer for the *Las Vegas Review Journal*, the morning paper, asked if he could take a picture of her feeding ducks by the lake at the end of the dock—the bucolic sort of picture newspapers frequently run when the weather is nice. She was feeling better. Her lawyer had told her he was going to drive up to St. George in person for a hearing before a judge, where he was going to ask to have the arrest warrants quashed. The county attorney would argue that there was enough probable cause to justify the charges, but Janet's lawyer felt certain he'd be able to clarify things in her favor. Janet told the photographer she didn't mind. He took her picture.

Two days later, the very day her lawyer was driving up to St. George, Janet's worst nightmare came true. She was riding her bicycle with a friend when the two of them were suddenly surrounded by three unmarked police cars. A voice came booming through a bullhorn.

"Pull over now! Get off your bicycle!" the voice commanded.

At first she feared she was being assaulted, uncertain of just who her assailants were, until the men identified themselves as police officers. Someone at police headquarters had seen her picture in the paper, which had given her name, and recognized her. She saw a fourth car pull up. To her surprise, a television crew from the TV show *Cops* got out and began filming, their camera lights shining in her eyes as she tried to explain to the police that the warrants for her arrest were supposed to be quashed that very day.

They didn't care. As far as they were concerned, the warrants were still current.

They bound her hands behind her back with handcuffs and led her to a car, the TV crew following her all the way. She felt humiliated, and she was furious. She was wearing shorts and a tank top that was somewhat revealing, and the TV crew was going for all the most provocative camera angles.

"You guys can't take me to jail like this!" she screamed.

"Have your friend give you her extra shirt, and let's go," a cop insisted.

At the Clark County Detention Center downtown, across from the courthouse, she was booked, fingerprinted, photographed, and thrown into a holding tank with fifteen other women who'd been arrested for things like prostitution or drug possession. It was the lowest point of her life. She was scared out of her mind but managed to put up a tough front. She couldn't believe this was happening, couldn't believe her bad luck. All she'd done was leave her purse in her friend's car. Ashamed and embarrassed, she called her father, who said that he'd contact the attorney and they'd get her out as soon as possible. But how soon was that going to be? The minutes crawled by, and each hour seemed an eternity as she waited for someone to come let her out. She felt as if she was going crazy.

She was held for three days and was released only after her attorney convinced a judge that she'd been a lifelong Las Vegas resident and thus posed no risk of flight.

Two days later, the county attorney's office in St. George called again to say that the accomplice of the woman who'd stolen Janet's identity had been reapprehended. He'd seen Janet's picture in a photo lineup and swore she wasn't the one committing fraud. Janet had to be driven to Utah, fingerprinted again, photographed again, and processed again. She was released. Finally, on June 2, 2004, eighteen months after her purse had been stolen, she received a letter bearing the judge's official signature, stating that she was innocent and the victim of identity theft.

Janet thanked God for having a father who was able to help her hire a competent attorney, though the cost of proving her innocence, totaling in the thousands of dollars, went beyond the purely monetary. She'd been in a kind of emotional jail, and the hardest part was losing contact with her son. Although the TV show *Cops* never ran the episode, it still stung to think of how she'd been so publicly humiliated and treated as if she were guilty. The perpetrator of the crimes against Janet was never caught. Every now and then, Janet still wonders how many other lives the woman is currently ruining.

HOW I WOULD HAVE COUNSELED JANET

Janet did not understand that identity theft is both a silent and an escalating crime. People will often not discover they have been victimized by identity theft until well after the thief has drained their bank accounts, destroyed valuable credit histories, and prevented the victims from rightfully obtaining credit and employment in their name. Even worse, as in the case of Janet, identity theft can result in a person being arrested for crimes he or she did not commit.

Many victims of identity theft, including Janet, fail to understand the nature of the "theft" they have experienced. It's easy to understand if you come home following a two-week vacation to find that your house has been broken into and all your possessions have been stolen. Yet, identity theft often has the same results. Just as a victim of a house burglary should change the locks on the house and install an alarm to thwart the burglar's easy reentry, victims of identity theft also need to change the access and identifying information associated with all their personal, financial, and health records.

Once you have discovered you're the victim of identity theft, you should assume the worst while still hoping for the best. In Janet's case, while filing a police report; canceling her credit cards; and obtaining a new driver's license, Social Security card, and health insurance card were good initial steps, it was not enough to stop the identity thief from ruining her credit or prevent her from landing in jail for a crime she did not commit. Two people had the keys to Janet's identity. Janet needed to change the locks to her identity.

If I had been counseling Janet, I would have advised her that in addition to the steps she had already taken, she needed to promptly notify each consumer credit reporting agency of the theft of her personal information. Janet should have called the 800 number of the consumer credit reporting agency and file an online report of stolen identity. The agency will ask personal questions to verify Janet's identity on her accounts. Once the agency red-flags Janet's credit reports, she can then move on to the time-consuming process of cleaning up her credit.

In addition, one of the most important keys to your identity is your Social Security number. This key should be carefully safeguarded. A Social Security number can be used to obtain driver's licenses and credit accounts. Janet should not have been carrying her Social Security card in her purse, or any other document listing this number, as the identity thief easily used this information to create a new identity to access Janet's personal, financial, and health accounts. If you lose your Social Security card, you should immediately contact the local authorities to report the loss or theft and the Social Security Administration to request a new card. You should also inform your credit card companies, bank, or any other financial institution that uses your Social Security number as a means of identification.

Janet's criminal difficulties presented a different set of hurdles. While Janet was fortunate to have the financial ability to retain a qualified attorney to guide her through the difficult criminal justice system, I would recommend such a course even for identity theft victims of lesser means who find themselves in similar circumstances. Any time you are charged with a crime—even if you are innocent—it's worth the effort to find a lawyer who will be willing to help. Ask friends and family members for a referral, or ask other lawyers to recommend a colleague who is known to handle identity theft cases. If Janet had been unable to retain an attorney because of lack of finances, I would have suggested that she call her local bar association and inquire whether there were any pro bono programs, in which attorneys donate their time to provide legal counsel to those who otherwise couldn't afford it.

Simply put, it's worth the time, effort, and money to find an attorney experienced with identity theft issues who will be more qualified than a lay person to jump over the hurdles necessary to quickly establish that you have been the victim of identity theft—especially when you must clarify that any criminal charges are attributable to the identity thief, not the identity theft victim.

While the particulars of each criminal matter may vary as to the crime charged and the state in which the crime was committed, I would have advised Janet to promptly file a report with her local police department the night her wallet was stolen. That would have established that she was a victim (or potential victim) of identity theft. In most states, the district attorney's office has an identity theft division that deals specifically with these types of crimes. This report would be in addition to the stolen property report that Janet initially attempted to file with the police. Janet should have been able to report the theft of her wallet whether or not her friend reported the car break-in.

Depending upon the requirements of the particular state, Janet may have been required to submit fingerprints, pictures, and other identifying information to the police to establish her true identity. Also, any victim of identity theft should call to file a report with the Federal Trade Commission (FTC), a federal agency that operates at both the federal and state levels to track identity theft. The FTC can give you information on where to report the details of your story and offer specific suggestions for help. Thereafter, when Janet learned of the criminal matter in another state, she could have requested that her FTC report and accompanying information be forwarded to the other state. While there is no guarantee that the other state would drop the matter simply upon receipt of the report, the fact that Janet filed her report prior to any alleged criminal activity would provide compelling evidence that Janet was the victim and not a criminal.

Most states have local task forces through their district attorney's office that investigate and assist victims of identity theft. Janet could have contacted her local DA and asked if there were such a program in her state.

Finally, I would have recommended that Janet hold on to the letter from the judge verifying her innocence and stating that she had been the victim of identity theft. In applying for jobs, credit, and even professional licenses and security clearances, Janet's prior run-in with the law may still show up on her profile. The letter will quickly answer any questions regarding Janet's innocence.

Chapter 2

FALSE ARREST, MISTAKEN IDENTITY

SHONDA DAILY, FORTY YEARS OLD AND A MOTHER OF FOUR, WAS COMING home from the grocery store on a Saturday night, the last day of May, when she saw the flashing lights of a police squad car at the end of an alley near her home. She was accompanied by her daughter-in-law, Vanessa, who was nineteen and married to Shonda's oldest son, James, who was twenty. At five foot ten, Shonda was tall, a light-skinned African-American woman with red hair, pulled back this evening in French braids. Shonda wondered what the trouble was this time. The apartment complex where she lived was in a bad neighborhood, perhaps the worst in town. She parked her truck behind her apartment building and went to see what the commotion was about. She was simply curious, or perhaps even nosy—but that wasn't a crime, was it?

She learned from another onlooker that a Hispanic woman had been mugged by two African-American girls. One hit her on the back of the head with a fist and took her purse. The other stomped on the woman's cell phone when she tried to dial 911.

Shonda was about to leave when one of the cops on the scene approached her.

"How long have you been standing here?" he asked her.

"I just got here," she said.

"What's your name?" He looked her up and down.

"Shonda Daily."

"Where do you live?'

"I live in this building right here," she said, pointing. She gave him the number of her apartment as well.

"This building here?" he asked.

"Uh-huh," she said.

"And where do you work?" he wanted to know.

"I work at the Silver Dice," she said. "I'm in housekeeping."

"Okay," he said. Then he asked her to wait a moment while he took her picture, the flash leaving a blue dot on her retinas. She didn't think much of it. After all, what was there for her to worry about? She'd done nothing wrong. She'd been completely cooperative. She felt bad for the woman who'd been mugged, but in this neighborhood, she was hardly surprised.

Three weeks later, on June 20, she was midway through her shift at the Silver Dice when she saw two men from house security approaching her. She liked her job, which made $800 a month plus tips—not enough to make her wealthy but enough to pay her rent and her utility bills and put food on the table for her three sons and her granddaughter.

It was her last day before her vacation. She was planning to take her youngest son, Roger, to a water park to celebrate his twelfth birthday, unless her daughter Angela, who was nine months pregnant and due any day, gave birth first, in which case the water park would have to wait. Shonda's dream was to stay with her job at the Silver Dice long enough to move her family into a nicer apartment in a safer neighborhood. But for now, life was good. She'd always performed her job conscientiously, and she wondered what house security wanted with her.

"There are some cops out back," one said. "They said they want to talk to you."

"Why do they want to talk to me?" she said, truly without the slightest clue.

"Shonda Daily," a cop said to her, grabbing her by the wrist and slapping a pair of handcuffs on her before she knew what was happening, in front of her coworkers and the men from house security, "you're under arrest for robbery and conspiracy to commit the robbery of Luisa Ruiz. You have the right to remain silent . . ."

"What's happening?" she said, bursting into tears.

"You have the right . . ."

It took her a second to realize they were referring to the mugging three weeks earlier.

"But I didn't do it!" she said. "Why are you doing this to me? I didn't do it. I didn't do it! Why are you doing this?"

"An officer on the scene questioned you and felt that you had something to do with it," a second cop explained, grabbing her by the arm and leading her down the hall.

"He felt like it?" she said. "What do you mean, he felt like it? Who cares what he felt like? I didn't do it! I was at the store."

At the county jail where she was taken, she was put into an interrogation room and questioned by two detectives, who tried to convince her that that things would go much easier for her if she cooperated and confessed, and that if she did, they could probably get her sentence reduced. "If you work with us, you're only looking at five to fifteen," one said. Shonda had no intention of confessing to something she hadn't done, and she felt confident that once the police realized they had the wrong person and had no physical proof (after all, how could they?), they'd let her go. She wanted to go home. She hoped that perhaps she'd be released in a few hours, unaware of how slowly the wheels of justice could turn, often stymied by a system that would rather make a bad arrest stick than admit a mistake.

She was taken to a temporary holding cell, which was so crowded there was nowhere to sit except on the floor, surrounded by exactly the kinds of people she'd told her kids to avoid at the apartment complex. She was supposed to have a public defender represent her at the arraignment, but he didn't show up. Bail was set higher than anything she could possibly afford. She asked one of the detectives why they couldn't release her on her own recognizance. After all, she had no previous record.

"I'll talk to the judge and see what I can do," he said, but it was a false promise. He didn't talk to the judge. He didn't care.

Shonda was in the "temporary" holding cell for two weeks. She missed her son Roger's birthday. Two days after her arrest, her daughter Angela went into labor but lost the baby two hours after delivery because of complications, and Shonda couldn't be there to comfort her little girl. The fact that she never saw the baby hurt her more than the experience of being arrested. Meanwhile, she learned that she'd been fired from the Silver Dice for "off-duty conduct that materially affects job performance and brings discredit to the company," even though she'd never had a complaint about her job performance. So much, she thought, for the concept of being innocent until proven guilty. A second public defender told her the district attorney was still convinced they had the right person, solely on the basis of the victim's positive identification of Shonda from the photograph the police had taken the night of the mugging and shown to Luisa Ruiz as she was leaving the hospital. She'd said at the time that her attackers were two dark-skinned African-American girls, in their twenties, or perhaps teenagers, about five foot six, and one of them had a red ponytail. Shonda was light-skinned, forty, and almost six feet tall. Her sole resemblance to the attackers was her red hair, which was in French braids and not a single ponytail. Ms. Ruiz had told the police she would "fear for her life" if she ever saw her attackers again.

Shonda was finally released on her own recognizance, on the condition that she report downtown once a week to be fingerprinted. That procedure cost her $10 a visit—no small amount to a woman trying to feed four people on a monthly unemployment check of only $341. Other bills began to pile up. Some she left unopened; what was the point if there was simply no money to pay them? Feeding her kids was the priority. She accepted handouts from her mother and from her sister-in-law, feeling both grateful and deeply embarrassed that it was necessary, even though she still knew she'd done nothing wrong.

Seven weeks after her arrest, on August 6, her oldest son's birthday, she was at the county courthouse with her third public defender, sitting on a bench in the hallway outside the courtroom, when she noticed a young Hispanic woman seated on a bench opposite her. The woman glanced over at Shonda, turned to her own attorney, and said, "Who is that?" The Hispanic woman was Luisa Ruiz, the victim, who said she'd fear for her life if she ever saw her attackers again. Shonda's public defender witnessed the exchange and reported it to the judge, who, after some deliberation, called Shonda into court and told her, with the court's apologies, that the case was being dismissed on the basis of mistaken identity.

Shonda was relieved, but her nightmare was hardly over. In some ways, it was just beginning.

When she got home, she found that her electricity had been shut off. There were threats of eviction from the landlord. She thought it would be a simple thing, now that the case was dismissed, to get a new job and begin digging her way out of the hole she'd fallen into. Yet, every time she filled out a job application, when she had to answer the question "Have you ever been arrested for a crime?" the only honest answer she could give was to check the box marked "Yes." What potential employer was going to give her a chance to explain her situation? Who was going to hire someone who had to say, "Yes, I was arrested, but I was never convicted," when they could simply hire someone who'd checked the box marked "No"? And whenever anyone ran a background check on her, the report came back: "Criminal History: Felon." Such reports did not mention that she wasn't convicted and never went to trial. The same reports denied her access to safer, more affordable living quarters when she appealed to the public housing authority. What she needed was to have her records sealed, but that required a considerable amount of paperwork, done in understaffed district attorney's offices where the public defenders had hundreds and hundreds of cases assigned to them to process. To Shonda, her situation was dire, but to the district attorney, Shonda's case had a very low priority. After all, she wasn't in jail, wasn't headed to trial, was free to do as she pleased—where was the urgency, when so many other cases were pressing?

The financial strain put an enormous amount of stress on her family. Her kids fought constantly. When she appealed to a local charity for assistance, she was denied on the grounds that she lacked potential employment opportunities. When she threw in the towel and applied to a program designed to help convicted felons get back on their feet and find work, she was told, ironically, that she didn't qualify because she wasn't a convicted felon.

The strain on Shonda herself was also enormous. She snapped at her children and fought with her mother and with her sister-in-law, even though they were only trying to help her. When her granddaughter needed a dollar for a Popsicle from the ice-cream man, she didn't have it. She heard gunshots outside of her apartment complex almost every night, it seemed, and she was desperate to move out but couldn't. One day a grown man tried to sell her youngest son marijuana. Another day, when all Roger wanted was to play outside after church with his new remote-controlled race car, he came in crying and said another boy had put a gun to his head and stolen it.

By the time she was finally able to convince an attorney to help her get her records sealed and to lay the initial groundwork for a lawsuit for false arrest against the metropolitan police department, she was too pessimistic to let her hopes rise. She met with her lawyer three times. He claimed to have placed a request to have her records sealed in the hands of the district attorney. Nothing happened. She began to doubt that her lawyer was telling her the truth.

The situation would have been unbearable, had it lasted only a few months.

Two years went by, and her records were still unsealed, and she still couldn't find a job.

All the time, her only comfort—and it wasn't much—was telling herself the simple truth of the matter: "I have done nothing wrong. I have done absolutely nothing wrong."

HOW I WOULD HAVE COUNSELED SHONDA

To put it simply, the system let Shonda down big-time. Even though the charges against her were dropped forty-five days after she was arrested, nobody told her—not the judge, not the district attorney's office, not her public defender, nobody—that she had the right to have her records sealed. Because nobody informed her of this, and because she did not have the finances to fight back, she lost everything: her job, her apartment, and her dignity. She was made to look, and perhaps even to feel, like a felon, even though she wasn't—even though the only "crime" she had committed was not minding her own business.

The system should have responded immediately. As soon as the case was dismissed, somebody should have said, "Shonda, you can now go up to the DA's office on your own and have your records sealed." One might think that in actuality, in this day and age of universally adopted computer technologies and the instantaneous transfer of electronic information, nobody should have to tell her that. It should be automatic. After all—why, when a court clerk is putting information into his or her computer that a case is being dismissed, isn't it just a matter of standard procedure to seal that person's record?

But it's not. The system still depends on human beings, and human beings are fallible. Public defenders and court officers often have hundreds of cases stacked up, each one demanding attention. In mistaken identity cases, it's almost impossible for the victim to make sense of the situation, and it can be equally confusing for an attorney, who is relying on the information provided by the client and investigators, to make sense of it for her. If no witness shows up to right the wrong of mistaken identity, the system can continue to process an innocent individual. Shonda did absolutely nothing wrong, other than unintentionally place herself in a position where she later found out she didn't belong.

If you are wrongfully arrested, and your case is dismissed, you need to be sure you follow through with the process of having your records sealed. You should note that while federal charges may be dismissed, federal records cannot be sealed. Ask the lawyer representing you to ask the judge for an order to expunge the record. Once your lawyer has this order, continue to follow up to be sure that the order is sent to the district attorney, who will ensure that it is disseminated to all the appropriate agencies. Make sure you get a copy of the order as well.

It is critical to make sure this happens. Once your records are sealed legally, it's as if your arrest never happened. You can fill in "no" if asked if you have ever been arrested. Because Shonda's records were not sealed, when she went to apply for a job she had to disclose that there was a felony case against her. The record stood, even though her case had been dismissed.

Unfortunately, the current practice of releasing electronic criminal record databases to companies that sell information for background checks means you can never be sure an arrest has been completely expunged from public record. Find out more about your state's criminal records policy by visiting www.sentencingproject.org/rights-restoration.cfm.

Shonda's case was made worse when her public defender didn't show up. If she could have afforded to hire an attorney or a private detective, the whole matter of mistaken identity might have been quickly resolved.

When I counsel someone who gets caught in this kind of mess, the most important thing is to put off all the woulda/coulda/shoulda lectures until the matter is completely resolved in the victim's favor. To tell a person in Shonda's fragile emotional state that she could have easily resolved the situation on her own would only complicate matters for her. She trusted that the system would give her the information she needed. The information was available, but she had to know who to ask and what to ask for. That's often too much to require of someone inexperienced with the legal system. There aren't any road signs along the way to tell you where to go or when to turn.

As time passes and the wounds heal, it is an attorney's duty to educate his client on how to avoid a similar situation, should it arise down the road. As Shonda learned, simply being in the wrong place at the wrong time can have devastating consequences. If you are ever falsely accused of a crime, you need to take two critical steps to keep a case of mistaken identity from ruining your life: immediately seek a lawyer's professional advice, and, once the charges are dismissed, be sure to request that the record be sealed.

Chapter 3

FALSE INFORMATION ON A BACKGROUND CHECK

AT FORTY-THREE, MONICA WALTERS KNEW SHE WAS GOING TO HAVE A TOUGH time getting back into the job market, but she never expected that it would take this long. When she and her husband left their childhood home in Brooklyn, New York, she was a twenty-three-year old newlywed with dreams of giving her future children a better life than she had experienced growing up in the dangerous neighborhood of Red Hook. The couple moved to Seattle, where her husband had found work as a computer programmer, and they could begin the family they both wanted. When they found a modest ranch house in Tacoma, they took a deep breath and made their first big purchase. Monica found a job to help defray the mortgage, and shortly thereafter their first child, a boy, was born. Three more children followed over the next eight years.

Monica felt incredibly lucky. No other members of her family had fared as well. Reports from back home in Brooklyn were that her younger sister was dabbling in drugs and gangs, and that her baby brother had refused to find a job and help out around the house when her dad upped and left. Gradually Monica lost contact with her family. The world she had grown up in was not her world anymore. She was proud of herself. She'd done all right, she told herself. There was no limit to how far she could go.

But that bright future disappeared just after the birth of her youngest son, along with her husband and more than half of their shared savings. Their marriage had been on the rocks long before Monica accepted her husband's lawyer's measly settlement offer of the house and half their savings. Frankly, she was glad to close the chapter on her marriage. Their relationship had not stood the test of time or children well. She was so desperate to be free of her husband that she would have let him go without asking for anything. When she found that their shared savings account had been drained to nearly nothing, she wasn't shocked. At least he was sending child support each month. But those checks stopped coming in the second year after the divorce. She'd gotten a court order to compel him to pay, but when no one could locate him or find a record of his being employed, she figured it was better to hang on to her modest savings rather than hire a private investigator to track him down and hire another attorney to force him to make payments.

Besides, although things were tight, they weren't dire. She had a good job and job security. As a civilian police administrative aide she'd become indispensable to the men and women detectives of the 14th Squad. After all, she'd worked there for nineteen years, practically the whole time she'd been in Tacoma. She'd begun by working part time. The chief had always been good about letting her have time off after each of her pregnancies, and she was always welcomed back. And after the divorce, she was able to increase her hours to full time. Sometimes there were even some part-time shifts on the weekends, and the chief was usually willing to let her have the overtime.

She sure wasn't rich, but she and the kids were getting by. But Monica's confidence took a big hit when the chief called her into his office one day and told her to shut the door. The city budget had been sliced, he told her, and his department had to make some hard decisions. He was being forced to cut the aide position back to less than half time. Monica was quick to reassure him.

"No problem, Chief," she said quickly. "I'm happy to go part time. I'm sure I can pick up something else to help make up for it."

The chief shook his head sadly. "You know I wish I could help you out here, but you've been here for so long, you've maxed out at your hourly pay. I've got to bring in someone junior, someone that I can pay less. I'm so sorry, Monica, but my hands are tied. I'll talk to the human resources people and see if I can get you some kind of severance. I'm so sorry."

Monica felt sick. Holding back tears, she assured the chief there were no hard feelings and returned to her desk at the front of the squad room. But her mind was racing. Where was she going to find another job with such a high hourly wage? Unemployment in Tacoma was at record-breaking levels. She consoled herself that, at least, she had a great track record—and a personal reference from the chief of police would certainly go a long way with any prospective employer.

For eight months, Monica sent out résumés and answered ads. The answers were always the same: she was underqualified for the high-tech jobs that employed most Tacoma residents and overqualified for regular secretarial work. While she worked hard to keep a positive outlook in front of the kids, Monica was growing panicky. She'd already gone through her modest savings and the severance from the police department. She'd refinanced the mortgage on her house. The interest rate was higher than she would have liked, and she'd already been using some extra cash from the refinancing to meet her new, higher monthly payment. But what could she do? She had a family to support.

A few months before Christmas, Monica saw the ad in the paper. A major shipping firm was looking for seasonal workers. The hourly pay was good, and Monica was sure she could put in enough hours to make it worthwhile. She sent in an application and got a callback the same week.

"Can you start on Monday?" Paula from human resources was chatty. "Nineteen years with the Tacoma PD, eh? I guess we won't have to worry about your background check."

On Monday, Monica showed up for work. It had felt great to drop the kids off at school and call out, "See you after work, honey."

She followed a supervisor down the industrial hallways to his temporary office. A mess of paperwork sat on his metal desk, and he shuffled through several folders before finding hers.

"Monica Walters, right?" he asked, glancing at the folder.

"Yes, sir."

"Hmmm, looks like we've got a little problem with your file, here," he said. "Can't start you today. We're missing your background check results. You'll have to go home."

The last thing Monica wanted on her first day at her new job was to be sent home. Taking a deep breath, she politely suggested that perhaps her paperwork had been misplaced. "Could you just check with human resources?" she asked.

The man checked his watched and frowned. He sighed loudly and picked up the phone.

"Any word on the background check for . . ." he looked at the folder again. "Monica Walters?"

Monica watched as he nodded silently and then hung up the phone.

"Sorry, Ms. Walters. We don't have your records. And in our experience, when the background check is delayed, it usually means a criminal history."

Monica began to protest, but he cut her off. Looking back down at the piles of paper on his desk, he told her to check back in at the end of the week. If the paperwork had turned up by then, she'd be able to start the following Monday. Then he strode to the office door and opened it.

"Thank you for your time," Monica said weakly. She didn't want to make a fuss and risk a bad impression with her future supervisor. She figured it would be best to do as he suggested and call on Friday to see what the problem had been. "I'll see you next Monday, then."

Her friends were reassuring. "Probably some stupid mix-up in human resources," they said. "That's what happens when you deal with these big international corporations."

On Friday, as she'd been instructed to do, Monica called the supervisor's office.

"Should I come in to work on Monday? Have you received the

background check for my file yet?" she asked the young woman who answered the phone.

The young woman was clearly uncomfortable. She informed Monica that they had received her background check, but she was sorry to have to say that the job had already been filled.

Monica couldn't believe her ears. "I was hired last week for that position. I'm supposed to start on Monday, now that my file is complete," she said.

The woman simply repeated that the job had been filled.

"You can't do that," Monica shouted. "You promised me a job. It's discrimination or something. You let me speak to your boss. You cannot do this."

"Sorry—company policy. That job went to an individual *without* a criminal history," the woman said snottily before hanging up the phone.

Monica stared at the phone. Criminal history? There had obviously been some mistake. She dialed the human resources office.

The man who answered the phone kept his voice cold and professional as he told Monica that it was against company policy to hire anyone with a criminal record.

Monica was dumbfounded. She didn't even have time to explain that it was all a mistake. She called back again, this time asking for Paula, the woman who had first processed her job application. After a few minutes, Paula's familiar voice came on the line.

"This is Paula."

"Paula, it's Monica Walters. We spoke a few weeks ago about my application."

Paula wasn't nearly so chatty as she had been the first time. "Yes. Your background check came back with negative factors," she replied.

"But you know that's impossible," Monica said politely. "We joked about how long I'd worked for the Tacoma PD. Don't you remember? This has all got to be some mistake."

Paula's voice softened as she admitted she did remember having that conversation. She was sorry, she told Monica, but the background check had clearly showed that Monica had a criminal record, so there was no way they could hire her. Paula apologized again. Taking advantage of the compassion she heard in the other woman's voice, Monica asked Paula to send her a copy of the background check.

A week later, Monica studied the background check, conducted by a Washington-based firm specializing in background and criminal checks. There it was in black and white: a six-year-old conviction for a misdemeanor and a sentence of one year in jail. It further noted that the jail time had been served in a Brooklyn prison five years ago—while Monica was still sitting at the aide's desk in the 14th Squad! It was perfectly clear what had happened when Monica read further: the crime had been committed by "one Monica Walters, also known as Sheila Hollis." Monica's sister had given her name and her birthday when arrested for the crime, and those facts had remained part of the record.

Despite repeated calls to the shipping company, Monica was unable to find a position with it. She was struggling to make ends meet and in danger of missing payments on her new mortgage. She didn't know what to tell her children about the grim prospects facing them in the coming holiday season. She was left considering her options. Perhaps she'd sell the house and try to move to another area. Whatever she did in the future, she wanted to know how she could be sure that prospective employers would never make this kind of mistake again.

HOW I WOULD HAVE COUNSELED MONICA

Upon being arrested, criminals often tell the police that someone else did the crime. In the case of identity thieves, they have "someone else" to lay the blame on—you. As Monica found out, even working for the police department did not prevent her from having a fraudulent criminal record in her name.

If I were counseling Monica, I would have first advised her that she should immediately file a police report with her local police department, verifying that she had been the victim of identity theft.

Monica should also file an identity theft report with the Federal Trade Commission. Monica would need to provide verification of her identity to the local police department, including fingerprints. This information should then be forwarded to the police department that issued the misdemeanor charges as well as the district attorney's office that handled the criminal matter involving Monica's sister, Sheila.

With criminal matters, I would strongly recommend that a victim of identity theft retain an attorney in the jurisdiction where the criminal charges were filed to ensure that the criminal matter is resolved as quickly as possible. This isn't a time to be counting pennies. It is better to spend a little money up front than try to "save a buck" and risk being arrested on any outstanding fraudulent criminal charges or, in the case of Monica, lose employment opportunities.

To find an attorney, Monica should contact the local or state bar association in the state in which the criminal matter is pending. These bar associations are found in every state. Depending on the state, the bar association generally provides for the licensing and oversight of attorneys in that particular state. Most of these bar associations offer lawyer referral programs to members of the public.

Criminal records are generally tracked first by real name and then by known aliases. As it stood, Sheila was using Monica's name as her primary name and using Sheila as her "alias." This should be corrected. Monica should request that Sheila's criminal record, including the databases in which the police department track these criminal records, list the name Sheila as her primary name. This should serve to minimize the occurrence of Monica's name being listed on a criminal background check.

Monica should also ensure that she receives a letter or other official document from the issuing police department and the issuing court verifying that the criminal matter did not involve her. Each state, including local police departments, may have different requirements for the correction of a criminal record. A local attorney who is experienced in both criminal matters and matters relating to false identities or arrests should be used for this purpose. Once the letter or official document has been obtained, it should never be destroyed, and multiple copies should be kept available in case any new problems arise relating to the prior fraudulent criminal matter.

While these steps may take care of the matter, there is the ongoing possibility that Monica's name will still appear on a criminal background search, as her name will most likely continue to be reflected as Sheila's "alias." To help prevent further difficulties in obtaining employment, Monica should be prepared to provide any prospective employer with the documentation verifying that the criminal matter related to the fraudulent use of her identity was resolved and that she was not involved in the alleged crimes. Depending on the type of employer, it may be advisable to warn the potential employer that this issue may come up during any background checks.

Chapter 4

CREDIT CARD FRAUD

CARL MARTIN AND HIS WIFE, MARION, HAD ALWAYS LIVED MODESTLY AND saved diligently. They were proud that they had been able to raise four children in their small, neat home, and they had even managed to amass some savings by relying on common sense and the careful budgeting of Carl's salary. But over the past two years the Martins had been swamped with credit card applications they hadn't requested and credit card bills for items they'd never purchased. Their carefully managed finances were in a shambles, and their future security was in jeopardy.

Carl, a tall, gray-haired, capable-looking man, blamed himself. Two years earlier he had been working as a court officer in Shreveport, Louisiana. Sometimes he pulled duty at night court. Night court could get quiet, so sometimes he'd bring in paperwork from home to work on during his breaks. He'd pay bills and catch up on correspondence—that sort of thing.

"I'd worked a night shift in early February, and it had been real quiet," he said. "I remember thinking that it'd be smart to get a jump on my taxes, so I brought a bunch of paperwork into the lunch room."

A month later, a Visa bill addressed to C. L. Martin arrived. At first he thought there had simply been some mistake. He and his wife had never used credit, he explained. They paid cash or went without. They had their mortgage and their car loan, both nearly paid off, and he had no intention of ever doing anything to ruin their perfect credit rating. He opened the bill, intending to get a number to call the credit card company, and noted that over $1500 had been charged to various stores up in the Dallas/Fort Worth area, several hundred miles away.

He called the credit card company, which noted the fraudulent charges. A few days later, another bill showed up in the mail. This one was from a department store in Dallas. Over $500 had been charged. The customer service person for the department store card was not as understanding as the one at Visa. "We have your information right here, sir. Your address, Social Security number, your last name—they all match up. You'll have to pay the charges." Instead of paying, Carl embarked on a letter-writing campaign with the store until the store finally agreed to drop the charges and cancel the card. No more bills arrived in the mail over the next few weeks, and Carl and Marion breathed a sigh of relief. They had read about identity theft and fraud. It could have been worse, they told themselves.

"In fact, we had no idea how bad it really was," Marion said.

A short time later, Carl and Marion applied for a mortgage through their local bank. With retirement on the horizon and the kids all living in different states, they were ready to downsize and find a home—maybe one with some land, where Marion could garden.

They began house hunting on weekends and soon found an adorable two-bedroom cottage on about a half acre in a quiet neighborhood on the other side of town. When the mortgage officer from the bank called back so quickly, they were thrilled.

"And then he told us that the numbers just weren't working out," Carl explained. "They couldn't give us the mortgage."

Carl was stunned. His retirement account, all of their personal banking—everything was through that bank. He immediately thought of the fraudulent credit cards and requested copies of their consumer credit reports. Sure enough, there were the reports from the Visa and department store cards, as well as charges on an unpaid gas credit card, a defaulted loan at a car dealership in Dallas, and a rejected bank loan request from a small bank in the Houston area.

It took nearly two years of letter writing and documentation to finally clear all the mistakes and clean up their credit. The credit card companies, the car dealership, and the bank had assured them in writing that their records were clear. Finally, Carl and Marion were ready to reapply for a loan. This time, they applied for a new construction loan, deciding to go ahead and build their dream retirement home on some land they owned along the Gulf.

Again the mortgage fell through. And again Carl requested their consumer credit reports. What he found was shocking. Despite the letter writing and fraud alerts, two of the credit agencies had not cleared the bad information. Only one of the three major agencies gave them a clean report.

At their wit's end, and unwilling to wait another two years to move out of their increasingly dangerous neighborhood, Carl and Marion hired a lawyer to sue the credit agencies that had not wiped the information from their report.

In the meantime, although they haven't received bills for any new charges, offers for various credit cards addressed to "C. L. Martin" arrive in their mail several times a week.

The irony isn't lost on Carl. "We can't get a mortgage," he said. "But the folks who ruined our credit ratings—well, they're welcome to apply for all the credit they can handle!"

HOW I WOULD HAVE COUNSELED CARL

We all know not to leave valuables out in plain sight. You watch your wallet or purse, cash, and jewelry like a hawk. Right? You understand that when left unattended, these items can be too tempting even for people you would have thought had absolutely no inclination for theft.

Everyone also knows not to leave documents containing a Social Security number, home address, date of birth, and other personal financial information lying around in plain sight. Right? Wrong.

Armed with this information, an identity thief can "create" a new you: a new you that *really* enjoys shopping and never thinks twice about figuring out how to pay for all the goodies. Don't make yourself an easy target for identity thieves.

As a rule, never take personal financial information to your place of work or to school, or leave them in your car. At work or school, we tend to forget about these documents and lose sight of them while attending to our work or studies. Leaving personal items in your car can be just as dangerous. One of the first things a car thief will do is search the car for money or other valuables. Remember, your personal financial documents can be as valuable as cash.

Another note: don't leave your car registration or insurance information in your car. Carry them with you in your purse or wallet. Why? If a thief has just stolen your car, then he will know where you live, be able to get there before you, and possibly break into your residence and further steal. You're on foot now, and he has your car; he will get there first.

If I were counseling Carl, I would have advised Carl that once he had learned of the first fraudulent charge, he should have immediately filed an identity theft report with the local police department as well as the Federal Trade Commission. Carl should have also placed a fraud alert on his credit file with each of the three separate consumer credit reporting agencies. Carl also needed to immediately obtain copies of his credit files from each credit reporting agency in order to determine whether any additional fraudulent accounts had been created or fraudulent charges incurred.

Carl should sign up for one of the various credit monitoring services offered by the credit reporting agencies as well as by several other private companies. In most cases, consumers can obtain information from their own credit profiles without triggering any negative scoring on them. I would recommend that Carl use a monitoring service that tracks all three of the consumer credit reporting agencies. These credit monitoring services offer, in many cases, immediate notification that a new credit account has either been requested or created under your name. If someone is creating fraudulent credit in your name, this is your first line of defense. You can immediately contact the merchant, advise the merchant of the fraudulent activity, and close the account before any charges are incurred.

In Carl's case, I would have recommended that he place an extended alert on his credit profile with each consumer credit reporting agency. An extended alert lasts for seven years and prevents any new credit from being issued without Carl's prior approval. Carl could follow this up by placing a password on his credit file and providing a telephone number where he can be reached so that the identity of anyone seeking to obtain new credit in his name can be verified.

There is a downside to placing an extended alert on your credit profile. An extended alert can inhibit your ability to obtain instant credit approval from some merchants, such as when you purchase a new car from a dealer. The merchant's policies may prevent you from making the purchase that day because of the extra requirements you have placed upon the issuance of new credit.

Since Carl pays cash for all his purchases, the extra requirement of identity verification due to an extended alert would probably not have much impact. For other people who use credit, the inconvenience of possibly missing out on a special promotion because of the additional time it takes to verify their identity can be offset by the knowledge that they have a far lesser chance of falling victim to identity theft.

Carl also should cancel all his bank accounts, including those held with his wife, and create new bank accounts with new passwords.

To stop the constant barrage of preapproved credit applications, Carl should request to "opt out" of any future unsolicited credit offers from any merchants that use a person's credit profile to send preapproved credit applications in the mail. Carl could request to opt out by calling the toll-free number listed at the end of this chapter. Carl would need to provide his Social Security number and his current mailing address. This is one time when it's okay to reveal personal information. When you are the one making a call to a known business entity, using your personal information to identify yourself may be necessary. If you *receive* a call from someone soliciting this information, you should never, ever give it out.

Instead of simply throwing them into the garbage, Carl should also shred any credit applications that arrive in the mail, because an identity thief can fill them out and seek credit in his name.

Carl should contact a lawyer who specializes in handling matters involving the Fair Credit Reporting Act, a federal law that applies to the issuance of credit and the rights and responsibilities of consumers and merchants with regard to credit issues. If the credit agencies do not correct Carl's records, the lawyer could file an action in court under the Fair Credit Reporting Act, which allows the victim to collect damages and attorney fees for falsely reported information. Generally, a victim of identity theft will need to write to the credit issuer (i.e., the merchant) to dispute the charges based on identity theft. The victim will also need to write to the consumer credit reporting agency to advise it that any particular credit account or charge is fraudulent.

Writing to both the merchant and the consumer reporting agencies should ensure that fraudulent charges and information are removed from your credit report. However, the charges can reappear on your credit profile if the merchant or credit agency finds that the charges were, in fact, legitimate. This process may take some time to finally clear all fraudulent charges from your credit profile, and the assistance of an attorney experienced in these matters can greatly diminish both the time and the cost of such efforts.

Chapter 5

YOUR CHILDREN AND IDENTITY THEFT

KATHY LEONARD'S HEART NEARLY STOPPED WHEN SHE SAW THE POLICE officers standing outside her screen door. Her immediate thought was that her ten-year-old daughter had had an accident while riding her bike to her friend's house down the street in the well-manicured cul-de-sac in the Miami neighborhood where they lived.

"Can I help you officers?" she managed to choke out.

"I'm Officer Taylor from the Broward County sheriff's office. We'd like to see Brian Daniels," the officer said, flashing his shield. His partner stood silently, one hand resting casually on the handcuffs attached to his belt.

Kathy's fear turned to slow-mounting irritation as she motioned the officers to step into the house. If Brian, her thirteen-year-old son, had been hanging out with those high-school kids down the block and had gotten into trouble, she'd kill him. As a single mother she prided herself on knowing where her teenaged son was, and what he was doing, nearly 24/7. She couldn't imagine what he'd gotten into. As the officers came through the front door she asked them why they were looking for her son.

"We'd just like to ask him a few questions, ma'am," the officer said reassuringly. "Is he here?"

Kathy thought for a moment. Maybe Brian had done something wrong. Brian's father, Hal, had a real sneaky streak to him, as she had found out during the long and ugly divorce battle they had fought nearly four years earlier. And if Brian were going to take after his father ... well, then, maybe now was the time to scare him straight.

"Follow me," she said, leading the officers back through the house to the room the family used as a study area for the kids. Brian was working at the computer, putting the finishing touches on a biology report that was due the next day. "Brian, there are some people here to see you," she said.

Brian spun around in the chair, and his eyes widened in surprise. Kathy thought she saw a flash of confusion across one of the police officer's faces as well. Brian stood up and looked from his mother to the police officers, and back to his mother again.

One of the police officers stepped forward. "Are you Brian Daniels?"

Brian nodded.

"We need you to come into the station with us. We've had a number of complaints about you and your little scam. You're looking at jail time, young man."

"Mom! What's going on?" Brian was pale and panicky.

Kathy held up her hand to stop the officers from marching her son out the door. Whatever they thought Brian had done, she was sure there had been some kind of a mistake. They had never said they were going to arrest her son. She had thought they wanted to only ask him some questions.

Kathy watched in horror as Brian was escorted to the squad car, put into the backseat, and driven off while the neighbors watched from their windows and backyards. She ran back inside, called her daughter's friend's house, and arranged for her daughter to stay there for supper. Then she grabbed her purse and raced off to find her son at the police station.

For Kathy, the rest of the night passed in a blur. She got to the police station but wasn't allowed to see Brian. She was told that he had not been arrested, but was being questioned in connection with a scam that had involved several homeowners in the Broward and Dade County areas. She called the lawyer who had handled her divorce and he agreed to meet her at the station. When he arrived, he was able to get a copy of the complaint against Brian. Kathy was stunned when she saw the file. There were at least ten complaints from homeowners for incomplete contracting work. And every complaint named Brian Daniels of Daniels and Son Contracting.

It wasn't until Kathy saw the address of the contracting company that she began to put two and two together. She told her lawyer of her suspicions—Brian's father must have used his son's name to sign these contracts. The address for the company was his address in Miami. Her lawyer left to check on the details of Daniels and Son Contracting, but not before getting permission for Kathy to see Brian.

When she finally got to see her son, Kathy hugged him tightly. "They said I used the computer to set up a fake business, to take money from people. But I didn't. I didn't do anything, Mom," he protested. She could see that he was working hard to hold back tears.

"I believe you, honey," she told him. "We're working to figure this all out."

It wasn't until after midnight that the police, under pressure from the lawyer, allowed Brian to go home with his mother. Kathy didn't even try to hide her anger as she took her shaken son home. She was angry with the police for their callous treatment of an innocent thirteen-year-old and furious at her ex-husband for thoughtlessly exposing his son to this kind of trauma. As the story continued to unfold she became even more concerned about the lasting effects on her son's future.

The lawyer was able to determine that "Brian Daniels" had obtained a residential contractor's license from the Florida state board. The Social Security number used was Kathy's son's. But the business address and other information belonged to her ex-husband. The Dade County police issued a warrant for Hal Daniels but were unable to locate him at his previous residence. Bank deposits from potential clients had gone into a bank account in Hal's name, but the account had been emptied and closed within the past month. Her ex had all but disappeared, and the police were telling her that Brian was liable for all the complaints filed against the business in his name.

Determined to make her ex accountable, Kathy visited his old apartment and was able to convince the landlord to give her Hal's mail, which had been accumulating over the past few weeks. She was shocked to see that there were more than six credit cards, all in Brian's name—and all seriously past due.

Realizing the extent of the identity theft that had taken place, Kathy contacted the credit bureaus and placed a fraud alert on Brian's Social Security number. She knew that this would help prevent Hal from applying for additional credit in Brian's name. Thanks to his father's actions, Brian, at thirteen, had acquired a credit rating far below what would be considered average—or even fair. No one would ever consider Brian a good credit risk. Kathy began the long process of writing to the credit bureaus. Because Hal had used Brian's Social Security number, and theoretically still had access to any of Brian's bank accounts, Kathy had to close and reopen Brian's college savings accounts, which were held jointly in his name and hers. Each time she made a change in any financial matter, she had to deal with fraud-alert paperwork and requirements that kept anyone else from using Brian's Social Security number.

As she spent months trying to repair her son's credit and plan for those occasions when he would need to use his Social Security number for identification, Kathy also considered whether she should try to track down and prosecute her husband for fraud. In the end, she decided she could not spend the kind of money necessary to hire a private investigation firm to track him down. She had already stretched her budget to the limit with lawyer's fees to get Brian out of a mess that he had not created. But she realized her decision would mean that she would never have peace of mind. How could she know that her ex-husband wouldn't try to appropriate their daughter's identity?

And Kathy wasn't the only one suffering sleepless nights wondering how, or when, the family might be plunged back into the bureaucratic and financial disarray caused by her ex-husband's deception. In the wake of his experience with the police, Brian began having terrible nightmares. His schoolwork suffered, and he became withdrawn and suspicious. He began to see an expensive counselor who specialized in treating traumatized adolescents. Kathy still struggles with her feelings about their ordeal. "I'm his mom," she said helplessly. "It's my job to keep him safe. What happened to him could affect him throughout his adult life. What about when he applies for credit? Or tries to buy a car, or a home? What could I have done to protect him from this?"

HOW I WOULD HAVE COUNSELED KATHY

Unfortunately, identity thieves can strike close to home. In the case of Kathy, it was her ex-husband who used her son Brian's Social Security number and personal information to fraudulently create a new business and obtain credit in Brian's name.

Preventing this type of identity theft is difficult when it's an "inside job." However, I would counsel Kathy that some of the steps to prevent this type of occurrence from happening in the first place would be to place a fraud alert on Brian's credit profile and put a password and contact information in his credit profile in order to ensure that no new credit is fraudulently created in Brian's name. Putting a password on a juvenile's credit profile is a simple step any parent can take to protect a child's future credit rating. Brian doesn't need credit at age thirteen, but he will when he begins college, or turns eighteeen and wants to buy a car. To be perfectly safe, Kathy should do the same for her daughter.

Fraudulent charges usually have lots of friends. When you find one, assume that more are on the way. It can take time for an identity thief to apply for new credit accounts with credit card merchants and then start charging the accounts. The delay time can amount to thousands of dollars in charges coming in month after month.

Kathy should invest in a monthly credit monitoring service that will track an individual's credit profile and promptly notify that person if any new credit is issued under his or her name. Since Kathy's ex-husband probably knows her Social Security number and other personal information, I would recommend that Kathy obtain the service for Brian, her daughter, and herself. Kathy could also place a fraud alert on her credit profile and use a password and contact information as well. If the ex-husband would commit fraud against his own son, then it's not a stretch to think that Kathy might be his next victim. Better safe than sorry.

Kathy should both write and call each of the credit card merchants from whom her ex-husband obtained credit cards and notify them of the fraudulent accounts. These accounts should be closed, and the charges should all be disputed. Kathy should also send a letter to each of the credit reporting agencies disputing the credit card charges as fraudulent. Once credit card companies are contacted, they will provide you with paperwork in the form of a sworn affidavit that names the disputed charges. The credit card company will investigate the charges. Once the investigation is complete and the charges are confirmed as fraudulent, they will credit your card.

With regard to the criminal matter, Kathy should also file a police report verifying that Brian is the victim of identity theft and forward the report to the contractors' licensing board and the local police department that issued the warrant for the arrest of Brian's father. Kathy should obtain written verification of both the receipt of these documents and the resolution of this matter. Kathy should maintain these records, including making multiple copies, as this matter might come up many years later when Brian seeks employment, applies to colleges, applies for a loan, or seeks other financial assistance.

Even though Brian was a minor, he had the right not to speak with the police and the right to request the presence of a lawyer during any interrogation. In some states, a parent must be present during any interrogation by the police. Unless he was to be actually charged and arrested, Brian would have been free to leave the police station. In this case, the presence of an attorney greatly assisted Brian in being able to leave the police station. As with any criminal matter, I would strongly recommend that everyone immediately obtain an attorney to protect his or her rights from the beginning of any criminal issues. Remember that asking to have a lawyer is not incriminating. Don't assume that because you are innocent you'll be fine without legal advice. Ask to have a lawyer immediately, and don't talk to the police without one present.

With regard to the contractor's license, Kathy should ensure that the license is revoked and a notation is placed in the file verifying that the license was fraudulently created. Each state generally has its own licensing entity for contractors. Kathy should determine which licensing entity issued the fraudulent contractor's license and send the written request to this entity. Kathy should request written verification that Brian's name has been removed. Once again, Kathy should maintain these records.

I would also recommend that Kathy request a new Social Security number for Brian. Since Brian is relatively young, obtaining a new Social Security number could prevent his father from ever using Brian's information again. You may apply for a new Social Security number by calling the Federal Office of Social Security, explaining your situation, and following its instructions. Once you have a new number, make sure you change it on all relevant information, including payrolls, bank accounts, driver's license (in some states), employer files, credit cards, taxes and other financial records, and health and life insurance policies. Be sure you notify all these agencies in writing and then follow up with each of them by phone or e-mail to confirm that you have changed your Social Security number.

While this will cause additional paperwork for Kathy, this is a preventive step that she should consider, given the fact that Brian's father probably cannot be trusted to "forget" Brian's personal information.

Chapter 6

IDENTITY: WHAT YOU NEED TO KNOW

IDENTITY THEFT IS ONE OF THE FASTEST-GROWING CRIMES IN THE UNITED States today. Don't wait until you are caught up in the system. Being proactive can prevent you from having to experience years of bureaucratic nightmares. The following are steps you can take to prevent the theft of your identity:

GUARD YOUR CREDIT—IT'S YOUR GOOD NAME

Reporting Agencies

Your credit profile or history is your good name to creditors, employers, landlords, insurers, and other private and government agencies. Don't let an identity thief trash your good name. Your credit profile, including your credit score, is tracked by three credit reporting agencies. These agencies are:

Equifax
P.O. Box 740241

Atlanta, Georgia 30374–0241
(800) 525–6285
www.equifax.com

Experian
P.O. Box 9532
Allen, Texas 75013
(888) 397–3742
www.experian.com

TransUnion
Fraud Victim Assistance Division
P.O. Box 6790
Fullerton, California 92834–6790
(800) 680–7289
www.transunion.com

These credit reporting agencies monitor everyone's credit histories and are used by businesses and government agencies to determine the creditworthiness of an individual. Your credit score, which ranges from 300 to 850, can determine what interest rates you receive for a mortgage or a car loan, as well as what rates you're charged for health and automobile insurance. The higher your score, the better.

You should monitor your credit report at least once every year, as this is one of the best ways to check for any fraudulent activity. You are entitled to one free credit report from each of the three credit reporting agencies each year. You can obtain the free credit reports by calling Annual Credit Report request center at (877) 322–8228, or get them online at www.annualcreditreport.com.

If, after reviewing your free credit report, you suspect fraudulent activity, there are two types of fraud alerts that you can place on your credit file: either an initial alert or an extended alert. The initial alert lasts for ninety days, and the extended alert lasts for seven years. Both alerts are designed to notify businesses that they must verify your identity before issuing any new credit because you believe that you are or could be the victim of identity theft.

You can also put a contact telephone number on your credit report and require that any merchant or other business personally contact you at the telephone number listed before authorizing any new credit in your name.

Shred Happens

Identity thieves love garbage. Before discarding any personal financial information, always shred each document. All personal financial documents that you do intend to keep should be stored in a locked (preferably fire-safe) container or safe.

I recommend that you shred bank statements, credit card statements, mortgage statements, health/insurance documents, and any other papers that contain your address, Social Security number, and/or account numbers, as well as any other documents that list any personal financial information, including e-mail addresses, telephone numbers, and family information. With regard to paper shredders, I recommend the confetti-type shredder for maximum destruction of the document.

Even those preapproved applications for credit cards should be shredded instead of merely thrown into the garbage. Identity thieves can find these discarded applications, fill them out, and obtain credit in your name. You can opt out of receiving these preapproved applications, including a substantial amount of other junk mail, by calling (888)5OPTOUT [(888) 567–8688] and following the telephone prompts. In a few short months, you will stop receiving all that junk mail. Your mail carrier will thank you, too.

Give Yourself an Identity Checkup

Today, many employers will conduct background checks on a prospective employee to determine whether the job applicant has any criminal history or other issues of concern to the employer. Depending on the type of work, these checks can include more rigorous security clearance checks, including fingerprinting. The type of information that shows up on a background check includes not only information relating to your credit history, but also information relating to any lawsuits, bankruptcies, or criminal matters.

You can give yourself a background checkup by using one of the companies that collect information from various public databases and offer this information for sale. This type of background information is called a public information profile, or PIP. Some of these companies are listed in the References section in the back of this book. For a fee, often less than $100, you can obtain a background check on yourself. This can be a very useful tool to determine whether someone has used your name relating to the commission of a crime or whether your Social Security number is being used by someone else. Knowing this information will allow you to take proactive steps to correct any errors.

Avoid Electronic Invasions

Limit your telemarketing purchases, including items purchased from television ads or the Internet. Avoid using your checking account to make purchases over the telephone or Internet, as identity thieves can use your account information to drain your bank accounts. If you must make a purchase over the telephone or online, do so with a credit card for greater protection against identity theft. Credit cards contain limited personal information and offer a means to dispute and recoup false charges. Never give your Social Security number, mother's maiden name, account I.D.s, or passwords to any telemarketer or Internet merchant. No exceptions!

If you just can't say no when telemarketers call, then make sure they don't call you in the first place. Depending on where you live, you can place your telephone number on a "Do Not Call" list to protect you from scam artists who might be looking to steal your money or identity. You can put your telephone number on the "Do Not Call" list by going to www.donotcall.gov or by calling (888) 382–1222. Registering your number will prevent telemarketing calls for the next five years. Be particularly wary of calls or e-mails from people offering to protect you from identity theft; these are sometimes the very persons who are perpetrating the crime.

Travel Light and Call Ahead

Put your wallet or purse on a diet. For most people, their wallet or purse is an identity thief's starter kit. Don't make yourself an easy target. Carry only your driver's license and a single credit card in your purse or wallet; everything else can stay at home in a secure location. If you must carry additional cards, make a photocopy of all the items in your wallet, and keep the copy at home. In case of loss or theft, you'll have a handy list of the companies you need to notify. Never leave your wallet or purse in your vehicle or office. It may be convenient, but it's also convenient for the identity thief.

Never carry your Social Security card in your wallet or purse. This document is almost never needed (most people memorize their numbers), and it is the one piece of personal information that an identity thief can use to create a false identity in your name. Leave home without it!

Don't carry any other documents that might contain your Social Security number, such as your driver's license or health insurance cards. If your driver's license or health insurance card uses your Social Security number as your I.D. or account number, request new cards that use different numbers. If these cards are lost or stolen, or if you have been a victim of identity theft, you can request a new Social Security number by contacting the Social Security Administration (see the References section at the back of the book for contact information).

When you travel, call your credit card companies before you leave, and tell them where you're traveling and for how long you will be gone. This way, they can flag any transactions made in the city or country you were visiting after you've returned home, in case someone reached into a wastebasket or cash register and retrieved the carbon copy from the credit transaction. When identity theft happens in a foreign country, it can be very difficult to stop, even after you know it has occurred.

Make sure you scrutinize the charges listed on your credit card bills carefully. People often pay the charges without looking carefully at each individual charge. If you see a transaction you don't remember, check with the credit card company to verify that this is a charge you actually incurred. You generally have sixty days after the first bill with the error was mailed to make this correction.

Tell your credit card company not to authorize any transactions in excess of a specific amount, say $100, unless the cardholder can verify a secret password the credit card company keeps on file.

Don't keep a list of your passwords or PINs in your wallet or purse. This might sound obvious, but you'd be surprised at how many people do this. Never give out your passwords or PIN numbers to anyone.

DON'T BE A VICTIM: TAKE QUICK ACTION AGAINST IDENTITY THIEVES

If, despite your best efforts, you discover that you are the victim of identity theft, you should act immediately in order to minimize the damage and any financial losses. Here are the steps you should take after you have discovered you are the victim of identity theft:

FILE AN IDENTITY THEFT REPORT with your local police department detailing your true identity. Also file a theft report if your wallet, purse, or other items were stolen at the same time. Keep multiple copies of these reports, as you will need to send them to the credit reporting agencies, creditors, and other business or government agencies. You should also contact the attorney general's office of your state as well as the Federal Trade Commission. You can find information on how to contact these agencies in the References section at the back of this book.

CLOSE ALL YOUR FINANCIAL ACCOUNTS, including bank accounts, credit card accounts, and any other accounts that hold monies, such as investment accounts. Reopen any such accounts using new account numbers, new passwords, and other identifying information. Do not use commonly recognized passwords, such as your mother's maiden name, date of birth, or any easily identifiable number sequences. It is also a good idea to regularly change your passwords and PINs.

PLACE A FRAUD ALERT ON YOUR CREDIT PROFILE. This will enable you to obtain free credit reports from all three credit reporting agencies. Carefully review your credit reports for fraudulent activity. If you suspect that an account has been fraudulently used and/or an account was fraudulently created, contact the merchant immediately in writing. Keep copies of all correspondence.

KEEP RECORDS OF ALL ACCOUNTS that you believe to have been compromised by the identity thief, and communicate with any merchants, banks, credit companies, and law enforcement agencies in writing. Keep copies of all correspondence and notes relating to any such communications. Take notes during any telephone conversation, and send a letter to the other party confirming the substance of each telephone conversation.

NOTIFY THE SOCIAL SECURITY ADMINISTRATION AND YOUR LOCAL MOTOR VEHICLE DEPARTMENT that issued your driver's license that you are the victim of identity theft, so they will be on notice if someone requests duplicate or new identification cards or driver's licenses.

CONTACT A LAWYER SKILLED IN IDENTITY THEFT MATTERS if you find yourself unable to handle this process following the theft of your identity. Each state has a bar association that licenses attorneys. Most of them offer lawyer referral programs, whereby the public can contact the bar association and be provided with the names of attorneys in a given area who handle a particular type of legal matter, such as identity theft, criminal matters, or creditor's claims.

CONTACT YOUR INSURANCE AGENT to see whether your policy covers losses, including attorney's fees, incurred in relation to identity theft. Be sure you understand the coverage and limitations of such a policy.

Part II

LOVE, FAMILY, AND RELATIONSHIPS

How to Keep Your Head in Matters of the Heart

Everyone should learn how to protect their families, their loved ones, and themselves from destructive outside influences, internal strife, or the consequences of poor judgment. The legal system can help you build firewalls around yourself and bring order to chaos, if you use it properly. If you don't, it can come back to bite you.

Someone once said, "There's no fool like an old fool." I would add that perhaps there's no fool like someone in love. Love is grand—don't get me wrong—but when it comes to decision making, love can cloud judgment. Worse still are relationships in which love and money mix.

When we're in love, we think, "What's money, compared with love? Who cares? Money comes and goes, but love lasts forever."

Actually—sometimes not. While it's true that some romantic relationships are dissolved with a minimum of messiness, the truth is that one partner or the other often tries to exploit the other's sympathy or pain.

And whether a couple is married or not, when children are involved and custody and support issues must be addressed, the stakes can become even higher.

But it's not just relationships that are ending that have the potential for disaster. There are also plenty of sad cases in which predatory individuals take advantage of someone else's heart. Yet, you don't have to be evil or amoral to do something stupid in the name of love. You just have to be in love, and who doesn't want that? In this second section we'll look at the whole spectrum of mistakes we can make in the name of love, romance, and family.

Chapter 7

CHILD CUSTODY RIGHTS

VIKTOR KARNOVICH STILL SPOKE WITH THE STRONG INTONATIONS OF HIS native Russia. Growing up in Vladivostok, a major Russian port city, he had spent his whole life working on docks and boats. But now, recovering from a recent hospitalization, his powerful longshoreman's build was wasted, and his gray hair and the deep lines around his haunted eyes made him look much, much older than his forty-six years.

For more than seven years, Viktor had been engaged in an interstate custody battle for his oldest daughter, a child he had fathered out of wedlock and, ironically, lost custody of because of his strong belief in the importance of family.

He had moved to the United States from Russia when he was just twenty. He'd quickly found work on the oil tankers that moved in and out of the port city of Newark, New Jersey. He'd been married in his early twenties and had obtained his green card. When the marriage ended a few years later, there were no hard feelings. He and his ex-wife both agreed that they were just too young to be married.

Viktor didn't spend much time mourning the end of his marriage. After all, he was a handsome man and made good money. When the time was right, he had no doubt that he'd find the right woman, settle down, and begin a large family. In the meantime, he signed on to shipboard jobs and traveled all around the United States. His trouble began while he was working on ships for an oil company that sailed from Newark to New Orleans.

"I was not even thirty, you know," he said. "Out having a good time on Bourbon Street, when I met the most beautiful woman." One thing led to another, and soon he was spending all his shore leave with Elizabeth Burns. To his amazement and delight, Lizzie was from New Jersey herself. Smart, beautiful, and from a good family, she'd grown up in the comfortable middle-class suburb of Montclair, only about twenty minutes from Newark, and her parents lived there still.

When Lizzie became pregnant, Viktor proposed immediately. But she turned him down, telling him that she just wasn't ready to commit to marriage. Viktor was willing to be patient, but he was concerned about Lizzie. Her behavior became bizarre. Sometimes she failed to meet him when she knew he would be in New Orleans. Other times she was moody, often weeping for no reason or picking a screaming fight. Finally, he convinced her to return to New Jersey with him. Even if she wouldn't marry him, she could be with her parents until the baby was born, and then they could figure out what to do.

But Lizzie's family hardly welcomed them with open arms. In fact they were shocked to see her at all. Her mother and father told Viktor coldly that Lizzie had mental health problems and a history of drug abuse. They made clear their relief that the two hadn't married. Frankly, they said, they wanted nothing to do with either Lizzie or Viktor.

Viktor convinced Lizzie to move into his small apartment in Newark. When their daughter was born, Lizzie showed no interest in motherhood. Viktor named the baby Anna, after his own mother. He took a leave from the shipping company and cared for the baby in his small apartment, not knowing where Lizzie was from night to night.

When Lizzie began to talk about going back to New Orleans, he told her he wanted to raise the baby. Lizzie agreed, and they went before a family court judge in Newark. On the basis of Lizzie's mental state and her willingness to relinquish custody, and Viktor's strong community ties and excellent work record, the court adjudicated him as the custodial parent.

Viktor delighted in his child, and she in him. One of his most treasured possessions is a picture of him holding a fair-haired smiling toddler on his shoulders. Although Anna was just four at the time, the family resemblance is striking. It's the last picture of Viktor with his daughter.

After Anna was born, Viktor took early shift work, rushing home from the docks to pick her up at day care. The money wasn't as good, but they were managing to get by. Just before Anna's fourth birthday, Viktor received a call from Joe Burns, Lizzie's father.

"My wife and I, we'd like to get to know our granddaughter," the older man said. "I suppose it's the only way we can share in our daughter's life, be a family again."

Despite his memory of the icy reception he had received years earlier, Viktor was touched. He brought his daughter over to the comfortable house where Lizzie had grown up and introduced her to her grandparents. To their credit, Lizzie's parents seemed to dote on the little girl. Soon they were watching her some weekends, allowing Viktor to pick up extra money by working overtime shifts.

Viktor was grateful for the help and happy that his daughter knew her grandparents. He even began to think of Lizzie's parents as if they had been his in-laws. Sometimes, stopping by to pick Anna up after work, he'd sit on the wide porch of their house overlooking the neat lawn and flowerbeds and have a beer with Joe. They'd talk man to man. Joe encouraged Viktor to think about his daughter's future. He stressed how important it was for Viktor to be able to provide for the little girl. He repeatedly said that nothing was too good for his only granddaughter.

These talks always made Viktor vaguely uneasy. He sensed that Joe wasn't impressed with the modest apartment they lived in and that he worried about Anna growing up in a city like Newark.

During one of these talks, Viktor mentioned that he'd seen an internal posting for a job aboard one of his company's tankers. The money was good, he told Joe. Viktor was sorry he couldn't take it. The next time Viktor dropped Anna at her grandparents' house, Joe took him aside. "I've been talking to my wife," he said. "And we'd like to help you." Joe offered to take care of Anna full time while Viktor took the assignment aboard the ship.

At first Viktor didn't like the thought of being away from his daughter, but the more he thought about it, the more it made sense. He could earn much more money, and Anna was very happy at her grandparents' house. He accepted Joe's generous offer and left the next week on a three-week trip.

When he returned, Anna was delighted to see him, but full of news of the kitten her grandparents had gotten for her and the new dresses her grandmother had picked out for her. Her visit was so successful that Viktor was happy to let her stay a second time, and then a third. Soon it became a matter of course for Viktor to be away for several weeks and for Anna to stay with her grandparents during that time.

Several weeks before Anna's fifth birthday, she said something that disturbed Viktor: "Mommy said she'd be coming with a birthday present for me soon." Viktor hadn't been aware that Lizzie had been talking to Anna, but with further questioning, it became apparent that they talked frequently while Anna was staying with her grandparents. He was annoyed that Joe and Betty had never informed him. In fact, he felt betrayed that they had decided to repair their relationship with their daughter without including him. He vowed to talk about it with them when he returned from this next trip.

When he arrived at Joe and Betty's house the weekend before Anna's birthday, Joe, instead of Anna, met him at the door. "Sorry, Viktor, Anna won't be going home with you. Not today. Not ever," he said shortly. Viktor stood there, stunned. Joe spat out, "Now get out of here before I have you arrested for trespassing." And he slammed the door in Viktor's face.

Viktor didn't want to make a scene while Anna was in the house, so after talking with several friends, he hired a lawyer to write a letter to Joe and Betty. What the lawyer found was shocking.

While Viktor had been away working on the ship, Joe had gone behind his back to a judge and claimed that Viktor had abandoned Anna. Joe and his wife filed a claim for emergency custody in the superior court. The claim was rushed through so quickly that Viktor suspected that Joe had called in some favors from old lawyer friends and retired politicians to influence the judge.

Victor went on to say that although there had been several court hearings, he'd never been present because all the notices had been addressed to him in care of Joe's home, and all the hearings had been scheduled for times when he was aboard the ship. The lawyer was able to find out that an employee of the New Jersey Division of Youth and Family Services had tried to locate Viktor but had found his apartment empty for weeks at a time and the child in the care of the grandparents.

Viktor showed his lawyer the ruling naming him the custodial parent, but according to his lawyer, that ruling had been overturned. Using his entire savings as a retainer to hire the lawyer, Viktor initiated a countersuit to regain custody. At the first hearing, he stood enraged as Joe's attorney testified that Viktor had simply dropped the little girl at Joe's house and was gone for weeks at a time before returning to see her. He said that Joe regularly saw Viktor drinking when he came to visit the child and painted Viktor as not much more than a vagabond, returning to a shabby rental apartment after weeks of carousing in different ports.

None of this was true, of course. Viktor loved his daughter and had cared for her as a single father for more than three years before Joe and his wife had made their offer to help take care of their granddaughter.

But Viktor thought he knew how the judge might compare the two men in front of him: the caring grandfather from a comfortable suburban environment, who was active in local politics and obviously well educated, and the longshoreman with a trace of a Russian accent who spent his days on the docks of Newark and aboard ships.

When Joe's lawyer requested a restraining order that would keep Viktor away from Joe's home in Montclair, and the judge granted it, Viktor felt that he didn't stand a chance of getting his daughter back.

Even his lawyer told him his case looked hopeless. When the retainer had been spent and the lawyer informed him that he'd need an additional $15,000 up front to continue the case, Viktor had no idea where he could get that kind of money. He dropped the suit. He consoled himself as well as he could, telling himself that his daughter was well taken care of. But he missed her and was very angry at Betty and Joe.

Viktor still tried to keep an eye on Anna, sometimes driving by the house to see whether he could spot her in the yard or on the way to school. He wondered what her grandparents could be telling her, what reasons they were giving for her father's seeming abandonment of her.

The constant stress and worry took its toll. Viktor began to have trouble sleeping. He suffered from chest pains and horrible stomachaches. Several months passed, and on one of his "drive-bys" past the Burns's house, he saw a moving van parked in the driveway. Forgetting the restraining order, Viktor slammed on the brakes, jumped from his car, and demanded to know where Joe was.

"The family's already left, man," the driver of the moving van said. "They flew down to Texas ahead of us. We've got to meet them in Dallas tomorrow."

That day Viktor's stomach pains were so intense that he collapsed at work, and an ambulance was called to take him to the emergency room. He was hospitalized for treatment of severe ulcers. When he got out of the hospital he began trying to locate his daughter. He wrote to Family Services and explained the situation; he wrote to the judge who had ruled against him; he wrote to senators, congressmen, even the mayor of Newark. He began writing letters to officials and legislators in Florida. Seized by an unaccustomed feeling of helplessness, he wrote a letter to the FBI, accusing Joe Burns of kidnapping.

Viktor's health continued to deteriorate, and he was forced to take an early retirement from his job. His union pension wasn't nearly as much as his salary. The only bright spot in his life was his new wife, who soon became pregnant and gave birth to their daughter and, a few years later, their son. Viktor brightened when spoke of his new family, but just for a moment. "If only Anna could meet her brother and sister," he said quietly.

The final straw, Viktor said, was when a letter arrived from the attorney general of the State of Texas, informing him that Lizzie Burns had filed a claim for past-due and ongoing child support. It had been seven years since Viktor had lost custody of his daughter. He felt he had been blocked at every possible turn and was out of ideas. "There is nothing I want more than to see this terrible injustice put right," he said. "I have done nothing wrong, and yet I am the one being punished."

HOW I WOULD HAVE COUNSELED VIKTOR

As parents we strive to provide for our children, protect them, and give them a better life than our own. Viktor was guilty of these noble ambitions. Unfortunately, while Viktor only wanted to provide the best for his young daughter, Anna, his attempt at making a better life for her only resulted in his losing custody and, ultimately, all contact with Anna.

Viktor's story highlights a central theme that guides courts in determining child custody matters—it's the time you spend with your children, not the money, that really counts. Although Viktor devotedly attended to Anna's needs until she was three years old, he lost his way when he began routinely taking extended absences on board a ship in order to make extra money for Anna. Before this time, Viktor was working the early shift and was always there to pick up Anna from day care. Viktor didn't need to be a rich parent; he just needed to be a parent who attended to his daughter and was there for her.

As a general rule, a court will determine issues involving the custody of a child by what is in the best interests of the child. It is arguable that leaving a very young child alone for weeks at a time, without either her mother or her father, is not in the best interests of the child. Viktor had placed more importance on earning more money for Anna than on being there day to day to raise her.

While Viktor had the benefit of the initial order granting him sole custody of Anna, this did not ensure that, at some later time, a subsequent court might find that Viktor was not the appropriate custodial parent. A common misconception of custodial parents is that once a court initially determines child custody issues, this custody determination will remain the same until the child reaches the age of majority. This is never the case. Whenever custody has been an issue, there is always a chance the dispute can resurface. Therefore, parents or guardians in this situation should remain aware of how their behavior could look in court.

Generally, child custody determinations are always subject to later review and modification based on a change in circumstances of the child's needs or the custodial parent's living, work, and/or social circumstances. Types of change can include drug and alcohol abuse, physical abuse, loss of employment, neglect, and any number of other issues that may arise with the custodial parent. The court will consider any change and its impact on what is in the best interests of the child.

If I had been counseling Viktor prior to his decision to begin accepting the lengthy ocean voyages, I would have advised him that such a course of action could jeopardize his custody of Anna. While Anna was with her grandparents, it could be argued that routinely leaving her for weeks at a time was very difficult for such a young child. A young child needs a stable home. As Viktor traveled more and more, the only stability Anna had was with her grandparents.

Since Viktor had managed to successfully raise Anna until the age of three without needing to go on these long ocean voyages, a court may be inclined to rule that Viktor's extended absences were not in the best interests of the child. I would have recommended that Viktor not take these trips.

Notwithstanding, it does appear that Anna's grandparents made misrepresentations to the court and deceived Viktor about their interests in Anna. If I were counseling Viktor, I would advise him to file legal papers with the Texas court in the jurisdiction where Anna currently resides. Viktor should, at a minimum, seek an order for regular visitation. While Viktor may have to spend money on travel arrangements to visit with Anna or arrange for Anna to travel to New Jersey for visitation, this course of action would enable Viktor to once again be with his daughter. Viktor is entitled to have regular visitation with Anna.

I would also advise Viktor to seek information relating to Lizzie's current mental health condition and whether Lizzie is currently using drugs and/or alcohol. These factors were extremely relevant when Viktor initially obtained custody of Anna. These same factors are also critical in determining whether there is a change of circumstances that would support a modification in the custodial arrangement. Furthermore, since Viktor is now married and has a more stable home life, this could also support a change in the custody arrangement.

I would strongly urge Viktor to retain an attorney in child custody matters in the jurisdiction where Anna resides. Child custody matters are extremely contentious and are fraught with special rules and procedures. An attorney will be able to properly jump through these legal hoops. Don't go it alone.

While Viktor may not have custody of Anna, or even a current visitation order, he is still responsible for supporting Anna until she reaches the age of majority. Viktor should not ignore the letter from the child support agency. He will need to make arrangements for the prompt and continued payment of any past and future child support. Failure to pay child support can lead to civil penalties and even jail time.

Chapter 8

CHILD SUPPORT FRAUD

It took Mike Flores and his current wife several years and cost them tens of thousands of dollars to prove that the child support he was paying to his ex-wife was for a child that didn't exist. In a case that made national headlines, Mike, a California corrections officer, had paid his ex-wife $20,000 in court-ordered child support before he was finally able to expose the unbelievable saga of mind-boggling fraud and incompetence of several government agencies.

After twenty-three years of marriage, things had gone pretty sour for Mike. Over the years, he'd come to realize that his ex-wife had spent most of their marriage manipulating him—and everyone else she came into contact with. He felt he had been used, and he was glad the marriage was over. He pointed out that he was still relatively young. It wasn't too late to start his life over.

The divorce wasn't friendly. Mike's wife, Angela, was bitter and vindictive. She moved out, convincing the couple's nineteen-year-old daughter, Carla, to move in with her and poisoning her attitude toward her father. Mike was dismayed. He'd never been anything but a supportive husband and father. Eventually he resigned himself to the fact that his ex-wife was going to make the end of their marriage as miserable as she possibly could.

But Mike never expected his ex to be able to turn his world upside down the way she did. As the case unwound, however, it seemed that Angela had been out to get Mike from the moment the divorce became final. The first indicator came when Mike received notice of his first payment of child support. The $300 per month child support he had agreed to had somehow become $800. When he protested the increase, a district court judge reviewed the original court document and determined that it had been altered. He ordered Mike to go back to paying $300 per month as agreed.

Mike assumed that would be the end of it. Angela had tried one last manipulation—and failed. He figured that as long as he made his child support payments on time, he'd never hear from her again.

But Mike had no idea what was in store for him over the next few years.

In December, the month when the child support payments went back to the original $300 per month, Angela informed the court that she had given birth to a daughter three months earlier, in September. She claimed that Mike had gotten her pregnant in the months before their divorce.

"I was shocked," Mike recalled. He told the court that there was no way he could have been the father. Not only had he had a vasectomy more than ten years earlier, but others recalled that Angela had chosen to have her tubes tied after the birth of her first daughter. It certainly seemed impossible that they could have conceived a child in the months just before their divorce. "I didn't see how anyone could take Angela's story seriously," Mike said.

Instead, the court ordered paternity tests. Mike and Angela both submitted saliva for a DNA sample. And Angela provided a swab from Mike's alleged infant daughter. The genetic testing company concluded that the parents of the child being tested were indeed Mike and Angela Flores.

Mike was completely puzzled by this outcome until the day he received the bill for the processing of his DNA sample. Although the bill was made out to him, it said that the money was due for the account of Carla Flores, his nineteen-year old-daughter. When he confronted Angela, she said that it was probably a billing error and accused him of trying to get out of his responsibilities.

Mike refused to pay child support, and Angela refused to provide the baby's birth certificate. A family court judge broke the deadlock by requiring a second round of DNA sampling. The result of the second round of testing was the same as the first: the individual being tested was the child of Mike and Angela Flores.

By now it was clear to Mike that something was not right. There was no doubt in his mind that he was not the father of this child. He hired a private detective to look into the details of Angela's story, and he continued to protest that he could not possibly have fathered a child. But according to the court, the DNA results were indisputable. Just a few months after Angela first made the claim of paternity, Mike was ordered to begin paying child support for his new daughter, Dominique.

Another person might have accepted the "facts" as the court insisted they existed. But Mike had spent years working in law enforcement, and he knew that the system wasn't always in the right. He continued to dispute the child support order, insisting that he had not had a child with Angela. But now Angela countered with documentation: a Social Security number, a Medicaid card—all in baby Dominique's name. The paperwork went into the system, and the system ground on, doing its job relentlessly.

The state human services child enforcement agency garnished Mike's paycheck, forcing him to pay the amount due each month. Mike appealed to the agency, asking to be shown its copy of the birth certificate for the child he was sure didn't exist. The agency said it would contact Angela and order her to bring the child and produce the birth certificate. When Mike asked about the outcome, the agency told him the investigation was closed. Instead of helpful information, all he received was a letter that read, in part, "We cannot help you any further in getting a copy of the birth certificate, but your daughter does exist, as I am sure you already knew."

As far as the child enforcement agency was concerned, it had a simple job to do: enforce an order from a judge. No doubt the agency didn't waste a moment considering whether there was a case to be made for this deadbeat dad. All the "evidence" pointed to him as the father, the court had ruled on the evidence, and it was the agency's job to make sure he didn't shirk his responsibilities to his ex-wife and their newest child.

That year, Mike's tax refund went toward meeting his child support. He'd been fighting to get someone to listen to him for over two years. He was fortunate that his new wife believed in him and was willing to stand by him as he doggedly pursued his right not to be victimized by the system.

When he got the report from the private detective he had hired, he began to put together the pieces of Angela's elaborate deception. The report suggested that the DNA samples had most likely come from Mike's daughter Carla. Furthermore, Carla had worked at the hospital, where a record of the baby's birth had been entered into the computer and faxed to the department of vital statistics. This hospital record and a baptismal certificate for the baby may have been the pieces of paperwork that let Angela obtain the other official documents. Unlike cases of stolen identity, Mike's disturbed ex-wife had created an identity out of thin air.

"I was trying to go on with my life," he said. "I had remarried, and my new wife didn't deserve to go without because of this lie. I didn't want her to have to live with all the threats and demands for payments. But I wasn't the father, and I wasn't giving in without a real fight."

Mike kept hammering away at the system that had let him down. He contacted news outlets, telling reporters about his unbelievable situation. Finally, five years after Mike's nightmare began, a reporter at a local news station took an interest in the bizarre tale.

Embarrassed by the attention, and no doubt desperate to prove that no injustice had occurred, the state court ordered Angela Flores to show up in court—and to bring her daughter, now about five years old, with her.

The court date was a media circus and a long-awaited vindication for Mike. Angela showed up, all right, but with a two-year-old toddler she had "borrowed" from a stranger just moments before her case was scheduled to be heard. Mike watched with a mixture of relief, anger, and pity as his ex-wife was arrested and the judge finally declared that five-year-old Dominique Flores had never existed.

Despite national attention and an investigation initiated by the governor, Mike Flores remains $20,000 poorer. His new marriage began and continued throughout this nightmare and though his wife was supportive, the stress was always present. And it could have been worse. If Mike had fallen behind on his payments, he could have been sent to jail. The system had worked against him every step of the way. Without his deep conviction that he was in the right and without his persistence in proving it, a bad situation might have been much, much worse.

HOW I WOULD HAVE COUNSELED MIKE

Part of being a responsible parent is providing for your children and ensuring that their needs are properly met. It's not just the morally correct thing to do—it's the law. When a divorce or separation occurs, this responsibility does not cease. In fact, often the responsibility increases because of the financial demands associated with maintaining two residences for the child. Of course, being a responsible parent does not mean providing for a child that does not exist, and that was Mike's problem.

While the dilemma that Mike confronted was extreme—his ex-wife, Angela, had "created" a fictitious child in order to fraudulently obtain child support payments—this situation is not without a close relative. A similar situation can occur when an ex-wife or ex-lover incorrectly claims that the child she gave birth to, and actually does exist, is your child in order to obtain court-ordered child support payments. The results can be the same: the man may be obligated to make child support payments for a child that is not his.

In any case in which the parentage of a child is disputed, I would advise the purported father to promptly obtain DNA testing to verify the actual parentage of the child. Provided the testing is done correctly, DNA testing should conclusively confirm or deny the parentage of the child. Either you're the father, or you're not.

In almost all cases, DNA testing will resolve the issue of the father's obligation to make child support payments. Today, courts generally accept these DNA test results as evidence of the true parentage of the child. As Mike found out, courts are reluctant to discredit the validity of proper DNA testing.

Unfortunately, in Mike's case, even DNA testing did not clear him from being ordered to pay child support for a "child" who did not exist. Angela cleverly obtained the DNA from Mike's true daughter, Carla, to fake the test results. The DNA testing correctly identified Carla as Mike's daughter. Since neither Mike nor the court was aware of the deception, Mike was properly ordered to begin paying child support payments for his "child."

Confronted with DNA testing confirming the parentage of a child, almost all courts and child support agencies will seek both the payment and enforcement of a child support order against the person identified in the DNA testing as the biological father. Mike needed another answer.

If I were counseling Mike, I would have advised him that while his persistent efforts in seeking additional DNA testing, hiring a private investigator, and repeatedly requesting copies of the "child's" birth certificate were good initial steps, his best course of action was far more simple. He should spend the afternoon with his "child."

Generally, the payment of child support is not a requirement for you to obtain reasonable visitation with your child. In ruling on matters involving the welfare of a child, courts are generally guided by the principle of what is in the best interests of the child. It is in the best interests of a child to visit and interact with both of his or her parents, regardless of whether the parent is current or behind in child support payments.

Assuming there are no issues of child abuse or neglect, parents are generally permitted regular unsupervised visitation with their children. Mike should have sought an order from the court requiring Angela to produce his "child" to him for regular visitation periods.

While the court was within its right to order Mike to make child support payments, based upon the fraudulent—albeit correct—DNA test results, the court would have permitted Mike reasonable visitation with his "child." If I had been representing Mike, I would have requested during the initial court proceedings that the court order Mike immediate and reasonable visitation with his "child." This tactic would have required Angela to promptly produce Mike's "child" for reasonable visitation periods. Since Angela would have been unable to do this, her fraud would have been uncovered much sooner and at much less expense to Mike in time, money, and aggravation.

Mike's case illustrates an important point relating to a parent's child support obligations. Until the child reaches the age of majority, and in some cases for several years afterward, a parent is required to provide monetary support for the child. Whether the parent exercises visitation or not, the child support obligations continue. Reimbursement for any past due child support payments may be taken from a paycheck, withheld from an income tax refund, and/or cause the suspension of licenses and other privileges. In some instances, a person can be jailed for not paying child support. Generally, even the filing of bankruptcy does not discharge a person's obligation to make past or current support payments.

I would advise Mike to seek an order from the court requiring the reimbursement by Angela of all child support payments Mike was forced to make for his "child," including all expenses associated with proving that baby Dominique did not exist. Depending on the state, I would request that the payment be in the form of reimbursement to

Mike for child support payments, wherein Angela would be subject to the same obligations and penalties for failing to pay the child support payments to Mike. After all, considering that Mike continued to make payments in good faith, despite everything he and his new family were put through, it would only be fair.

Chapter 9

BLINDED BY LOVE AND TAKEN FOR A RIDE

MILTON AND HIS WIFE, SONDRA, HAD MOVED TO LAS VEGAS WHEN THEY sold their successful Dunkin' Donuts franchise up north and took early retirement. They didn't have a lot of savings, but they'd made a good profit on the sale of their business, and Sondra had inherited some property in Las Vegas when her father died a few years earlier. They agreed that if they were careful with their money, they'd be able to enjoy a comfortable life. They moved into one of Sondra's properties, a stucco house on Mendoza Court, a family-oriented street in a nice neighborhood near the center of town.

Not long after they'd settled in to their new home, Sondra told Milton that she felt too young to just retire, and she set about making herself even busier than when they had been small business owners. She joined a health club, got a golf club membership, and took up tennis. She and some other women formed a book club that met twice a month, and it wasn't long before she was out of the house more than she was at home.

At least that's how it felt to Milton, who began to fill up his empty time with visits to the casinos. He played a little blackjack a few mornings a week and liked to bet on the NASCAR races, maybe play a little golf. He got into the habit of going to one of the local casinos on the nights when Sondra was out with her girlfriends. It was better than going home to an empty house, and he came to enjoy the status and special treatment that came with being a regular customer. It was at a casino that he met Rachel.

Rachel was redheaded, long-legged, and about fifteen years younger than Milton. She told him she had recently relocated to Las Vegas from Chicago. She said she'd been a broker for a big commercial real estate firm and had gotten burned out on the job. She had some savings and was bartending just enough to get by while she jump-started her career in Vegas, she told him. Milton found himself looking forward to his chats with Rachel. She was sharp and liked to talk about business. Milton felt energized when he was around her.

Before long, he was swinging by to pick her up after her shift and take her out to a late dinner. He'd offer her career advice, and they'd talk for hours about the market and the potential in neighborhoods around them. Milton told Rachel she made him feel ten years younger, and Rachel admitted that she found Milton's knowledge and experience to be very sexy. "It had been a long time since anyone had told me that," he laughed. "How could I resist?"

At Rachel's urging, Milton finally confessed to Sondra about his affair. She immediately asked for a divorce. Milton felt so bad about how he had treated his wife that he quitclaimed any interest in her investment properties. They divided up their finances, and Sondra, in what Milton admitted was an incredibly gracious and generous act, deeded him the house in which they had lived on Mendoza Court.

Sondra moved out, and Milton quickly moved Rachel in. For the next two years, life felt exciting to Milton. Rachel cut back on her shifts at the bar, saying she would rather spend time with him before she jumped back into restarting her career, which she was sure would be very high-pressured. And Milton agreed, wanting to keep her to himself for as long as he could. He knew Rachel didn't make much on the shifts she worked, and he wanted her to have nice things. Though they never talked about whether he would support her, they opened a joint checking account, and he named Rachel as authorized user on his credit cards.

"I never knew what a pretty girl like her saw in an old guy like me," Milton confessed. "But we were very happy together in those days." In the back of his mind, he worried that she'd find someone younger or more successful. So he bought her gifts: a new Caddy that she titled in her name, furniture for the house that she had admired, and jewelry.

What Milton didn't know was that Rachel was being very generous with herself as well.

After they had been together about two years, Rachel began spending less time with Milton. She told him she was taking night classes to get her real estate license in Las Vegas and needed to quit her shifts at the bar. She moved his things down to the guest bedroom at the end of the hall, telling him that his snoring was keeping her awake and making her too tired to focus on her studies.

About this time she first suggested that he refinance the house. "She told me that she'd been watching how hot the market had become since she had first moved to the neighborhood—and that we were sitting on a gold mine," Milton said. He figured that since Rachel had been in the real estate business, he ought to take her advice. Milton refinanced the house, taking out a substantial amount of cash, which he deposited into their joint checking account. He was so pleased with Rachel's advice that he bought her an expensive chandelier that he knew she had been wanting for the dining room. "She was very affectionate in her thanks," he said, and he admitted that this was a change in her behavior, which had become very distant.

Over the next three years, Milton refinanced the house two more times, always at Rachel's urging. After each refinancing, she'd go on a buying spree for things for the house: a flat-screen TV for her bedroom, a new entertainment center for the living room, a hot tub for the outside patio. If Milton complained, she accused him of being ungrateful for her advice and efforts and would be very cold to him.

Milton didn't know what to do. He loved Rachel, but he didn't know how to make things go back to the way they were when they had first met. He became depressed and uncertain about their future together.

When Rachel suggested refinancing the house for a fourth time, Milton was shocked to find his application turned down. His credit report showed that his cards were maxed out—he was more than $50,000 in debt and behind on several payments. When he confronted Rachel about her credit card use, she became very angry.

Rachel screamed and sobbed and accused Milton of not trusting her. She told him that she knew he had just used her for sex and that he had never wanted her to better her life. Milton was stunned. He told Rachel that none of that was true. He asked her how he could prove to her that he still loved her, that he only wanted what was best for both of them.

Rachel told Milton that they could refinance the house one more time and pay off the credit card debt, but that he would have to put the title of the house in her name because she had a good credit rating. "She told me she had a friend at the title agency who could push things through for us, that it was just a matter of paperwork. She promised that once we used the money from the refinancing to pay off the credit card debt, she'd be careful about her spending," Milton said.

Milton signed the paperwork, which included a grant, bargain, and sale deed, and passed the title on the house to Rachel. As she had promised, the refinancing sailed through. Again, they deposited the money from the refinancing in their joint account, and Rachel promised to pay off all the credit cards immediately. Milton celebrated by taking them out for a luxurious dinner at the most expensive restaurant on the strip. Rachel moved his things back into their bedroom, and it seemed almost like old times again.

Milton was relieved that he had been able to save the relationship that had meant so much to him. Rachel was being affectionate and sweet to him again—right up until the day he came home and found his clothing and possessions stuffed into trash bags and piled on the lawn. He tried to open the front door, but it was locked, and his key no longer worked. Using the garage door opener inside his car, he was shocked to find the garage filled with a weight bench, pool table, and suitcases and boxes full of men's clothing.

Rachel came to the door and shouted at him. "She had a box with all my toiletries in it," Milton said. "And some huge guy was standing behind her inside the house."

Rachel introduced the stranger as her boyfriend, shoved the box at Milton, and told him to get out of her house. Fighting back the urge to strangle her, and cursing loud enough to bring the neighbors to their windows, Milton stuffed his belongings into the trunk of his car and left.

For a few weeks he stayed with friends. Rachel gave the creditors his cell phone number, and they began hounding him for overdue payments. She had never paid off the credit cards, and the debt had grown to surpass $60,000. The money in their joint checking account was nearly all withdrawn, although the account remained open. Milton was forced to hire a bankruptcy attorney to negotiate a payment plan with his creditors. His depression worsened, and he sought clinical treatment. He decided to fight to get back his house and whatever he could of the money Rachel had blown through over the course of their relationship. Drawing on his last resource, he cashed out two of his IRAs and retained lawyers to file a complaint.

"I don't know what will happen to me. I have no house, no savings, no credit. But you know what is almost worse?" he said sadly. "I believed she loved me as much as I loved her. How could I have been so blind?"

HOW I WOULD HAVE COUNSELED MILTON

Don't be a Milton. The easiest lesson to learn from Milton's story is not to cheat on your wife. The more practical lesson to learn is to be very careful spending significant amounts of money on someone, or giving someone access to your money, when you really don't know the person. It's easy to get carried away in a romance. Don't let your hard-earned money and assets get carried away too.

Share your heart, but keep your money separate. Unless you're married or in some other type of legally recognized relationship, I would strongly recommend against placing any money into either a joint account or an account to which your romantic partner has access. This would include checking and savings accounts, credit accounts, investment accounts, and, as with Milton, transferring ownership in a house.

Milton's story highlights an important point. Many people ignore their monthly bank and credit card statements. While most people will check to see what is owed on their credit cards, many people fail to check each charge to ensure that it is accurate or to track their monthly purchases. Milton would not have been surprised by Rachel's excessive spending—over $50,000 worth—or that she had failed to pay the monthly bills had he been diligently monitoring his monthly credit card statements.

If I had counseled Milton before he lost everything to Rachel's excessive spending, I would have advised him that unless he was willing to separate his romantic self from his financial self, he would not stop "wanting her to have nice things" until he was broke. Given Rachel's history of excessive spending, there was no reason to believe that with each successive refinancing of Milton's house she would curtail her spending. She was clearly in the relationship for the money.

I have counseled numerous older clients, both men and women, in Milton's situation. In the majority of the cases, these older men and women spend and continue to spend their life savings on their new younger love interests based on a desire to either show their newfound love a nice lifestyle or to keep the younger person interested in the relationship. Don't be a Milton. If the relationship is only as good as the last gift, how real is the relationship?

While giving relationship advice appears to be outside the job description of an attorney, surprisingly, much of the law is based on relationships and the interaction between the parties to relationships. Married couples, business partners, and even next-door neighbors share special relationships to which the law applies certain legal principles in deciding the rights and obligations of each party. Because Milton was not married to Rachel, much, if not all, of the money and property Milton gave her would be considered gifts.

If I had counseled Milton after he had lost everything, which is usually the point when a person first seeks the assistance of an attorney, I would have regretfully had to tell him that generally a person does not have any obligation to return a gift. Almost everything Milton gave Rachel, including, for example, the Cadillac, were gifts. Milton had no expectation that Rachel would return these items to him. There is little, if anything, Milton could do to seek the return of these items.

However, I would advise Milton to promptly close all joint bank accounts and remove Rachel as an authorized user on any credit accounts. I would also advise Milton to change the addresses, account numbers, and passwords on any bank or credit accounts, including any retirement or investment accounts. Unless Milton were to remove Rachel as an authorized user from his accounts, she could continue to incur charges that Milton would be obligated to pay.

As for the house, generally oral agreements regarding the transfer of an interest in a house are not valid. When it comes to real property, such as a house or land, courts generally require that any agreement be in writing and signed by the person against whom you are seeking enforcement of the agreement. This legal concept, described as the statute of frauds, is designed to prevent fraudulent sales or transfers of real property without the written consent of the original owner.

In Milton's case, he relied on the advice of Rachel, who was supposedly a commercial real estate broker, in agreeing, without a written contract, to transfer the house to Rachel's name in order to secure the fourth refinancing of the house. This "agreement" was required to be in writing. While the "agreement" was required to be in writing, nevertheless, I would advise Milton to sue Rachel for fraud and other equitable forms of relief under the legal theory that Rachel's promise regarding the retransfer of the house back to Milton was made fraudulently and was merely designed to enable her to take Milton's house for herself.

Separately, while Rachel may have legal "title" to the house, Milton appears to be the only person on the mortgage. Milton is paying for a house he does not own. In addition to the lawsuit, I would recommend that Milton place a certain type of lien on the house. The lien is called a *lis pendens*. However, in most states, you must file a lawsuit at the same time, for the lien to be legally effective. This type of lien affects the title on the house and makes it difficult to sell by giving notice to potential buyers that there is a dispute on the property. By doing this, Milton could complicate Rachel's ability to sell his house and may give him time to pursue other legal actions.

Chapter 10

FAMILY VICTIMIZED BY CHILD PROTECTIVE SERVICES

DENISE ROBERTS LIVED IN AN APARTMENT THAT WAS SMALL BUT HOMEY. The stucco walls were painted in soothing earth tones, and scattered throw rugs hid the worn tiles on the floors. The walls of the apartment were decorated with framed photos. Some showed Denise as a child. Another showed her as a teen, flanked by her parents and siblings and posed in front of a white farmhouse that looked as if it had come straight from a movie set. But the most numerous and most prominently displayed photos showed a chubby, smiling baby and toddler, his mischievous eyes peeking out from under straight black bangs.

Denise had grown up in Iowa, the oldest child of seven in a farming family. After graduation from high school, she had left her small hometown, hoping to find success as an actress in Los Angeles. She had made it as far as Las Vegas, where she had met her boyfriend—now fiancé—Joseph Chavez, and traded in her dream of being an actress for motherhood.

She was happy being a mother. Her fiancé, Joe, was supportive, and although an old back injury and the pregnancy weight she'd never managed to lose made her a bit slower and less active than she used to be, she was still proud of how she took care of Nicky, her active two-year-old. She would have told anyone who asked that she was a good mother. In fact, that's exactly what she told Nevada's Child Protective Services (CPS)when they showed up to remove her son from their home.

The nightmare started one morning after Denise had gone into Nicky's room only to find his mattress stuck between the slats of his crib. "I really wasn't even that surprised at the time, to tell you the truth," she admitted. "Nicky's a real handful, very active and athletic." In fact, Denise and Joe had talked about moving Nicky to a "big-boy" bed, but since Joe worked nights at one of the casinos, Denise was afraid Nicky would get out of bed and she wouldn't be able to get to him fast enough. "I really did think he was safer in his crib," she protested.

Denise got Nicky out of the bed and was shocked to see that he had dark ugly bruises on the right side of his face. They were not round but looked more like lines or stripes. Her first thought was that he had banged his head on his crib somehow.

Denise woke up Joe, and they checked Nicky carefully. He wasn't crying, there was no other swelling on his head, and his pupils seemed normal. Just to be sure, Denise called her mom in Iowa and asked her if she thought she should take Nicky to the emergency room. "My mom is better than any book on parenting," she said.

Denise's mom was reassuring. As long as Nicky was acting like himself, there was no need to worry. "Kids get themselves banged up all the time," she told her daughter. "It won't be long now before he starts climbing out of that crib and causing real trouble."

Even though Nicky seemed to have escaped serious injury this time, Denise was determined to prevent it from happening again. That day, she and Joe went out and ordered a toddler bed for the daredevil two-year-old. The store promised delivery by the end of the week, and Denise decided that Nicky could sleep on his mattress in her and Joe's bedroom until the bed came. She wasn't risking anything with that crib again.

The next day, she got Nicky ready for day care. Because Joe needed to sleep during the day so he could work his night shift and because

Denise had a part-time job in a hotel gift shop, Nicky spent part of the day in a preschool program run by a neighborhood church. Although they didn't attend the church, Denise was glad Nicky could be part of the program. She knew how much he loved running around with other kids, and between her weight and her back troubles, she knew she was not the most active playmate for her son.

When she dropped Nicky at day care, Denise made sure to let them know about the bruises on his face, telling his teacher that the boy had banged his head on his crib. Denise remembered the teacher making a comment about how Nicky sure did seem like a little boy who hurt himself a lot, but she shrugged it off. It was true—Nicky was the kind of kid who always seemed to be bumping his head, or scraping his knees.

Joe picked Nicky up on Monday afternoon and remembered the teacher commenting on the bruising as well. The teacher asked him how Nicky had gotten the bruises on his face. "Didn't Denise tell you?" Joe asked. But the teacher didn't respond, just turned away to help get another child into his coat to go home.

On Tuesday, Denise dropped Nicky at day care and went back home. She had intended to do housework, but her back was bothering her, so she took her prescription painkiller and sat down on the couch, elevating her feet as her doctor had advised her to do. "I must have dozed," she said. "Because when the doorbell rang, I was disoriented."

Denise was shocked to see two Las Vegas police officers at the door. They informed her that Nicky had been taken into protective custody at day care by CPS and began to ask her questions about the marks on his face as they peered around the apartment.

The sound of voices woke Joe, and he came out of the bedroom, rubbing his eyes at the sight of two police officers standing in his living room. For the next hour, Denise and Joe cooperated with the officers, showing them the crib and explaining how they had found the mattress pushed between the bars. They explained that they had ordered a bed and that Nicky was sleeping in their room until it arrived. The officers took notes, but when Denise frantically asked how they could get Nicky home, they told her that she needed to contact CPS.

It was late afternoon, but Denise called CPS immediately. She was told that yes, there was an open investigation involving Nicky Chavez, but the social worker who had begun the investigation had gone home for the day. Denise was frantic, crying and screaming into the phone, trying to get information as to her son's whereabouts. The CPS worker told Denise that Nicky was in protective custody pending an ongoing investigation. She then asked Denise several questions about Nicky and the bruises on his face, which Denise tried to answer as calmly as possible, although she couldn't stop herself from crying throughout the interview.

Joe couldn't afford to miss his shift at work, and Denise barely slept that night, wondering where Nicky was and how he would fall asleep without his beloved stuffed hippo.

On Wednesday morning, bleary-eyed from lack of sleep, Joe and Denise told their story to a different CPS worker who arrived at their house in late morning, despite Denise's repeated calls to the CPS offices to find out where her son was and how she could bring him home. They showed the woman the crib and explained, yet again, how they had found the mattress pushed between the slats. Joe, his temper short from lack of sleep and lack of answers, demanded to know who had called CPS. "I know it was that teacher," he told the social worker. "She's got no business interfering with my family in that way."

When Joe left the room to answer the phone, the woman rattled the bars of the crib. "There's no way a baby falling against these could bruise himself as severely as your son was bruised," she told Denise. The woman glanced at the doorway as if fearing Joe might reappear and told Denise her only hope was to figure out what had really happened to her son. "You won't get him back until you can convince us that he won't get hurt again," the woman from CPS said.

Before leaving, the CPS worker handed Denise a notice that explained that Nicky had been placed in protective custody in a foster home because police and CPS investigations had determined a risk of future physical injury to the child. A hearing to determine whether he could return home was scheduled for the following Monday at 10:00

a.m. Until the judge made his final determination, Denise would be allowed only daily one-hour supervised visitations with Nicky.

Denise spent the rest of the week calling the CPS offices. She learned that although an advocate would be appointed to represent Nicky's interests, she was not eligible for a public defender to represent her at the hearing. She could request a continuance, in the hope of having enough time to find a way to afford a lawyer, but to her, that option just meant that more time would pass before her son could come home.

On the Monday of the hearing, Joe was asked to wait outside the hearing room while the judge heard from CPS and Denise. Afraid to make any kind of bad impression, Denise told Joe she'd be fine and went into the hearing alone.

At the hearing, a different CPS worker from the one who had visited Denise at home spoke to the judge. She shuffled through her papers and read portions of several reports she attributed to various "sources." According to these reports: "The mother seemed disoriented, prescription medications were observed within reach of a child, both parents were sleeping during daylight hours, parents claimed to have toddler bed, but child sleeps on floor, the child's facial injuries are severe, other injuries to the child's person have been observed, and in initial telephone contact with CPS, the mother appeared emotionally unstable." The woman finished with her conclusion that on the basis of these reports she could not recommend returning the child to the home environment.

Denise was near hysteria. She didn't know how to explain that the facts were being distorted. That the only wrong thing she could possibly have done was to buy the wrong kind of crib. Joe, who had been listening outside the door, burst into the hearing room, demanding to know what was happening. The judge ruled that Nicky should stay in protective custody and told Denise and Joe that CPS would continue its investigation to determine whether further court action was necessary.

He explained that CPS could decide to work with Denise and Joe to reduce the chances of Nicky's being hurt again. Or it could decide to file a formal petition with the court, and there would be another hearing within thirty days of that petition being filed, at which Denise and Joe would have an opportunity to address the allegations against them. If they wished to admit to the allegations at that time, the judge would then determine whether Nicky remained in need of protection or could return home with them.

If Denise and Joe wished to deny or contest the allegations, then another hearing would be scheduled, so the judge could rule on custody. He told Denise and Joe that if they were not awarded custody, they might be expected to continue to attend review hearings for as long as nine months while Nicky remained in foster care, after which point the court would review the progress made by them as parents and decide whether Nicky could go home permanently.

Denise and Joe were devastated by the news that Nicky could remain in foster care for so long. "We're good parents. We love our son, and we didn't do anything wrong," Denise said. "They're telling me they can keep my baby away from me for nearly a year. How can the very system that is supposed to help children cause such damage by taking them away from the parents who love them?"

HOW I WOULD HAVE COUNSELED DENISE

If only Nicky had been able to speak for himself, he would have said: "I was just playing in my crib!" He could have told his teacher, CPS, the police, and the judge what his loving and devoted parents had been truthfully saying all along. It was the crib. What was meant to protect him from danger as he slept had caused his separation from his parents.

While child abuse in any form is both criminal and reprehensible, Denise's story highlights the difficulty of parents confronted with inaccurate reports of suspected child abuse. Whether the allegations of suspected child abuse turn out to be either true or unfounded, for practical purposes the investigation and handling of a claim of suspected child abuse follow the same course of action. If there is any objective doubt as to whether the child has been abused, generally CPS will remove the child from the home and place the child in protective custody. A court will then determine when, or if, the child can be returned to his or her parents and under what conditions.

For a parent dealing with an incorrect claim of suspected child abuse, the process will undoubtedly be both traumatic and confusing. Not only can the parent lose custody of the child, but the parent may not even be able to spend time with the child unless supervised by the watchful eye of a foster parent or a CPS worker. Because it is usually in the best interests of the child for things to move slowly, and because CPS workers are mainly concerned with the child's welfare, friendly cooperation may be more effective than an adversarial approach. If I had been counseling Denise and Joe, I would have advised them that this process will take time. It will involve checking into their backgrounds and making an evaluation of their own personal living habits and their parenting skills and habits in raising Nicky. This is not a time to be confrontational with CPS and the court. The parents need to work within the system to get Nicky back as quickly as possible.

As with the other areas covered in this book, I would strongly recommend immediately retaining an attorney experienced in handling matters involving suspected child abuse. While the court will retain a lawyer to act on Nicky's behalf as a *guardian ad litem*, a parent is not afforded this protection.

As Denise and Joe found out to their dismay, their understandably strong emotional response to having Nicky taken from them was actually used against them in court! While this may seem incomprehensible to the average parent unfamiliar with the court system, in determining whether a child may be returned to a parent, a court will generally consider what is in the best interests of the child. A lawyer can provide strong advocacy for the parents' interests without being criticized for being "emotionally unstable."

Obviously, the primary concern for Denise and Joe was getting Nicky out of foster care and back home. When an active case is pending with CPS, and the child has been placed in a foster home or another protective setting, getting the child back quickly can be a daunting task. Once your case is in the system, the wheels of justice—or, in this case, injustice—tend to roll rather slowly.

If available, I would have recommended that Denise and Joe obtain approval from CPS and the court to have a local relative, such as a grandparent, aunt, uncle, brother, or sister, take custody of Nicky during the time the case was pending. Provided the relative is a responsible adult, has a safe home, and has no record of prior problems, both CPS and the court should permit Nicky to be transferred from a foster home to the home of a local relative. Generally, there is no motivation on the part of CPS or the court to have a child in a foster home when a responsible local relative lives within the jurisdiction of the court. It is in the best interests of the child to be with a local caring relative rather than in the impersonal surroundings of a foster or group home.

However, even with placement with a local relative, this relative may still be required to be present during any visitation with the child's parents. Again, this is far better than having a stranger watch you visit with your child.

It is understandable that Joe was very unhappy about someone reporting him to CPS. Joe believed it was Nicky's teacher. Most states mandate that certain classes of persons, such as teachers, child care workers, and medical personnel, among others, are required to report any instances of suspected child abuse. Generally, anyone with a duty to report suspected child abuse is also immune from any civil liability for reporting—even if the suspected child abuse turns out to be incorrect. Again, the law generally tends to err on the side of caution when it comes to the littlest members of society.

To help them further strengthen their case, I would have recommended that Denise and Joe check for any product recalls by the manufacturer of the crib. This can be done by contacting the manufacturer of the crib. This is a good idea even before the purchase of a child's crib, bed, car seat, and/or stroller. It can be difficult to determine all the ways in which children can hurt themselves with these products. If a product has a history of causing these types of injuries, even under normal use, the parent should know this in advance and not purchase the product.

Chapter 11

CASH SETTLEMENTS AND DIVORCE

AFTER ALMOST TWENTY YEARS OF MARRIAGE, JIM O'ROURKE FELT THAT HE was living a nightmare. He was ready to do anything to get out of his marriage; he'd already moved from Pennsylvania to Iowa to California and completely changed his career. But despite all his attempts to make a new start, it seemed his wife was determined to ruin his life.

During his marriage, Jim had worked hard to build a thriving dental practice and had helped raised two sons and a daughter. He'd tried to do his best as a father and a husband, but over the years his wife, Danielle, had become increasingly difficult to live with.

"First, she became paranoid, convinced I was having an affair with my secretary—which I was not," Jim said. Danielle would lurk in the parking lot of Jim's office building and question his patients as they walked to their cars. Sometimes she would come into the office and begin to harass the receptionist and the people in the waiting room until Jim was forced to leave work and take her home.

The situation grew unbearable, and Jim's practice began to suffer. His two sons were away at college and had moved out of the house, although his youngest child, a daughter, was still living at home. He knew his wife needed help and suggested that they seek couples' counseling, or that she begin therapy on her own. But she insisted that everything was fine; she didn't need help of any sort.

Jim was at the end of his rope. So he did the only thing he could think of. He told Danielle he wanted a divorce.

His request enraged his wife. She made it pretty clear that she would fight divorce proceedings every step of the way if Jim dared to initiate them. She told him he was obligated to take care of her and that she was entitled to a huge settlement because she had stayed home with the children and he had always been the breadwinner.

As his wife's bizarre and harassing behavior escalated, Jim continued to suggest that it would be better for both of them if they separated. Finally Danielle agreed. But she indicated that she would be the one to set the terms and conditions of the separation. She demanded that he close his dental practice, deed the house over to her, and immediately give her the lump sum of $250,000.

"She told me that she thought a quarter million would be a fair cash settlement for her support and the support of our daughter, who was still a minor." Jim said. And while he did not obtain a divorce at that time, his wife told him that he was free to do as he pleased. She wouldn't bother him anymore.

As she was apparently intent on her campaign to destroy his practice, and he wanted nothing so much as to move on from the nightmare the marriage had become, Jim agreed to her terms. Accompanied by his oldest son to serve as a witness, he went to the bank, cashed out one of his IRAs, and presented his wife with $250,000 in cash.

Jim packed up his things and with a sense of relief, and the blessing of his three children, relocated to a small town in Iowa. He opened a modest local dental practice, helped support his sons through their college years, and flew his daughter out for summer vacations. He was there for four fairly happy years—and then the phone calls started. His wife was beginning another campaign of harassment, reminding him that he had said he would give up his practice, and accusing him of shutting her out of the vast sums of money she was sure he was making.

Jim's small practice was hardly showing a profit, and he certainly couldn't afford to pay his wife another quarter million to get off his case. So he moved again, this time to a town on the California coast. Wanting to completely change his life, Jim took a course and became certified as a building inspector. He found that he enjoyed the work and was good at it. Before long he was promoted to a supervisory position.

The phone calls from his wife stopped, and reports from the kids led him to believe that her mental state was more stable. But if his emotional life was finally calm, his physical state was now one of turmoil. Jim suffered a serious back injury, requiring a spinal fusion. The dramatic change in his lifestyle—chronic pain, limited mobility, and the threat of future surgical procedures—made him realize how unpredictable life could be. It also made him realize how important the girlfriend who had stayed by his side through all his medical nightmares had become to him.

He'd been separated from his wife for nearly ten years when he retained an attorney to procure a divorce so he could marry the woman he now loved. Jim asked his wife to sign a paper saying she had been given $250,000 in cash at the time of their separation. But when he brought the topic up she became irate, screaming at him that he would never get his divorce. Jim was so desperate to be free of this woman who had ruined so much of his life that he simply dropped the subject entirely. He told his lawyer to do whatever it took to get the divorce and then left him to talk it out with his wife's lawyer. To Jim's great relief, the divorce seemed to go through quietly enough. A settlement was reached, and papers were signed. For three years Jim enjoyed his new life.

Then Jim was notified that a suit had been filed in Pennsylvania, charging him with delinquency in child support. He contacted the attorney who had handled his divorce, who recommended a colleague who could take the case. Despite the tremendous discomfort travel caused his back, Jim and his attorney flew to Pennsylvania, gave depositions, filed responses, and listed witnesses—the secretary his wife had harassed; the receptionist who had fielded so many phone tirades from her; and his son, who had been with him when he handed over $250,000 in cash to his then wife. After much time and expense, Jim returned home to California.

When he finally received notice of the court date, Jim's back injury had flared up. He'd had another operation, and the recovery had been long and painful. There was no way he could travel to Pennsylvania again. He sent the judge documentation of his medical history and letters from doctors stating that he was not able to travel. He reminded the court of the witnesses he had ready to testify to the amount of cash he had already paid to his ex-wife.

Despite all of this documentation, the case proceeded through the Pennsylvania court without Jim or any of his witnesses being called. The court awarded a judgment of nearly $200,000 to Jim's ex-wife and ruled that she was eligible to collect part of his retirement savings.

Enraged, Jim tried to file for bankruptcy, but the pending judgment complicated the filing, and he was unsuccessful. Money was extremely tight—following surgery he was on partial disability and was working in his office only a few hours a week—but despite the expense, Jim hired a lawyer and appealed the ruling in the Pennsylvania court. His medical and legal bills were rapidly eating away at his limited savings, and he was beginning to worry about his future and retirement. Despite the concerns of his new wife and the strain on his health, he began to increase his hours at work.

Not long after increasing his work hours, he received notice that a suit had been filed in California to collect the child support that was due under the ruling he was appealing in Pennsylvania. His lawyer told Jim that if the California family court judge ruled in his ex-wife's favor, his paychecks would be garnished to satisfy the original judgment from another state.

"From the very beginning, I tried to do the right thing for my ex and my kids," Jim said. "Isn't there any way to make her uphold her end of the bargain?"

HOW I WOULD HAVE COUNSELED JIM

It's always good to get a receipt. Or, in Jim's case, he should have insisted on a written agreement reflecting the terms of his "settlement" with his ex-wife. Without this document, Jim was faced with the classic "he said—she said" scenario. Just because Jim was trying to do the right thing for his ex-wife and young child in agreeing to her initial demands, it didn't mean that his ex-wife had the same benevolent plans. She didn't. Jim was experiencing separation anxiety; instead of agreeing only to be "separated," Jim should have gone all the way and obtained a divorce. When the marriage is over—make sure it's really over.

Sometimes married couples decide to "separate" instead of filing for divorce. There are many reasons for this, including perhaps a hope that they can reconcile at a later date, a wish to keep the breakup confidential and out of the courts, or a desire to minimize the impact on the children. Often the motivation is strictly financial, as there are certain financial benefits to being married, such as the filing of joint tax returns and favorable health insurance coverage, among others. Breaking up can be very expensive. But, as Jim found out, breaking up the wrong way can be far more costly.

A separation can be brief, lasting only until one spouse ultimately decides to file for divorce, or it may last years, even decades. While each state has different requirements for legally separating, generally legal separation may be informal or court arranged. In an informal separation, both parties agree to split and live apart, and there is no binding agreement about how finances are handled or how payments and support are met. A formal legal separation is obtained by a petition to the court, and payment arrangements such as child or spousal support are mandated. Generally, a separation ends each spouse's entitlement to any future earnings or community property of the other spouse. Because of the complexity of the laws applicable to the dissolution of marriage, as well as issues relating to spousal and child support, I would strongly recommend that anyone contemplating separation or divorce consult an attorney experienced in family law matters. Even if you can afford only an initial consultation with an attorney, the advice you will receive will help you avoid the pitfalls that Jim experienced. Don't go it alone.

As a general rule, you should always get the terms of any agreement, whether related to marital issues or otherwise, in writing and signed by every party to the agreement. Memories may fade, people may pass away, or, in many cases, people may simply lie about the terms of the agreement. While it was extremely generous of Jim to deed the house to his ex-wife and give her the $250,000 lump sum payment for all future spousal and child support, by failing to document the settlement, his ex-wife was free to seek more later. That is exactly what she did to Jim, but it was preventable.

Jim must appeal the Pennsylvania judgment. Generally, once there is a final judgment setting spousal and child support obligations, this judgment can be taken to any state in which the ex-spouse is located for collection of the debt. Jim cannot hide from these obligations. If Jim doesn't make the required payments, his paycheck can be garnisheed, his income tax refund can be withheld, and he is even subject to jail time for failing to pay the required support payments.

Unless the court in Pennsylvania continued the hearing on his court date, Jim was required to attend. Even "sick notes" from your doctor may not secure a continuance. Remember, while this may be Jim's only divorce case, it is likely only one of hundreds that the assigned judge is handling. While an attorney can usually obtain a continuance of court dates based upon the medical condition of the client, there is no guarantee. Because Jim failed to appear in court, the judge excluded Jim's evidence that he already paid his ex-wife in settlement of her claims.

Depending on the length of the marriage and the relative earning ability of each spouse, an ex-spouse can be required to pay spousal support for years after the end of the marriage. In some cases, the spousal support can last for the remainder of the ex-spouse's lifetime and may be stopped only if the ex-spouse remarries.

Unless Jim truly wished to stop being a dentist, he should not have closed his dental practice. In determining both spousal and child support obligations, a court can assign a certain level of income based on the ex-spouse's ability to work and earn a living. Because Jim was a dentist, the court could assign a higher level of earning than what he currently earns as a building inspector. In such case, Jim would be required to pay this amount, which could result in a higher percentage of his income being used to pay for the support payments.

In my experience, in many instances when a vindictive ex-spouse has intentionally switched jobs in order to make less money—sometimes substantially less money—the ex-spouse's motivation is usually the same: he or she is under the erroneous belief that a reduction in income will force a court to order lower spousal and/or child support payments. Wrong. Unfortunately for the ex-spouse, courts generally frown upon an ex-spouse voluntarily reducing his or her work schedules or intentionally switching to a job that has less earning potential in order to reduce the ex-spouse's spousal and/or child support obligations. If you are in the midst of a divorce or custody battle and are considering changing jobs—for any reason—my advice to you is to remain in your current employment until all spousal and child support obligations are determined and agreed to by all parties.

Chapter 12

UNMARRIED COUPLES, JOINT FINANCES, AND SHARED PROPERTY

WHEN LIZA MET BRYAN SHE WAS SWEPT OFF HER FEET INSTANTLY—OVER the phone. The two were introduced by a friend of Liza's, who had traveled to the West Coast to do some business with the firm Bryan worked for. Bryan was from Australia and was charming, sensitive, and smart. Liza was a successful hair stylist with a thriving practice and a devoted clientele in the small city where she had lived most of her life. She had recently left the salon where she had worked for years and had started her own high-end salon. Business was good, and she was putting away money and planning for her future.

After several months of heartfelt and romantic phone conversations, Bryan invited Liza to fly out to Los Angeles to visit him. When she finally met Bryan in person, Liza couldn't believe her luck. He was fun, he loved to go out, and he had tons of friends. For the two weeks she was in L.A. it was like being at a constant party—a party where she had the most attentive date.

Bryan was equally smitten, and soon Liza was flying out to L.A. on a regular basis to spend time with him. He told her he was divorced; his wife had come to the United States with him when his company had originally sent him to work abroad, but she had grown bored while he traveled on business and had had an affair. She had returned to Australia and ended their marriage. "He was heartbroken," Liza recalled. "He said how much he missed being in a committed relationship, how he worried that the long distance between us would hurt our love affair."

Bryan told Liza that he needed to stay in L.A. because of the conditions of his work visa, but that he wanted her to come and live with him. Despite cautions from her friends and family, Liza decided to move. She wanted to be with Bryan, no matter what it took. "I knew he was my soul mate," she said.

She found someone to take over the lease on her business, sold the salon furnishings to the new leaseholder for a nominal amount, and referred all her clients to the new owner. Bryan gave her the name of his bank and advised her to open a checking account in her own name, explaining that since he had his own accounts, he wanted her to have a private account as well.

Right before she left for California, he suggested that she deposit the proceeds from the sale of her business along with her other savings in a second account that she could put his name on. Bryan told Liza he was worried that something might happen to her on the trip out west and he would need to be able to get money to her quickly. Liza was touched that he was so concerned about her traveling alone, and she opened the joint account.

Liza settled in to her new life in L.A. Bryan did work long hours, but Liza spent time decorating the apartment and getting used to her new home. "His place was such a bachelor pad," she said. "I must have spent a couple of thousand dollars on turning it into a nice home for us."

After they had been living together for a month, Liza began to grow restless. Bryan still wanted to go out and hang out with his friends every night. He drank too much and flirted with other women, and Liza and Bryan often fought when they got home. The relationship became very tense, with Bryan showing a fierce temper, followed by romantic gestures and lavish gifts by way of apology. He suggested that Liza needed to become more independent and told her they should lease a second car. "You should sign the lease agreement," he said. "You've got a good credit rating, and you're a citizen. If you handle this, we'll get the best deal." Any worries Liza might have had about putting Bryan on the lease vanished when he offered to put down the $6,000 deposit—in cash. Bryan drove the new car, claiming that it was more reliable for the travel he needed to do for work, and Liza used his old Honda to run errands around town.

Shortly after they leased the car, the company Bryan worked for folded. He told Liza that he was going to be able to get another job with a company based in the United States but that he would have to go back to Australia, reapply for a work visa, and then return to L.A. He didn't want to be without her that long, he said. "Come home to Australia with me and meet my parents," he pleaded.

A trip to meet Bryan's family seemed like a very positive sign to Liza, and she thought it would be just what they needed to get their relationship back on track. Bryan had talked about marriage, and this seemed to her to be a sign of his serious intentions. She purchased two tickets to Australia and lent Bryan $2,000 as a retainer for his lawyer, who would work on his visa while they were away.

The trip to Australia was wonderful. "It was like when we first met," Liza said. "We would go out, Bryan was fun and charming; I met so many of his friends, and they all loved him so much. I remembered why I had fallen in love with him."

While in Australia, Bryan took Liza to a popular vacation resort, where they struck up a conversation with the woman who managed the condos at the resort. The woman told Liza and Bryan that three of the units were available for sale.

Bryan told Liza that they should buy one of the condos. It was a deal at just $275,000, he told her. "It would be perfect as an investment property," he said. "We could rent it out to cover the mortgage and then use it for ourselves for a vacation once in a while." When he told Liza that it could be their retirement home, she agreed to the idea.

With only a few weeks in Australia to make the deal, they had to act fast. Liza wired money from her account in L.A., and Bryan borrowed from his parents for the deposit. Because his parents had lent him the money, Bryan insisted that they give his father power of attorney. That way he could look after the property for them while they were in L.A. and take care of anything that came up.

Bryan's lawyer assured Liza that she would have the opportunity to sign off on any actions proposed by Bryan's father. Nothing could be done without her knowledge. Liza granted Bryan's father her power of attorney. With only a few days left of their stay, Liza used her credit card to furnish the condo for future renters, and they returned to L.A. "I felt great at the time," she said. "Like we were really planning for our future together."

Unfortunately, once they had been back in L.A. for a few weeks, Bryan's behavior returned to the way it had been when they left. Liza began to realize that his temper and bad behavior were linked to his alcohol use. When she confronted him about it, he became abusive, and she realized that she needed to leave him.

Over the next few weeks, Liza quietly began making plans. When she went to the bank to transfer her money back east, she made a shocking discovery—her savings account was nearly empty. "I asked Bryan what had happened to the money, and he told me it was what he had used for a deposit for 'our' car," Liza said.

As Liza made her plans, Bryan became suspicious. The car dealership had called him to confirm that he, as a cosigner, had agreed with Liza's request that they cancel the lease on the new car. That night he beat her so badly the police were called to their apartment.

As the officer left the apartment with Bryan in handcuffs, he gave Liza some advice: "Get out right away. If you don't press charges, we can't keep him in custody too long."

It was all she needed to hear. She called a moving company, arranged for them to come and pick up her things the next day, and booked a ticket on a flight home. She figured she would deal with the loose ends of her former life in L.A. once she was safely back east.

Once she was back at home, she tried to undo all her ties to Bryan and L.A. She called the car dealership but was told that she was responsible as the guarantor on the lease and that she would have to continue to make payments until Bryan returned the car and paid the early cancellation penalty. She tried to reach the Australian attorney who had handled their purchase of the condo, but because of the time difference, she finally resorted to contacting him via e-mail.

His reply was completely unexpected. The attorney told Liza that he was glad she had called. That he'd been trying to reach her but did not have her new contact information. The condo had been sold. Liza was shocked to find out that Bryan's father had signed the sales contract, using his power of attorney, and was claiming an agent's fee out of the proceeds. Liza found that Bryan's father had covered the mortgage payments during times when the condo was empty and that he expected to be fully reimbursed for all of his out-of-pocket costs as well.

Still afraid of Bryan, Liza doesn't know how or whether to fight to get her investment back. Often she feels as if she is starting over again. And she still feels a horrible mixture of anger and embarrassment when she thinks about how she gave up everything—her business, her home, and her friends—for a dream of true love with a soul mate that ended in a financial and psychological nightmare.

HOW I WOULD HAVE COUNSELED LIZA

When it comes to new love, we're all millionaires. Most people never think about money when they're in the throes of a new romance. Buying expensive gifts, dining at fancy restaurants, taking extravagant trips, even "lending" money to our newfound love interest. We're in love, right? What's the harm? Plenty. Just ask Liza.

You might be surprised to learn that Liza's story is not unusual. It happens all the time to people from all walks of life—even those who really do have millions in the bank. Our emotions get the best of us, and we think that our new partner is our soul mate and that any decision will be in our future best interest. For a "soul mate" like Bryan, thinking like this can mean taking advantage of someone else and draining that person's bank account in the process. Don't be an easy target.

While it's easy to look back and see that Bryan was merely using Liza for her money, Liza could have taken several steps to prevent Bryan from stealing her hard-earned savings. The easiest thing Liza could have done was keep her money in a separate bank account. Generally, unless you're married, there is never a need for either having a joint bank account or making someone an authorized user on your separate bank account. Don't mix and match.

It's easier to keep your money in your bank account than try to get it back after it's already gone. Liza was surprised to learn that the $6,000 down payment Bryan so graciously offered to put on the new leased car had actually come from her bank account. Liza would not have been surprised to learn that Bryan had spent the money in her savings account if she had been regularly checking her monthly bank statements. Most people never read them. Read them. Carefully. It's your money.

When "lending" money to your romantic partner, get it in writing, as uncomfortable as it may seem. Is it really a loan? Or is it a gift? Being clear about which it is can mean the difference between possibly getting the money back—or inadvertently being a really generous person. With their relationship over, and Liza's money gone, is there any doubt which scenario Bryan will claim? Liza should have made Bryan sign an agreement confirming both his receipt of the "loan" and his agreement to repay the money. Armed with this document, Liza would have had a much better chance at recovering the money from Bryan.

If you're sizing up a potential romantic partner for marriage, you should first consider his or her financial history before you make the plunge. Generally, when you marry someone you marry his or her debts and financial obligations. In retrospect, it was obvious why Bryan had bad credit and Liza had good credit—one was responsible, while the other was not.

The problem with entering into long-term agreements with a romantic partner you're not married to is that the terms of the agreement may last far longer than the relationship. While married couples can be jointly liable for debts even after the end of the marriage, generally the same rules do not apply to unmarried couples. Even though her relationship with Bryan is now over, Liza is still saddled with the monthly obligation of the leased car. If your romantic partner has bad credit and cannot qualify for a long-term agreement without your assistance, give him or her a short-term answer. Just say no.

While the condo in Australia may or may not have been a good investment, giving Bryan's father power of attorney was not a good idea. Generally, a power of attorney grants power to someone else to conduct either your personal or your financial affairs, or both. This type of power should never be given to someone with whom you have only a casual acquaintance, as this person will rarely understand how you wish your affairs to be handled. Even though the person with power of attorney must act in your best interests, this is not always the case, as Liza found out.

At a minimum, Liza should immediately revoke the power of attorney and promptly advise Bryan's father and the attorney in Australia in writing of the revocation.

The attorney advised Liza that nothing could be done with the condo without her prior approval. Unfortunately, the attorney could not contact Liza because she had failed to give the attorney her contact information. Even if you decide to run away from a bad love affair, you should never lose touch with your lawyer. This is a common mistake. Always make sure that your attorney has your current contact information, including your postal address, telephone number, and e-mail address. Had the attorney been able to contact Liza before the sale of the condo by Bryan's father, she would have had time to stop the sale, or make other arrangements that were in her best interests, such as revoking the power of attorney she had given to Bryan's father.

Unless there was an agreement allowing Bryan's father to act as the "agent" in the sale of the condo, I would have advised Liza that any such payment be withheld. However, to the extent that Bryan's father paid part of the mortgage and upkeep on the condo, these monies may be recoverable by Bryan's father. The key point is that Liza, as the owner of the condo, should have kept track of the monthly expenses and the rental status of the condo. This was her responsibility as owner.

Chapter 13

LOVE, FAMILY, AND RELATIONSHIPS: WHAT YOU NEED TO KNOW

LEGAL BATTLES ARE NEVER SO MESSY AS WHEN THEY'RE INITIATED OVER love that's gone sour. Here are some ideas on how to better get along with your family, significant other, and friends before, during, and after a breakup or divorce:

CHILDREN AND FAMILIES

They're your kids—nobody else is going to take care of them. Right? Being a parent means not only watching out for your children but also providing a stable home, giving them proper nutrition, and ensuring that they attend school and stay out of trouble. In return, your children will "bless" you with years of enjoyment and love. However, if you fail to uphold your end of the bargain, you might have to deal with the potential loss of custody of your child and the bureaucratic hoops inherent in your local Child Protective Services (CPS) agency. Here are some suggestions for staying out of trouble and helping to ensure that your children get a positive jump start on adulthood.

Child Support Obligations

As a parent you have an obligation to provide for the financial support of your children until they reach the age of majority (commonly age eighteen or nineteen in most states). Your obligation is not extinguished even if you and your spouse divorce and your spouse is awarded custody of your children. Unfortunately, most noncustodial parents quickly realize that not having custody of their children actually substantially increases the costs associated with raising them—another benefit of staying happily married.

In most states, child support obligations are calculated on the basis of a mathematical formula adopted by the state legislature. The calculation takes into account your income, the number of children, and the amount of time each parent has custody of, or visitation with, the child. The mathematical formula and the associated support amount are generally binding and will be modified only on the basis of well-presented arguments that the set number is financially unworkable or that the particular child requires more or less support because of the circumstances.

Today, many states offer online child support calculators (see the References section in the back of this book) based on the same mathematical formula used by the courts in setting child support obligations. You can also check your state's department of social services Web site to see whether your state offers this service.

Failure to pay child support obligations can lead to fines, wage garnishments, and even jail time. Pay your child support payments on time, and make sure you maintain complete copies of all payments. Keep copies of canceled checks and bank statements in your records. You should never pay support payments in cash, since you will not have a record to show the court should your ex-spouse claim he or she did not receive the payment. It is surprising how often this issue comes up in court. If you insist on paying your support obligations in cash, make sure you get a signed and dated receipt from your ex-spouse confirming receipt of the payment. Don't lose the receipt—keep it with your other financial papers.

Keeping In Touch with Your Children

You're supporting them; you should at least get to see them. Visitation is a right of any noncustodial parent. While there may be issues relating to the safety of the child —for instance, when the noncustodial parent has a history of violence, criminal activity, or even child abuse—generally a noncustodial parent is entitled to reasonable visitation with the children. Even noncustodial parents who are behind in child support payments are generally permitted full visitation rights.

Any divorce or separation agreement or decree should provide a framework for the noncustodial parent's visitation. These agreements can be as simple as designating a number of days per week or month when the child will be with the noncustodial parent, or as complicated as specifying the exact dates and times when the child will be with the noncustodial parent. Your particular circumstances will dictate the level of detail required for your visitation agreement. It's best to get these agreements in writing and have them signed by each parent. This will help prove the intent of the parties should you wind up back in family court over visitation issues.

Use your visitation time with your children. This seems obvious, but many parents simply fail to exercise their right to be with their children. Not only is this bad for the child, it may prejudice your rights if the custodial parent later decides to decrease or modify the visitation schedule. When dealing with children, a family court will always consider and rule in a manner that it believes is in the best interests of the child.

Child Protective Services

While there are legitimate cases in which a child is injured through no fault of the parent, in other cases parents can be neglectful of their children. According to the perceived harm to the child, CPS may require monitoring of the home, parenting classes, or, in severe cases, removal of the child from the home pending a resolution of the matter with the court.

I would never recommend that anyone faced with the removal of a child from the home deal with CPS without the assistance of an experienced lawyer. Information you provide to the authorities, while perfectly truthful, may be interpreted in a different light by CPS. The key is to always remember that CPS and the court base their decisions not on your wishes but on what they believe is in the best interests of the child. You need to work within the system and not try to fight the process.

BREAKING UP IS HARD TO DO

A Divorce Lawyer—Do I Really Need One?

Child custody issues tend to be the most difficult, time-consuming, and emotionally draining aspect of any divorce or separation proceeding. Unfortunately, one spouse may use the children to get back at the other spouse. Don't do it. This course of action usually results in creating division within your child's mind and usually has a negative effect on your child's emotional and educational well-being and maturation.

If you are embroiled in a child custody dispute with your ex-spouse and the matter has spilled into the courts, I would recommend that you at a minimum consult—or even better, retain—an experienced lawyer to handle the matter on your behalf. Many lawyers will handle routine divorces; however, fewer lawyers will handle divorces involving child custody and support issues. Find one who is experienced in child custody and support issues. Places to look for a lawyer include the following:

➤ Your state's bar association is the organization responsible for the admission, administration, and discipline of lawyers in your state. Most state bar associations have a Web site, and many offer lawyer referral programs. You can get the contact information for your state association through the American Bar Association (listed below and in the References section at the back of this book.)

➤ The American Bar Association (ABA) has useful information for the public on various areas of the law, including child custody and support obligations. The association is located online at www.abanet.org.

➤ The Martindale-Hubbell Lawyer Directory at www.martindale. com is also a good resource. This comprehensive resource lists literally thousands of lawyers, legal professionals, consultants, and other service providers.

Alimony and Protective Orders

Alimony, or spousal support, is generally provided by one ex-spouse to the other ex-spouse to alleviate any income disparity resulting from the marriage, for instance, when one spouse worked and the other stayed home and raised the children. The amount of spousal support is generally set by formulas in each state and is designed to place the supported ex-spouse in a similar, if somewhat lower, financial position as during the course of the marriage. The length of any spousal support payments can vary widely, based on the length of the marriage: the longer the marriage, the longer the potential term of spousal support. Spousal support payments may be terminated by the death or remarriage of the supported ex-spouse.

Protective, or restraining, orders are designed to protect someone from a reasonable likelihood of personal injury caused by another, generally a spouse, romantic partner, or family member who has a history of violence toward the protected person. These types of orders must be issued by a judge and supported by facts showing that the one person is likely to injure the other person without the issuance of the protective order. The protective order generally prevents the restrained person from being within a certain distance of the protected person, and any violation of the order will usually result in the restrained person's being sent to jail. If you believe you need a protective order, you should promptly go to your local police station and obtain the necessary paperwork to obtain one.

Community Property—Share and Share Alike?

It's good to share, isn't it? We're taught early on that sharing helps us socialize and learn the value of compromise. When you're in a relationship with another person, whether married or just dating, sharing is an important component of a happy and successful relationship. However, until you're married it's best to keep your finances separate. You'll lose your heart in a breakup. Don't lose your finances, too.

Unless you're married (and maybe even then), keep your money and finances separate from those of your significant other. Here are some helpful tips:

➤ Do not open a joint checking or savings account. "Joint" means that both of you will have complete and unlimited access to any money in the account without the other having prior knowledge. Keep separate accounts.

➤ Don't enter into any long-term contracts or agreements, such as lease agreements, installment agreements, or credit contracts. If you're inclined to do this anyway, stay clear of significant purchases such as houses, cars, or other high-value consumer items. Remember, if your name is on the contract, you will be fully responsible for the bill if your significant other leaves you and decides not to pay.

➤ The law considers the person who holds the title to be the legal owner of a piece of property or a vehicle. Don't place the title of anything you own in the name of your significant other. Sometimes the motivation is to either reduce or increase your assets for purposes of obtaining a loan or financing or for other means. Aside from the possible civil and criminal liability you may incur in fraudulently converting your assets, the result of transferring the title may be that your significant other takes full possession of the property—and kicks you out!

➤ Assets held in joint title with your significant other can be obtained and sold by your significant other's creditors. It is common for unmarried couples to purchase a car in both their names. Don't do this. If it's your car, it should be in only your name.

➤ Are you being generous, or are you a shrewd business-person? That is the question a court may ask if required to rule on whether money or property you gave to a former significant other was a gift or a loan. As a rule, gifts are not expected to be returned or repaid. A loan must be repaid, and the best indication that the money or property was a loan, instead of a gift, is a written agreement signed and dated by the recipient confirming his or her agreement to repay the loan. If you're giving someone something you expect to get back someday, get that agreement in writing.

Breaking Up 101

If you're finished with the relationship, make sure you can move on with your life without all the baggage. Here are a few things to keep in mind:

➤ Legal separation is less than a divorce and is designed to end the accumulation of any community property of either spouse. There may be financial or social reasons why a couple may not want to officially divorce. Besides preventing the further accumulation of community property, legal separation enables both spouses to know that they're working for themselves again. Many states require a formal written legal separation agreement that is filed with the court. You should check with a family law lawyer in your state for your state's requirements.

➤ If you want to get remarried, you will have to obtain a legal divorce. Each state has certain requirements for the filing of divorce. Generally the primary issue is that the spouse must meet certain minimum residency requirements before filing for divorce. Once again, a family law lawyer will be able to guide you in this process.

➤ If you have minimal assets and no children or support issues, a couple can obtain an uncontested divorce rather quickly with little effort and in most cases without the assistance of a lawyer. Most courthouses in larger cities also offer information packets and blank forms for filing for divorce. Some of these forms can be found online. Check to see whether your local courthouse offers this service.

➤ In most states, when you file a divorce action and the split appears to be uncontested and straightforward, the court may appoint a mediator to meet with both parties in an attempt to limit both court time and attorneys' fees. A mediator will deal with property resolution, alimony, child support, custody, and visitation. A mediator will have the power to attempt to resolve the issues among all parties and make recommendations. Mediation is nonbinding and can be court appointed or requested by either or both parties. Using a mediator can help divorcing couples put emotions aside in order to resolve issues quickly, saving everyone enormous amounts of money and time.

Part III

MONEY, FINANCES, AND DEBT

How to Steer Clear of Major Financial Hassles

Protecting your savings, your credit, and your investments begins by avoiding so-called deals that end up costing you much more than simply the money you owe. Whether it's reaching beyond your budget to purchase a new car or deciding to take on a significant mortgage to buy your dream house, it's easy to make emotional purchases with credit. But what can give you such positive feelings in the short term can cause negative feelings later. You need to fully understand how credit works so you can choose to spend wisely, with your eyes wide open.

While everyone knows the old saying "You can't buy happiness," I can tell you that it's probably more important to say that you can't borrow happiness. That is, you can't (and therefore shouldn't) put happiness on a credit card, or take out a loan to buy something that makes you happy now. It may seem like the easiest thing to justify at the time, but your good feelings may be short lived when the easy road takes some unpleasant detours.

It's just as tempting to take the easy way in other areas of our lives as well, like choosing inexpensive health insurance without reading the fine print, or putting hard-earned money with an investment advisor who promises unbelievable returns but can't show you a track record. You probably think I'm stating the obvious when I tell you that if a deal seems to good to be true, it probably is. Yet, hundreds of people find themselves in financial ruin when they believe the hype and make impulsive, poorly researched decisions about how to spend and where to invest their hard-earned money.

Chapter 14

REFINANCING FIASCO

LIKE MOST MIDDLE-CLASS AMERICANS, SANDRA AND LEE BAILEY WERE working hard and providing for their family. They were getting by, but their financial situation was more precarious than they wanted to acknowledge. Lee worked long hours as a driver for a trucking company that made deliveries for a big-name electronics superstore. Sandra was a stay-at-home mom, who took care of their three school-aged kids. They lived in a modest four-bedroom home in a nice family neighborhood in a small North Carolina town. Sandra had a minivan, and Lee drove a used Jeep. Their biggest indulgence had been to install an aboveground pool to keep the children occupied over the hot summer months.

They certainly weren't extravagant spenders, but even maintaining an average lifestyle for a family of five could be expensive. Sandra tried to stay within their budget, but with three school-aged children, she felt as if she was always buying groceries, or play clothes, not to mention the latest toys and gadgets for the kids on their birthdays or for Christmas. "We tried to save," Sandra said. "But it was never easy."

When Lee's delivery route was cut back, the family felt the financial pinch almost immediately. Both Lee and Sandra felt it was important for her to be home with the kids. Lee figured he'd be able to make up the slack eventually—maybe take a second job. They agreed that they would try to get by without having Sandra look for work.

With money tight, like most people today, Lee and Sandra turned to their credit cards. They didn't change their lifestyle to reflect their new monetary concerns. They figured they'd use their credit cards to get by until their income picked up again. Only now, when they used their cards to purchase necessities like groceries or fuel, or to pay the cell phone bill, they were adding the charges on top of the luxury and impulse buys that they were still trying to pay off. Before long their bills began to snowball, and Sandra and Lee were forced to juggle their finances—managing to pay some bills on time, but falling behind on others.

Sandra dealt with all their creditors directly, calling them and telling them of the couple's financial hardship and making arrangements to pay what she could on each of the credit cards. After they had fallen several months behind on their mortgage payments, Sandra called the financing company to see what options they had.

"They offered me a deal that was supposed to help us out," she said. "Instead, it nearly put us into bankruptcy." The mortgage company representative told Sandra that she and Lee were facing foreclosure because they had fallen months behind on their payments. Between the back payments and the fees that had accrued, they owed the mortgage company thousands of dollars. The customer service person told Sandra that they could save themselves from foreclosure proceedings by refinancing their house. The company would work with them to establish a short-term plan that would allow them to make the payments that were in arrears, and then they would continue to pay the newly refinanced mortgage. The woman urged them to take the highest loan amount they were eligible for.

The Baileys agreed to the plan and began to make the higher payments. At first the extra money from the refinancing seemed to help. They paid off the most urgent bills and were able to meet their monthly mortgage payments. Their lean budget was still an issue, but they no longer had the same sense of panic.

After a few years of skimping and pinching pennies, the Baileys had caught up on the payments that had been in arrears and had begun making regular payments on their mortgage. "Then we got a notice from the mortgage company that said we owed them $3,000 in unpaid fees from the refinancing," Lee said. The mortgage company claimed that the Baileys were in default on their loan agreement and notified them that their house had been placed in foreclosure.

When Sandra called the company, she talked to a sympathetic representative, who offered to help them refinance the loan again, to cover the $3,000. To a couple used to relying on credit to cover their bills, the offer seemed perfectly logical. They never stopped to think that they had reached the point of borrowing to pay for what they had borrowed. And so, once again, the Baileys refinanced their house, filling out the endless paperwork and taking on an even higher interest rate, simply to pay the $3,000 in fees.

"The one bright spot," Sandra said, "was that after the refinancing, the customer service person told us we wouldn't have to make a payment for sixty days." This meant that although the Baileys closed on the refinancing in June, they didn't have to send a payment until September. "It was nice to have that extra cash around," Lee admitted. They even splurged and took the kids to the beach for a few days—the first family vacation they'd been able to afford in years.

In September the Baileys mailed their mortgage payment. The finance company promptly returned it along with a notice of default, and a second notice informing them that they were liable for legal fees related to the foreclosure proceedings. Sandra began calling the company, but to no avail. The people who were so willing to help with refinancing didn't seem the least bit interested in correcting a clerical error.

The stress of a threat of foreclosure began to take its toll on the family. Although Sandra and Lee never talked about their financial problems in front of the kids, they began arguing with each other more frequently. Lee would criticize Sandra's spending on things like groceries, and she would retaliate by telling him he didn't earn enough money. The kids, picking up on the tension, began to act out, both at school and at home.

Lee told Sandra that he thought she should try to get a job, but she argued that trying to straighten out the mess the mortgage company had caused them was practically a full-time occupation.

Sandra called the company several times a day. Every time she got someone on the phone, she would be transferred to some other person, and then that person wouldn't be available. Then she'd get bounced into the automated system, and it could be days before she was able to get a person on the line again. "I tried for weeks to try to talk to someone named Fred, who was supposedly the one person who could help straighten this out," Sandra said.

When Sandra finally spoke to Fred, he told her that the company had put the house into foreclosure and that there was nothing he could do to help her. Tired of the runaround, Sandra and Lee agreed to take money out of their 401K, and they hired a lawyer who specialized in foreclosure prevention. Their attorney told them that according to the records of the mortgage company, the Baileys' house had been in foreclosure more than ten times. Furthermore, because each foreclosure had been reported to the credit bureau, their credit rating was in a shambles. There was nothing he could do for them.

Panicked and desperate, Sandra and Lee dipped into their retirement savings again and sent the company a check for the three months in which they had supposedly been in default, along with the amount the company claimed they owed in fees. Sandra continued to call the company daily, sometimes several times a day, trying to confirm that they had received the payments and reinstated the mortgage. No one returned her calls. After about a month, when they hadn't heard anything, Lee and Sandra just figured "No news is good news."

Their relief was short lived. On the same day their uncashed check to the mortgage company was returned via Federal Express, an officer from the county sheriff's office appeared at their front door and served them with a notice of eviction. The mortgage company had foreclosed on their house. The Baileys had to be out within thirty days.

"It was the last straw," Lee said. The long hours he was working at both jobs began to take their toll. He found that he would rather go out with his friends for a few beers after work instead of coming home and watching as Sandra began to pack up their lives.

"It was the worst thing that had ever happened to us as a family," Sandra said. She became seriously depressed. All she wanted to do was sleep. She didn't feel as though she could deal with anything, whether it was packing the kids' lunches for school, or doing the laundry, or even walking the dog. Only when her doctor prescribed medication was she able to take control of their lives and begin to do what had to be done.

With their credit rating in ruins, and their savings seriously depleted, the Baileys couldn't afford to buy a new house. They searched for a rental that would accommodate the whole family. "We had to give away our dog," Sandra said sadly. "I don't know if the kids can ever forgive us for that."

Sandra and Lee began seeing a marriage counselor to try to repair the damage that had been done to their relationship and their family. They were both devastated. "We've lost our home, our savings, and our peace of mind," Sandra said. "We didn't do this to ourselves. We were victims."

Just two weeks after they moved out, Sandra and Joe watched as a SOLD sign went up on the lawn of their beloved home. The same week, Sandra picked up their mail only to find an offer from a company that specialized in mortgages for people with poor credit. Having lost their house, their savings, and their hopes of a secure future, neither Lee nor Sandra could say whether they would ever trust a mortgage company again.

HOW I WOULD HAVE COUNSELED THE BAILEYS

For most people, their house is their single greatest asset. Not only do those monthly mortgage payments keep a roof overhead, they build equity that can be later used for unexpected expenses, a child's college tuition, and even retirement. Yet, in today's era of quick loans and "cash out" refinancing, it's easy to think that the equity in our homes will always be there to protect us from any financial crisis. As the Baileys found out, failing to protect their most significant asset resulted in the loss of their home, causing considerable strain on their marriage, disruption of their children's lives, and lasting damage to their formerly good credit rating.

The Baileys' story is not unusual. There are many reasons why we might suffer temporary or long-term financial difficulties, such as a reduction in working hours, reduced commissions or tips, a disability, layoffs, or even being fired. The financial strain of raising a family today can be daunting even to those with above-average incomes. Without savings and by living month to month, we are only one car or house repair, one medical bill, or one unexpected expense away from a financial crisis.

The Baileys' response to the loss of Lee's delivery route and the reduction in their income was not unusual, either—they did not change their lifestyle to reflect Lee's reduced income. This was their biggest mistake.

If you're unable to afford your current monthly mortgage payment, it is unlikely you will be able to afford an even higher monthly mortgage payment after refinancing your home in order to pay off outstanding debts. This was the Baileys' problem. While having the extra cash on hand to pay off some of their debts initially helped the Baileys, they were not likely to be able to afford the higher monthly mortgage payments.

Being late on your mortgage payment is one of the most damaging marks against your credit rating. If you can't afford to pay for the place you live in, credit reporting agencies generally assume that your finances are in for a serious downturn.

With real property, such as a house or land, everything must be in writing. This would include buying or selling a house, getting a mortgage to purchase a house, and refinancing the mortgage on the house.

If you've ever been through any of these situations, the piles of paperwork can be intimidating. As part of their refinancing, the Baileys should have received from the lender a disclosure statement reflecting the total fees, interest, and associated costs for each refinancing of their mortgage. The $3,000 in fees from the refinancing should have been detailed in the disclosure documents, including whether the fees were to be paid separately or included in the new loan amount.

If I had counseled the Baileys, I would have requested that they immediately contact the lender in writing and request copies of all disclosure documents reflecting the outstanding or overdue amounts and the basis of the alleged deficiencies. If the $3,000 were charged to the Baileys in error by the lender, requesting documentation verifying the alleged deficiency can often lead the lender to "correct" the alleged deficiency.

While each state has different requirements for a lender to foreclose and force the sale of a house to pay off the existing mortgage, generally the lender must provide written notice to the homeowner at each stage of the foreclosure process. During this process, most states allow the homeowner a certain amount of time in which to stop the foreclosure by paying the late mortgage payments and any interest, penalties, and other associated fees. If you find yourself in a foreclosure situation, you should consult a lawyer to determine the time period allowed in your particular state.

It is unlikely that the Baileys were not provided with written notice regarding the ten prior foreclosures. Don't throw away notices that look official or legal because you "don't want to deal with them" or think that you can ignore the situation. If you are not provided with proper notice, generally a lender is prevented from seeking the foreclosure of the house. Once again, consult a lawyer to determine whether you have been provided with proper notice, what steps you should take in your state to contest any improper notice, and what rights you may have to stop the foreclosure.

When dealing with a lender or with any person or financial institution regarding collection issues, get everything in writing. Never rely on anything that someone on the other end of the telephone tells you unless that person is willing to back his or her statements up with a letter confirming the same. Don't trust the roof over your head to the word of a customer service representative for the lender. The Baileys should have requested that the lender provide them with written verification that no payment was due for sixty days.

Given the Baileys' financial situation, and the impending foreclosure sale of their house, I would have recommended that they immediately consult a lawyer experienced in bankruptcy matters or other possible legal remedies available. While filing for bankruptcy is a last resort, in the Baileys' situation, it might have prevented the loss of their home and provided them with additional time to catch up on their late payments.

Chapter 15

BANKRUPTCY AND DIVORCE

IN HER WILDEST DREAMS, JANE ADAMS NEVER THOUGHT SHE'D BE NEARLY fifty and living with her four kids at her elderly parents' house. When her husband abruptly ended their twenty-four-year marriage, he had left her not just heartbroken but financially destroyed as well. Not only had she and the kids been forced to forfeit their privileged lifestyle, but given the circumstances, she realized that they were lucky to simply have a place to call home.

Jane was a tall, thin, attractive woman. Her dark hair, once colored and cut in a chic style, was streaked with gray and pulled back in a messy ponytail. Her nails were chewed ragged, and dark circles under her eyes made her appear pale and exhausted. "You might not believe it, but I used to have it all," she said. "Beautiful kids, nice house, two cars, vacations twice a year—if I wanted something, I just went out and got it."

Jane and her husband, Paul, had been married for twenty-four years. Paul had worked his way up from stock clerk in a supermarket to a high-level executive position at a large national drug company. Jane was a typical suburban housewife, happily chauffeuring their four kids from soccer games to Little League, from horseback riding to dance lessons.

"Paul was always very concerned with appearances," she said, admitting that she, too, always wanted the best. When they bought houses, they always considered the best neighborhoods. Jane spent freely on decorating and landscaping, and Paul always backed her up on her choices. As the kids grew older, Jane and Paul sent them to private schools, telling themselves that they should spare no expense for their children's education.

Money never seemed to be a worry. Paul and Jane had four or five major credit cards, in addition to Paul's business cards. Their credit was excellent, and they never hesitated to borrow against their large home equity line of credit to pay for a new project or to cover an unexpected expense.

Jane admitted that having savings was never a priority. They had plenty of credit and had no problem making payments on time. "Our philosophy was to live for the moment," she said. With Paul's career doing so well, she had always assumed there would be plenty of time to put money away for a rainy day.

And as far as Jane could tell, her husband was on the fast track to even greater success. Though she could admit that they had grown very distant with each other, she told herself—and the kids—that the long hours and endless traveling were how Paul paid for their comfortable lifestyle. "What I didn't fully realize," she said, "was how the days on the road were taking their toll on Paul."

The pressure to earn more and more income to support their spending habits was becoming nearly unbearable for Paul. He began going out with guys from his sales force after work, telling himself that he was entitled to relax after his intense workday. What began as an occasional night out turned into a regular habit of visiting gentlemen's clubs and strip bars. He became secretive about his after-work activities, and Jane began to suspect him of having an affair.

When she confronted him with her suspicions, Paul exploded, telling her that he couldn't handle her demands. Then he just walked out of their home. A few days later his lawyer called with the news: Paul wanted a divorce.

Jane was stunned, but she acted quickly to protect herself and the kids. She got a lawyer who she knew would fight for a good settlement. Jane's lawyer told her that Paul would continue to maintain the house payments and make all credit card and loan payments, as well as provide child support. Jane was relieved. Paul had been acting polite and decent, and she was optimistic that—especially for the sake of the kids—they'd be able to continue to work things out amicably.

But Paul quickly realized that he had not gained any freedom by getting a divorce. If anything, he felt more trapped than ever, because he had to continue to pay all the bills without being able to enjoy the comforts of the lifestyle he and Jane had built up. Living in a bachelor apartment not far from his old house, Paul grew increasingly bitter and angry toward Jane. Jane felt that he was blaming her for the divorce. "He couldn't even take responsibility for his own decision to tear his family apart," she said.

What Jane didn't know then was that long before walking out on his family, Paul had been struggling to continue to meet all the financial obligations he and Jane had taken on. Without telling her, Paul had worked out an arrangement for his company to reduce his salary and make up the difference by paying him huge cash bonuses and commissions. Each paycheck was smaller, but he would receive several large windfalls throughout the year. Now he tried to use his smaller paychecks as a way to prove that he couldn't afford to pay all the bills he had been ordered to pay.

Jane was sure he was only seeking revenge, so she continued to spend freely. It seemed to her that nothing had changed. Paul still had the same job, and she still had the same expenses in running a home and raising children. Besides, the judge had ordered that Paul continue to maintain the house and lifestyle she and the children had always known. So the kids remained in their expensive private schools, and Jane retained all the household help she had always used—the housecleaner, the gardener, the pool service company—and the bills continued to pile up. Jane simply forwarded them to Paul, sure that the court would continue to make him pay.

When Jane received the notice that Paul had filed for bankruptcy, she was furious. She thought that he was trying once again to shirk his responsibility to the family he had walked out on. When she began to receive calls from collection agencies regarding their credit cards, she was merely irritated. When she received a notice from the mortgage company saying that the house had thirty days until foreclosure, she panicked.

She contacted her lawyer to force Paul to do whatever he had to do to cover the bills. But her lawyer's reply to her was grim: now that Paul was in bankruptcy, Jane was responsible for all of their joint debts, including the mortgage and all their credit cards. Jane was stunned. "How could I be responsible for all these payments?" she said. "I've never even had a job."

Her lawyer advised her to scale back her lifestyle as much as possible. He suggested that she sell the house and transfer the children to public schools. Jane was devastated, but she realized she needed to take drastic steps. With only weeks until the threatened foreclosure, she began the process of putting the house on the market. Houses in their neighborhood were in high demand. She figured she would make enough profit from the sale to be able to put a down payment on a more modest house in a nice, but not luxurious, neighborhood. She was shocked when the real estate agent called to tell her that there was a tax lien on the house and that any profit left over from paying off the existing mortgage would go to the IRS.

Jane found out that for years Paul had never reported any of the bonuses from his company to the IRS. As a result, even before the divorce there were hundreds of thousands of dollars in arrears on taxes. Since the divorce, most of Paul's bonus checks had gone directly to the IRS. Without the extra income, his weekly paychecks were truly insufficient to pay the maintenance the court had ordered.

Without savings and with her credit destroyed, Jane could not stop the foreclosure. She and the kids moved in with her parents while she began to search for a job that would help her support the family. Now Jane and Paul barely speak. His children don't want to see him, either.

The kids blame him for what has happened to them. Jane doesn't know what her future holds. When she agreed to give Paul a divorce, she thought Paul was agreeing to take care of her and the kids. Now she wishes she had understood more clearly what was involved in ensuring their financial security.

HOW I WOULD HAVE COUNSELED JANE

When times are good, it's difficult to picture things going bad. However, reality has a way of quickly focusing our vision once again. How many times have you heard someone remark, "I would never have guessed that 'so-and-so' were having problems." For Jane, she surely knew things were becoming unsettled just under the surface—they were living on credit, they had accumulated no savings, and Paul was becoming increasingly distant. By growing accustomed to her carefree spend-now-pay-later lifestyle, Jane was trapped in life's most common truism: things do change. Unfortunately, it was not a change for the better.

Unless a couple is fabulously wealthy, a divorce is never profitable. Paul quickly found out what most people realize soon after filing for divorce—it's almost always more expensive to be divorced than to be married. Freedom has its price. The costs of maintaining two residences, especially if there are minor children, can be significant even for formerly well-heeled ex-spouses.

Jane should have kept track of her family's income and expenses. Generally, married couples are jointly liable for all debts incurred during the marriage. Without adequate savings, it was no surprise—except to Jane—that Paul was forced into bankruptcy. Jane should have realized that since she and Paul were both able to use the credit cards, they were also jointly liable for these debts. It was only a matter of time before the creditors circled overhead and laid their sights on Jane.

Regardless of Paul's current financial situation, he must still provide economic support to Jane and the minor children. Depending on the length of the marriage and the laws of the state where the couple live, Paul may be required to provide Jane with spousal support payments until she remarries, or for her lifetime. Paul will be obligated to provide support for his minor children until they reach the age of majority or, in some instances, several years afterward.

The amount of support, either spousal or child support, that a court will order is based on the financial ability of the ex-spouse and the financial needs of the ex-spouse and the minor children. You might be surprised to learn that many states use a set of mathematical formulas and variables to determine the amount of support. These formulas take into account the income of the ex-spouse, the financial obligations of each party, and even the amount of time the minor children are with each parent. Generally, the parent with primary custody of the minor children will receive more financial support from the ex-spouse. It pays to spend time with your children.

Paul's self-imposed "salary reduction" not only offended the IRS but also should offend the family court. Paul is attempting to use his "lower" salary to reduce the amount of money Jane and the minor children receive in court-ordered support payments. However, Paul is still making the same amount of money he earned during the course of the marriage, and that "true" salary should be used by the court in calculating his monthly support obligations. While Paul will be required to continue to support Jane and the minor children, invariably, the amount of these payments will afford Jane a more modest lifestyle than she was previously accustomed to. Remember, now there are two separate households to run from the same amount of money.

The actual amount of support payments calculated by the mathematical formulas can be altered, sometimes significantly, on the basis of several exceptions to these formulas, often called either upward or downward "departures." A "departure" can be obtained because of any special financial needs of either the ex-spouse or the minor children, whether the ex-spouse is considered a high-income earner, or any other factors that the court deems relevant to the calculation of support payments.

Even though Paul filed for bankruptcy, this does not extinguish his requirement to make court-ordered support payments. Generally, support payments are exempted from a person's ability to discharge the debt through bankruptcy. If I were counseling Jane, I would argue that one basis for her to seek an "upward departure" of any court-ordered support payments is that Paul's filing for bankruptcy now makes Jane solely responsible for all the family debts. Jane needs more money. Paul needs to pay.

By filing for bankruptcy, Paul has made Jane solely responsible for all the marital debts. Jane may be entitled to partially offset these increased debts by receiving a greater share of community property accumulated during the course of the marriage. However, since Jane never worked, it appears unlikely that she will ever be able to either make the required monthly payments or pay off the debt. Like Paul, Jane will likely need to seriously consider filing for bankruptcy in the future.

While no one can avoid death and taxes, Jane may be able to argue that she was an innocent spouse and was unaware of Paul's failure to properly report his income to the IRS and pay the required taxes. If successful, Jane may be able to avoid all or part of the tax obligation. As with the other areas covered in this book, it is strongly recommended that an attorney experienced in tax matters be retained to represent your interests. Alternatively, Jane could seek an offer in compromise of the outstanding income taxes through a one-time reduced payment to the IRS.

Chapter 16

HEALTH INSURANCE

DAN PETERSON WAS ONLY SIXTY-ONE, BUT HIS RECENT ILLNESS HAD LEFT him looking more than a decade older. He and his wife, Karen, lived in a tiny Florida condo, filled with books and decorated with silver-framed photos that documented their life of travel and adventure. In the photos, Dan, a tall, robust, redheaded man, was always smiling or laughing. It was hard to believe that the white-haired, pale, weak man in the wheelchair was the same person.

For the past twenty years, Dan had owned a very successful small marketing company, and he and Karen had enjoyed an active and adventurous lifestyle. It was clear they considered themselves a great team. They worked together, played tennis frequently, and eagerly traveled around the world in search of new experiences.

In fact, it was on their latest trip that Dan became ill. "We went to the Amazon to celebrate my sixtieth birthday," he said. "It was a great trip. We really did some roughing it. It was the vacation we'd talked about taking our whole lives."

When they arrived back from their travels, Dan told himself that the tiredness and stomach pain he experienced the first few weeks at home were just the hazards of taking an exotic trip. But the symptoms didn't go away, even after a few months. In fact, Dan felt worse. He lost his appetite and suffered from an almost constant feeling of nausea. Finally, he scheduled an appointment with his doctor.

"Ordinarily, I would have said it was too expensive to see a doctor about a stomachache," Dan said. In the small business he owned, his insurance premiums and deductibles had always been a major expense. However, with an eye toward retirement in the near future, Dan had recently scaled down his marketing business. He had kept just a few clients and had cut back on expenses. He moved his office into a smaller space, had Karen do all the company paperwork, and changed health insurance carriers. At a trade show for small business owners, Dan had purchased a new health insurance policy from a salesman representing a carrier that claimed to specialize in health insurance for small-business owners. It was a great deal: the premiums were about 25 percent less than what he had been paying, and the benefits were extensive. Even the co-pays were lower.

Dan expected that his doctor would check him out, tell him he had an intestinal virus, and prescribe some Pepto-Bismol. Instead, Dan's doctor gave the couple a shocking diagnosis. Dan had contracted hepatitis B, probably while on the trip. He needed to start on medication immediately.

The next year was a nightmare of paperwork and red tape. Karen tried to stay on top of all the bills and forms, but it wasn't easy. The doctor's office would send them a bill, and she'd forward it to the insurance company. A month or two later, they'd get another copy of the same bill, and she'd forward it again. Then she'd call the insurer and be told that the doctor's office had just used the wrong code, or that the insurer had just done the billing for that month. Each time the insurer reassured her that the office would take care of it.

And Karen was happy to let them handle it. She had more important things than paperwork to worry about. Despite the aggressive medical treatment, Dan was not getting better. He was forced to close his business. Fortunately, Dan had taken out disability insurance a few years earlier. Although it was only a minimal policy—he never figured he would need to use it—he and Karen were grateful to have any money at all coming in. After all, it was more important than ever to stay current with their health insurance payments.

Nearly eighteen months after he returned from his dream vacation,

Dan was placed on the liver transplant list. Karen put her secretarial skills to work, wading through the endless masses of paperwork required by his doctors, the insurance company, and the hospital.

When an official-looking letter arrived from the hospital saying that Dan had been removed from the transplant list because of a lack of insurance coverage, Karen was sure there had been some mistake.

"I went back through all my files. We'd always paid our premiums on time. I'd always forwarded the bills to the insurance company. I'd even noted when I'd called them to ask about the status of a bill. Our insurance shouldn't have lapsed. I was confident there had been an error."

Karen called the insurance company, but there was no answer. With a growing feeling of dread, she made phone call after phone call. Finally she called the trade organization that had sold Dan the insurance more than two years earlier.

When Karen finally spoke to a woman at the trade organization, she received some shocking news. The organization had just found out that federal regulators had closed down the insurance company that had sold Dan the policy. The woman told Karen that all the policies that had been sold were bogus and that claims had never been honored. "I'm sorry," the woman said. "But we've been scammed, too."

Karen was stunned. She mentally calculated the cost of Dan's treatment to date. There was no way they could pay the doctor's bills that had piled up, never mind find the nearly half million dollars that a liver transplant would cost. Karen couldn't bring herself to break the news to Dan. His health was so fragile, and she knew he would need all his strength to fight for his life.

Karen called the hospital and asked to speak with an administrator. She explained what was going on. She explained that her husband, Dan, was on the waiting list for a new liver. She told the administrator that he'd been sick for so long and that this was a matter of life and death. But in the end, the hospital officials said that although they were very sorry for her situation, there was nothing they could do.

For the next few days, Karen made round after round of harrowing phone calls. She simply was not going to take no for an answer. Karen waged a one-woman publicity campaign, writing the governor, their congressman, even the president. She called local news stations and told them that the hospital was refusing to treat a dying patient because he had lost his insurance. "We believed we were insured," she said. "It wasn't like we were trying to scam anyone. We were the victims."

In the end, the hospital agreed to put Dan back on the transplant list and perform the surgery. The hospital even agreed to absorb part of the costs, with some of the doctors waiving their fees for the operation. Dan and Karen were grateful, and their faith in the medical profession was somewhat restored by the generosity of those involved.

Dan's operation was successful, and he was resting and looking forward to regaining his strength. But the future that he and Karen had worked so hard to ensure was destroyed. Their doctor's bills from when Dan first became ill and received treatment totaled in the tens of thousands, and they still owed nearly $250,000 for the transplant operation.

Dan admits that his life is far from the easy-living retirement he had envisioned. But despite losing so much to the callous con artists that sold him insurance policies, Dan knows that he and Karen have held on to what is really important. He's still alive. They still have each other.

HOW I WOULD HAVE COUNSELED DAN

Everyone loves a great deal. No one can blame Dan and Karen for trying to save money by switching to a lower-cost health insurance plan. With the high cost of health care these days, having health insurance means the difference between seeing the doctor for that persistent cough or having to rely entirely on some over-the-counter medicine. Con artists know this, too. If the deal is almost too good to be true, it's probably a scam. Be careful, and do your homework before writing that first premium check.

There's an expression: "You pay a premium for bogus insurance." Sometimes the cheapest deal is the worst deal. Regardless of how attractive the quoted premium and benefits sound, you're just wasting your time and money if the insurance company is not legitimate.

If you're shopping around for health insurance, or any type of insurance, it's best to deal with established companies. While the lure of a low quote can be extremely tempting to anyone on a fixed budget or someone just looking to save money, you must be careful in dealing with unfamiliar companies. I recommend that you contact the National Association of Insurance Commissioners [(816) 842–3600, or online at www.naic.org)] to find whether the association is aware of the particular company and if it has received any complaints regarding the company's business practices. Before giving anyone a check, check them out first.

Most fraudulent insurance companies follow similar patterns of operation. Learn the signs and avoid them. First, they aggressively sell their "insurance coverage" through e-mail, mass mailings, and often at trade shows or conventions. Second, pushy salespeople usually require the unsuspecting victim to sign up for insurance coverage on the spot or within a short time frame; otherwise the "special offer" will no longer be available. The advertised "premiums" are usually significantly lower than those any legitimate insurance company can offer. Last, after enough premiums are collected, the con artists vanish along with your money.

More sophisticated scam operations will sometimes use unsuspecting and legitimate claims-processing companies in order to delay payment of claims, or even pay out small claims, in order to encourage "policy holders" to continue to make the monthly premium payments. This appears to be the tactic used in Dan's case.

Another problem associated with these scam operations is that the con artists will also obtain your personal information in order to steal your identity. That's another reason to check out the insurance company before even applying for coverage.

If you're still uncertain whether the insurance company you are considering is legitimate, I would also recommend checking with your state insurance commissioner whether that particular insurance company is permitted to sell insurance in the state, whether it has a history of financial problems, whether there are numerous complaints regarding the payment of claims, or whether it is suspected of being a fraudulent business.

If I were counseling Dan, I would recommend that he contact the federal insurance regulators regarding filing a claim against the fraudulent insurance company and its operators. In the case of Dan's "insurance company," the federal regulators likely have frozen the assets of the con artists. This may be one avenue for recovering some of the premium payments.

Unfortunately, Dan is likely out of luck with regard to his outstanding medical bills. He didn't have real insurance. While filing a lawsuit against the fraudulent insurance company and its principals is definitely an option for Dan, it is highly unlikely that he will be able to recover money from these individuals. However, I would recommend that Dan look into claims against the salesman and claims against the processing companies used by the con artists.

By contacting the state attorney general's office and filing an initial complaint, Dan will begin the process of discovering whether there are other complaints against the company. If these people were involved in the scam, or had sufficient information to determine that the "insurance" they were selling or processing was fraudulent, then Dan may be able to sue these individuals. Unfortunately, however, in many cases, these scam corporations have no money, so even if you can initiate—and win—a lawsuit, you may still lose, because you will likely never get your money back. When your health is at issue, protecting yourself from insurance scams is a *preventive* issue.

Sometimes even legitimate insurance companies go out of business because of financial problems. If your insurance company goes out of business, in many states there is a fund set aside to pay out claims to policyholders. While the limits of any payout are generally small and can vary from state to state, this is an additional way to obtain payment of any outstanding claims.

Chapter 17

HIGH-RISK INVESTMENTS

DAVE RANDALL NEVER THOUGHT HE'D BE FACING THE POSSIBILITY OF being forced to return to work after retiring in order to support himself, but after an unscrupulous investment firm pressured him into making bad financial decisions, the retired firefighter didn't see what choices he had left.

His city pension wasn't huge, but he figured as long as he was careful, he was going to be all right. But advice from an unscrupulous investment advisor left his financial future uncertain. Instead of retirement being a new chapter in his life, Dave worried that he faced having to start all over again.

A widower, with grown children living several states away, Dave had always been careful with his monthly budget. But when a fishing buddy told him how he had made more than $6,000 in a month by investing only $2,500 of his savings, Dave was intrigued. His friend, Craig, told Dave that he had used this one broker to invest in the precious metals market. He bought gold bullion and sold it for a good profit a few months later. After Craig told him how easy it was, Dave thought it would be a good way to enhance his savings.

Dave called the number his friend gave him and was connected to a sales agent. He talked with a woman named Annette Raymond.

She told him that it was great he was thinking of investing but that he would be making a mistake if he were too cautious.

Dave explained that he was a retiree and on a limited budget, and Annette told him that that was precisely the reason he needed to be more aggressive in his investment strategy. She repeated over and over that by using a small amount of money he could purchase shares in the futures market and be able to quickly realize vast profits. Although Dave was unfamiliar with some of the terms she used, he listened as she explained that silver was selling at $11 to $12 an ounce and that if he invested in silver futures there was the potential to make enough money to secure his retirement. "She was a great salesperson," Dave said. "I'll give her that."

Following Annette's advice that he act quickly, Dave followed her instructions to go to the company's Web site, check the box indicating that he had read its disclosure statement, and wire $50,000 from his retirement account to the broker's attention. "I told her that I wanted to start small," Dave said. He wanted to invest just $10,000 initially, but Annette told him that if the market were on a streak and he wanted to invest more, it was easier for her if the additional cash was on hand. She told him that she'd put it in a special account managed by the company and that all his profits could be deposited to the same account. She took all of his information over the phone and told Dave he could call her anytime to place an order or check on his account.

During that phone call, Dave told Annette to go ahead and buy $5,000 in silver, as they had discussed. He told her that he wanted her to put in stop-loss orders close to the purchase price. So, if the value of the shares fell below the purchase price, the company would sell the shares quickly in order to limit his losses. "She told me she would buy silver—it was at $11 an ounce—and I could check in with her if I had any questions about the account."

Dave began following the markets online and in the newspapers. For a few days, the price of silver went up, and he mentally calculated his earnings. "I'm not much of a gambler," he said. "So I was ready to get out after the price had gone up a few dollars."

Dave checked in with Annette almost daily by e-mail or by phone. At first she was very understanding, telling him that her dad was retired, too, and she understood how folks had to look out for their financial security.

After the first week, she became cool to him, suggesting that perhaps he didn't need to be in contact quite so much. She told him that she'd call him if anything major happened, and he should just relax and let his money do the work. Her tone made Dave feel as if she thought he was just an old retired guy with nothing else to do. She made him feel he was being pushy.

Taking Annette's advice to heart, Dave took a long weekend and went on a fishing trip with his friend. When he came home on Tuesday and logged on to his computer, he was shocked. The precious metals market had crashed, and the price of silver had fallen to just $6.00 an ounce. He checked his e-mails—there were no messages from Annette. He checked his cell phone, having had no reception up at the lake; no messages were waiting for him on the phone, either.

"I was so relieved that I had put in a stop-loss order," Dave said. Realizing that he could have lost more than half of his retirement money really made him reconsider his investment decisions. Dave decided to close the account and put the money back into something safe, like a nice mutual fund.

Dave called the company and asked to speak to Annette. Both times he was told she was at her desk, but both times his call rang into her voice mail. He sent an e-mail—no answer. When he finally got Annette on the phone, she confirmed that the silver market had crashed. "She told me that it was a gamble I had to be prepared to take; that in order to make a lot of money, you had to be prepared to lose some," Dave said.

From Annette's casual tone, Dave assumed she had executed his stop-loss order and sold his holdings as the market was going down. Annette told him not to panic; she was sure the market would go back up, and she asked him if he wanted to get back in at the same levels. She told him it was what she would advise her own father to do.

"She seemed so confident," Dave said. Annette told him that now was the time to bet big and make up his losses. And he thought maybe she was right. Dave admitted he was worried about the loss, but the way Annette talked to him made him feel that he was acting like some old man scared about his future. Besides, Dave figured he still had the balance of the $50,000 in that account at the brokerage. After some thought, he told Annette to go ahead and get back in to the market for another $10,000.

The price of silver continued to inch downward. And again, Dave was unable to reach Annette by phone or e-mail. Several days after placing his second order, Dave received a Western Union MailGram from the trading company. The message said that his account with the company had fallen below trading approved levels and that he needed to immediately wire a minimum amount of $5,000 to restore the account and to cover outstanding brokerage commissions and fees.

Dave immediately called the company. By his own reckoning, he still had more than $30,000 in his account. He had invested only $15,000 and had placed stop-loss orders that should have limited his losses. For days, Dave phoned the company, trying to get Annette on the phone. Eventually, after threatening to get on a plane and show up at the company's offices, he was transferred to a trader named Jerry.

As Dave listened in stunned silence, Jerry told him that no stop-loss orders had been placed on his account. Annette wasn't a trader; she was simply a salesperson whose job it was to process the orders and pass them through to the traders. According to Jerry, Dave's initial $5,000 and subsequent $10,000 had purchased highly leveraged futures shares in the silver market. The remainder of Dave's money had been held in his margin account—the "special" account Annette had referred to. Because Dave's account had been so highly leveraged, the amount he lost as the price of silver went down was multiplied exponentially. Each point the market gained or lost was equal to 250 leveraged points. So each time Dave thought he was losing $1, he was actually losing $250.

Dave protested that Annette hadn't explained this to him. But the guy on the phone just asked him if he had signed the disclosure agreements. When Dave told him that he had checked off the box on their Web site, the guy said that by doing so Dave had agreed to their terms and conditions of trading. He told Dave that he had chosen a risky investment and that any losses were Dave's own responsibility, not the company's. Before he hung up, he reminded Dave that he owed the company thousands of dollars in unpaid commissions.

Dave felt sick. He had just thrown away a lifetime of work and the security it represented. That night as he lay in bed he could feel his heart racing. He couldn't sleep and got up, thinking he'd watch a little television to take his mind off things, if only for a moment. Sitting in his armchair, Dave struggled to catch his breath. "I felt as if an anvil was pressing down on my chest," he said. Afraid he was having a heart attack, Dave called the paramedics and was transported to the hospital.

The doctors told him it was just a panic attack. Dave felt foolish, but he was afraid it would happen again. Or that the next time it really would be a heart attack.

Unnerved by his medical condition and too embarrassed to tell his kids or friends of his predicament, Dave slipped into a depression. For months he was unable to do anything but sit in his chair in front of the television. He made excuses to keep visitors away, and he lied to his kids, telling them he was fine each time they called to check on him.

Finally, one of his fishing buddies, worried about Dave's change in behavior, simply showed up at his house. "I guess he was pretty shocked," Dave said. "I'll admit that I hadn't been keeping up with the house—and I guess I'd gained some weight just sitting around the way I had been."

Concerned, Dave's buddy called Dave's oldest son, who flew out and demanded to know what had happened. It was humiliating for Dave to have to tell his son what an idiot he felt like. But his son wasn't critical. Instead, he simply said, "Dad, you've been taken advantage of, and now you have to get off your butt and fight these thieves."

Dave was desperate to get his initial investment back. He felt that Annette had misrepresented her authority to invest his money. He sent a letter to the company, with copies to the National Futures Association and the Better Business Bureau of the state where the company was located. The company sent a letter back stating that investing in the futures market was considered risky and that by accepting the disclosure statement, Dave had agreed to assume the risk for his investments. The letter went on to say that in accepting the disclosure statement, Dave had also agreed to go to arbitration instead of suing the company. The company also had the nerve to send him a bill for unpaid commissions.

Dave still doesn't know whether he should spend the money to hire a lawyer. On one hand, he feels that the company deliberately misled him. The company bought futures instead of actual silver, leveraged his account without his authority, failed to put in stop-loss orders, and charged him outrageous commissions. On the other hand, hiring a lawyer would be expensive, and there's no guarantee that he will be able to get even his initial investment back.

HOW I WOULD HAVE COUNSELED DAVE

We've all seen them. Beautifully typed, single-spaced pages filled with endless and confusing words that are supposed to "disclose" the warranty or terms of use for that new product or service we just purchased. Or, in Dave's case, what his "stockbroker" was going to do for him. The term "disclosure statement" really doesn't do it justice. A more appropriate term would be a "no matter what happens—it's not our fault" statement. Be careful.

Now, my advice to Dave, and everyone else, is going to get me into a little hot water. Here it goes anyway: read every word of those darn disclosure statements! If the disclosure statement is online, print off a copy and sit down and read it. Nobody reads them. You will be surprised at how many rights you're giving away. These "disclosure statements" are really contracts whereby you agree to purchase the product or service conditioned upon your acceptance of the terms of the disclosure statement. Don't be surprised later. Read each disclosure statement.

One of the most common rights you give away is the right to sue. Virtually all investment brokerage disclosure statements contain an agreement that both sides, the investor and the stockbroker, agree to arbitrate any disputes. Arbitration is a method by which parties agree to resolve their disputes outside of court. It's usually quicker and cheaper than going to court.

Disclosure statements are typically written by teams of lawyers that are skilled in predicting all types of problems that may arise following your purchase of any product or service. Since the lawyers are armed with this knowledge, the disclosure statement is written to ensure that the provider of such a product or service is immune from any liability. Depending on the type of product or service you are purchasing, including the amount of the purchase, it may be advisable to have the disclosure statement reviewed by your own lawyer before you agree to its terms.

It's uncanny how otherwise intelligent people will follow the "financial advice" of just about anyone with a smooth voice and the promise of making easy and significant profits. Never make any substantial "investment" based on a telephone call, even if the caller was referred to you by a "friend." If anyone tells you that you can make easy money in the stock market, walk away. Don't let a slick salesman con you out of your hard-earned money.

The term "aggressive" usually means "high-risk." Being on a limited budget, Dave should not have been playing the market with high-risk investments. While Dave did check the box saying he had read the disclosure statement, if he had actually read the whole thing he would probably have found that the disclosure statement described the highly leveraged type of investment he was contemplating as extremely high risk. Had Dave thoroughly read the disclosure statement, he probably would have thought twice about investing on his limited budget.

Dave should have received a written confirmation for each and every trade he made and the terms of each trade, including whether a stop-loss provision was included. By reading these statements, Dave would not have been surprised that he was losing money. Never rely on the word of the stockbroker; get each trade confirmation in writing. If he had followed up on each trade, Dave would have quickly realized what he was getting into and stopped his "investment" before losing his entire savings.

If I were counseling Dave, I would advise him that he should, at a minimum, seek the full return of his money from the brokerage firm on the basis of the fraudulent misrepresentations made by Annette regarding his investment. She misrepresented her role and the nature and risk associated with the "investment." Dave did not make an informed decision. It is clear that Annette was representing herself as a stockbroker and giving investment advice. This is illegal. Not only did Dave not get the requested stop-loss protection, but his money was being invested in high-risk "leveraged" trades. While Dave did not understand this term, it was incumbent on Annette and the brokerage company not to mislead Dave into thinking his investment was low risk.

If you are confronted with a dispute with your stockbroker, I would strongly urge you to retain a lawyer experienced in securities law. Securities law, which covers the obligations of a stockbroker to a client, can be extremely intricate and confusing, even to lawyers. Don't go it alone.

Chapter 18

DEBT REPAYMENT AND DEBT MANAGEMENT PLANS

TOM AND MAUREEN CAVANAUGH BOTH HAD GOOD JOBS. HE WORKED AS foreman at a plant that manufactured high-tech electronic circuitry, and she had recently completed her training as a dental hygienist and had started working part time for a practice not far from their house. They considered themselves solidly middle class, but their drive to get ahead and attempts to climb out of an ever-deepening pit of credit card debt had driven them to the edge of bankruptcy.

Neither Maureen nor Tom had ever gone to college, but they were hard workers, determined to make a good life for themselves and their future family. Although both of them were in their late twenties, they both looked and acted older, possibly because neither could remember a time when they hadn't held some kind of job. As youngsters, Tom had had a paper route, and Maureen had babysat half the kids in the neighborhood. They had both worked at a neighborhood Italian restaurant while they were in high school. "We fell in love—the busboy and the waitress," Tom said, a smile momentarily softening his craggy features.

They were married two years after they finished high school, and

Tom began working at the factory. He was well liked and diligent, and over the course of the past five years he had slowly but steadily worked his way up. Maureen had worked at a variety of restaurant and office jobs before deciding to train for a career that had potential for good earnings.

They bought a house as soon as they were married and stretched their budget to be sure that it was a good-sized home in a good neighborhood. They were eager to have a family home for the rest of their lives.

To furnish their new house, Tom and Maureen held several joint credit cards. And they used them frequently. "We had two different Visas and a Discover card," Tom said.

"And department store cards: Macy's, Sears, Penney, Home Depot, Target, Best Buy . . ." Maureen added.

Because they were both earning good incomes, the credit limits on the cards kept increasing. They bought furniture, electronics, and other household items. They bought appliances and clothing. It all went on the cards without a second thought. Each month they made the minimum payment on each card.

When Tom got his first promotion, they celebrated by buying a new car, financing an Explorer at a friend's dealership. When Maureen graduated from dental hygienist school, they bought her a snazzy little Mazda to commute to work.

"And then one day, we were just overwhelmed by the bills," Maureen said. "I can't even explain how it happened. One day we were making the minimum payments; the next we had run the cards up to the limit and were thousands of dollars in debt—and even the minimums were too high for us."

Both Tom and Maureen were dismayed each month when the bills arrived. Their creditors began charging them late payment fees and overlimit fees. "Even when we weren't using the cards anymore, we were being charged a couple of hundred dollars each month, between interest and fees and penalties," Tom said. "We felt as if we were drowning in debt."

Even as their income seemed to be shrinking, their family was growing. Maureen became pregnant. When morning sickness forced Maureen to cut back on her hours at the dental practice in the first few months of her pregnancy, money became even tighter. Tom sold his motorcycle, and Maureen asked her parents for a short-term loan. But those small infusions of cash only kept them afloat week to week. They were not making any progress at all on their debt.

In desperation, Tom searched the Internet for advice on debt consolidation. His search turned up several companies that offered to consolidate debt and to repair credit. He filled out forms at a couple of the sites, requesting more information on their programs.

The first guy who called was a really slick salesman. "Our company can get your creditors to simply forgive some of your debt," he told them. Tom and Maureen were suspicious. The promises the company made just seemed too good to be true.

However, when a representative from BankCard DebtSavers called, Tom had a different reaction. "This guy took his time explaining things to me," Tom said. He told Tom how the company would negotiate with the credit card companies to take cents on the dollar. He said the company had teams of skilled lawyers who would go up against the credit card companies. He explained that because the companies just wanted money, not hassles, they would deal with their lawyers. He said that the company usually negotiated for 40 cents on the dollar, although he bragged that one of their lawyers had just negotiated a huge debt down to just 15 cents on the dollar! He also told Tom that BankCard DebtSavers was a nonprofit company, which was paid by taking a few more cents on each dollar, and that the company had an ironclad money-back guarantee if it could not resolve their debt situation.

Tom and Maureen agreed that this seemed like the best possible plan. If they could reduce their debt by up to half, it was worth doing. They added up all their debt—over $45,000 in total—and sent BankCard DebtSavers a $4,500 money order to cover their 10 percent enrollment fee.

The BankCard DebtSavers account representative told Tom and Maureen to stop paying all their credit card bills for the next three months. He said that this would give them leverage to bargain with the credit card companies. He said if the credit card companies thought they were going to get nothing from Tom and Maureen, then a percentage—no matter how low—would seem like a good deal.

Tom and Maureen stopped making payments to their creditors. The phone calls began after the first missed payment, and they intensified. Then the letters began to arrive from collection agencies. As instructed, Tom and Maureen forwarded all correspondence to BankCard DebtSavers. They invested in caller I.D. and answered their phone only when they knew exactly who was calling.

"It was incredibly stressful," Maureen said. "I was so sick and moody, and Tom was picking up extra shifts to try to make ends meet. We fought all the time."

After three months, Tom contacted BankCard DebtSavers to inquire about the settlement plan. He was told that the representative he was asking for no longer worked for the company. Furthermore, according to the new representative he spoke to, there was no record of their account.

Tom and Maureen began calling each of their creditors. Each told them the same thing: No, they had never been contacted about debt settlement, and they had never heard of BankCard DebtSavers. In fact, each creditor continued, the account is in collection, and you face serious consequences.

"Those were the hardest calls to make," Maureen said. "We were so shocked, we couldn't even think of anything to say or how to offer to begin to repay our debts."

With their debts mounting quickly, and their savings $4,500 lighter, Tom and Maureen swallowed their pride and told Maureen's parents what had happened. Maureen's father lent them the money to hire a lawyer, who helped them file a claim against BankCard DebtSavers in small claims court and won a judgment against the company. But BankCard DebtSavers appealed, and Tom and Maureen haven't even gotten their enrollment money back. "They basically stole $4,500 in cash from us," Tom said. "And I don't know what we can do."

Tom and Maureen tried to refinance their house, but because their credit rating was ruined from not paying their bills, no bank would approve their application. And they knew they were going to face harder times when the baby came and Maureen wasn't working.

Maureen was particularly upset. "I had always wanted to be a stay-at-home mom, at least for a few years," she said. "Now the kind of life we worked so hard for is going to be taken away from us. I'm afraid we'll lose everything, even the house."

Tom and Maureen never looked for the easy way out of anything in their lives. And they can't believe that the one time they tried to make it easier on themselves, they created such a nightmare.

HOW I WOULD HAVE COUNSELED THE CAVANAUGHS

You can't sleep at night. Your credit card bills are piling up, and you're using a cash advance from one credit card to pay the minimum monthly payment on another credit card. Then you see the television ad promising significant reduction on the amount of your credit card bills and associated interest rates—all you have to do is just call that 1–800 number. Be very careful before you give someone money in the hope of reducing your debt.

The Cavanaughs' story highlights the fact that there are many fraudulent "credit counseling" companies that will seek an initial large "fee" in order to get you into their "program" that promises to quickly reduce your credit card debts and help you avoid paying all that interest. It's not that easy. In the end, they just take your money and increase your debt. Don't be fooled. While there are many legitimate credit counseling companies, you need to make sure you're dealing with one of them.

As a rule, don't use any credit counseling companies that require an initial "enrollment fee" of more than a minimal amount of money, generally under $100. Legitimate credit counseling agencies will not charge any fee, or will charge only a minimal fee. If the credit counseling company you are considering requests a large fee or a payment representing a percentage of your outstanding debt—walk away. The company is probably not legitimate, and dealing with it will only increase your money woes.

Never work with any credit counseling company that does not have a written agreement detailing the scope and costs of all services offered. All legitimate credit counseling companies will have written agreements reflecting how they will pay your bills, the costs associated with any such payments, and what notifications you will receive regarding your credit accounts. As with any contract or agreement, always request a written copy, and read the agreement. It's your money.

You should request a written statement reflecting the terms of any reduced payment plan and stating that the credit card company agrees to accept a certain amount as full payment of any outstanding balances. I would suggest that you obtain this written confirmation from both the credit counseling company and your credit card company for each debt. Also, make sure you get copies of documents reflecting the actual monthly payments to your creditors.

If you can't learn to manage your finances, you're doomed to repeat your spending patterns, even after successfully reducing your debts through the use of a legitimate credit counseling company. You should only use a credit counseling company that actually provides debt counseling to teach you how to manage your income and expenses. This will help you stay out of trouble in the future.

When picking a reputable credit counseling company, you should consult your local Better Business Bureau or another consumer agency, like your state attorney general's office, to determine whether the credit counseling company you are considering has any history of problems. If the company does, avoid it. Never pick a credit counseling company merely on the basis of an advertisement on television, or one that contacts you through an e-mail or telephone solicitation. Do your research before sending your money to anyone, no matter how quick a fix that person promises.

One additional word of caution: the designation "nonprofit" does not mean the credit counseling service is legitimate. Again, do your homework—check out the company.

Never solely rely on the credit counseling company to pay your bills. While most credit counseling companies require that you pay them a certain amount per month toward payment of your bills, don't simply take their word that they are actually making the payments to your creditors. In the Cavanaughs' case, the credit counseling company never paid their creditors. And even in the case of legitimate credit counseling companies, sometimes errors can occur. You should regularly contact all your creditors to make sure that they have agreed to accept the monthly payments proposed by the credit counseling company; to ascertain that the monthly payments are, in fact, being made by the credit counseling company; and to check the amount of your current outstanding balance.

Nothing is free. Generally, having your bills compromised and paid by a credit counseling company will result in a lower credit rating. In some cases, it can be a significant reduction. If the credit counseling company has negotiated a reduction in your total debt and you are not paying the full amount of your bills, your credit rating will be reduced to reflect your inability to timely pay all your financial obligations.

Chapter 19

MONEY, FINANCES, AND DEBT: WHAT YOU NEED TO KNOW

IN OUR CONSUMER-DRIVEN SOCIETY, IT'S EASIER THAN EVER TO GET INTO real trouble by overextending our credit and jeopardizing our savings. To keep from finding yourself in bankruptcy court, take the time to think about the following simple facts that can help protect your savings, home, and investments.

HOME AS EQUITY

Your Home Is an Investment—Don't Bet the Farm on a Bad Mortgage Company

For most of us, our house is our biggest investment—and our biggest expense. We scrimp, save, and then ultimately borrow the vast majority of the purchase price of the house. That means one thing—most of us have to deal with a mortgage payment and mortgage companies. Most mortgage companies offer legitimate services and faithfully work to get you into your new home or refinance your current mortgage with an eye toward lowering your monthly payments and enabling you to afford some of life's other big expenses—college tuition, that new car, and maybe a new kitchen. Unfortunately, there are unscrupulous businesses that prey upon the uninformed.

Here are some tips to avoid falling into the mortgage trap:

➤ When choosing a mortgage company, try to stick with established companies with long histories of providing mortgages. Many Web sites, like www.bankrate.com and www.eloan.com, list mortgage companies throughout the United States. These Web sites provide listings of loan companies and show terms and rates for the most common loan types. They also offer useful financial tools such as various loan calculators and mortgage information for new home buyers.

➤ Be wary of mortgage companies that offer substantially lower interest rates, no requirement for income verification, or terms and conditions that vary greatly from those of other traditional mainstream mortgage companies. These companies may be fraudulent, merely attempting to obtain your financial information in order to steal your identity. Mortgage companies must generally be licensed by the state to offer mortgages in your state. Check with your state real estate division to verify the status of the mortgage company.

➤ Check with your local Better Business Bureau (BBB) to find out whether the mortgage company is a member and whether it has any history of complaints. You can find your local BBB online at www.lookup.bbb.org. While not all businesses are members of the BBB, most large consumer businesses are members and consider a good reputation with their customers to be as invaluable as the products and services they offer to their customers. If a mortgage company has a history of unresolved consumer complaints with the BBB, walk away.

➤ Avoid mortgage companies that send you unsolicited e-mails or telemarketing calls. These are often scams. You can learn more about mortgage scams from the Federal Trade Commission; its Web site is www.ftc.gov.

➤ If you're considering refinancing your current mortgage, compare your old interest rate with the new interest rate. Make sure that the offered rate terms are at least equal to, or better than, your current rate. You should also calculate any closing costs or prepayment penalties for both the old loan and the new loan. Finally, make sure that the greater total interest you're going to pay on the new mortgage does not offset any monthly savings you'll achieve by refinancing your current mortgage.

➤ If you're running out of options and do not qualify for a refinance of your mortgage, you may be headed for a foreclosure. Each state has its own set of laws with regard to how and when a lender may foreclose on your mortgage. If you are confronted with this situation, I would recommend that you immediately consult a lawyer who is experienced in debt management and counseling. In most cases, the foreclosure process, which begins with a notice of default and ends with a foreclosure sale of your property, can take months to complete. Generally the law provides for a safety period in which you can pay any back payments and retain your home.

PROTECTING YOUR INVESTMENTS

Making Money While Avoiding Scams

As long as people have been trying to make money, there have been people trying to con them out of their hard-earned cash. The old adage is true: if it sounds too good to be true, then it probably is a scam. A little research can avoid many of the traps unwary investors fall into when searching for a secure investment.

Here are some places where you can find out about the company you are considering investing in:

➤ If you're looking at stocks, bonds, or mutual funds being offered by a brokerage company or individual, you can check out the company and individual through the National Association of Securities Dealers (NASD) online at www.nasd.com. You may also contact the United States Securities and Exchange Commission (SEC) online at www.sec.gov. Make sure that the broker or financial advisor you are dealing with is licensed to sell the investment product you are considering and also does not have a checkered history of consumer complaints. If he or she does, invest your money elsewhere.

➤ If you have a dispute with your broker or financial advisor, most investment contracts provide for the binding arbitration of disputes. You will not have the right to file a lawsuit and go to court. Arbitrations are more informal than court proceedings but allow for final resolution of the dispute. Information regarding resolving claims against your broker or financial advisor can also be found online at www.nasd.com. General information about the arbitration process can be found at the American Arbitration Association's Web site, www.adr.org.

➤ If your financial matter does not involve securities or other federally regulated investments, and the amount of your loss is less than $5,000, you may be able to sue the person or company in your local small claims court. You do not need a lawyer, and the time period from filing your complaint and having a judge decide your case can be relatively short—sometimes only a month or two. Many state courts now offer information online regarding small claims procedures, online forms, and fee information. Check your local court Web site or call your local courthouse to see what information is offered at the courthouse and online.

➤ If you're purchasing insurance, make sure you contact your state's insurance commissioner's office to ensure that the agent and the insurance company are both licensed and admitted to sell insurance in your state. While licensing is probably not required for most nationally recognized insurance companies, when you are dealing with an unknown insurance company or if the offered premiums seem too low, this may be a sign that the insurance is a scam. Check out the company before you send in your first premium payment. The National Association of Insurance Commissioners Web site at www.naic.org has links to your state's insurance commissioner's Web site. Purchasing insurance through a licensed and admitted insurer means that you may be entitled to recover some benefits under your state's insurance guaranty fund if your insurance company becomes insolvent. Once again, you can check your state's insurance guaranty fund by linking to your state through www.naic.org.

DEALING WITH DEBT

It's something everyone has and nobody wants: debt. For most of us, our debts are manageable and enable us to own a home, buy a car, and obtain our education. Sometimes, though, we're hit with unexpected medical expenses, the loss of a job, or the death of the primary income earner, and our debts become a burden that we're unable to recover from without help. While there are ways to find help with your debts, make sure that you don't fall prey to the unscrupulous person or company that seeks to steal your remaining money or credit at a time when you can least afford it.

Debt Counseling: Getting Outside Help

If you're having trouble paying your debts, you may seek the help of debt repayment counseling. Here are some things to keep in mind as you look for help with managing your debt:

➤ If you're watching television these days, you will see ad after ad for debt counselors offering to reduce your interest rates and help you to get your bills paid. While many of these businesses offer legitimate help, some are merely scams designed to take your remaining savings or credit. Steer clear of companies that require set percentages of the total amount of your outstanding debt as their "fee."

➤ Also, make sure that the company truly offers credit counseling to ensure that you learn the proper steps to prevent yourself from experiencing debt problems in the future. You should contact your local BBB to find out the names of reputable credit counseling companies in your area.

➤ Often, a simple call to your credit card company requesting a reduction in your interest rate will achieve the same result as a credit counseling service. Most credit card companies are willing to arrange payment options for you to pay your balance in order to avoid your filing for bankruptcy.

➤ Be wary of companies that offer "credit repair" services, whereby they offer to increase your credit scores so that you can qualify for credit or more favorable interest rates. If there are legitimate bad marks on your credit history, no "credit repair" company can have them removed. If there are errors in your credit report, you can have them removed yourself through your own efforts. The Federal Trade Commission offers free advice on "credit repair" companies at www.ftc.gov.

Paying Uncle Sam

We all have to pay our taxes. Many people feel that they should not even file their tax returns unless they have the money to pay the tax bill. Wrong. You should always file your tax return on time and seek assistance from the IRS if you need special payment assistance. You can find information online at www.irs.gov. Sometimes, when you are confronted with an outstanding tax bill, the IRS may accept less than the full amount through a provision called an offer in compromise. Each taxpayer's situation is different, and I would recommend that you consult a tax lawyer or tax professional before considering this approach. Generally, a taxpayer has only one opportunity in his or her lifetime to do an offer in compromise, and there are stringent restrictions and rules that apply.

Bankruptcy: The Final Frontier

In October 2005, the federal bankruptcy laws were substantially changed. One important change limited the number of people who qualified to entirely eliminate their debts, as opposed to debtors who are required to repay a portion of their debts over three to five years.

If you are contemplating bankruptcy, you should consult a lawyer experienced in bankruptcy matters in your state. Most state bar associations offer lawyer referral programs. You can also research local bankruptcy lawyers in your area at www.martindale.com.

Part IV

YOUR HOME

How to Live in Your Home Without Ruining Your Future

Whether you rent or own your home, you always have a great feeling when you are finally moved in. You closed on the mortgage without a hitch, you managed to expertly avoid any major hassles with the neighbors, your furniture arrived on time and intact. You should be in the clear—right? In this section, we'll examine the perils of finding and maintaining the place you call home.

Home should be a place where you feel safe. If you make smart decisions and understand the responsibilities involved, most likely it will be. Unfortunately, some folks learn the implications of home ownership the hard way. When you own a home, you are responsible for all the things that happen on your property—things that are sometimes unavoidable or not your fault, but for which you have to pay anyway. If you own a home, you immediately take on a lot of potential liability.

Some people purchase homes as investments, opting to become landlords and assuming that the benefit of collecting rent will outweigh the responsibilities of essentially maintaining a home for your tenants. This section of the book will deal with all the things that can go wrong between a landlord and a tenant, and the ways you can protect yourself and your property before the situation goes south and relations sour.

Finally, most of us like to feel that home is the one place where we get to have things our way. However, if you live in a neighborhood governed by a homeowners' association, you may find that very stiff penalties are attached to "having it your way" if your way doesn't meet the association's rules and restrictions.

Chapter 20

HOMEOWNERS VS. HOMEOWNERS' ASSOCIATIONS

MARGARET AND WILLIAM BRADLEY HAD SUNK EVERY LAST PENNY THEY HAD into their retirement dream house in the new development of Nine Palms in Tampa, Florida. They had planned to spend years together watching their grandchildren play on the neat back lawn and enjoying their view of the lake from the two deck chairs on their small dock. They never expected to be talking about finding a new home.

For a few years, their dream house had been everything they had hoped for. But when William was unexpectedly hospitalized, Margaret fell behind on her bookkeeping. That led to a simple oversight that turned their lives upside down.

For weeks, William had been having terrible headaches. Instead of working in his garden—a spectacular collection of terra cotta containers that held everything from tomatoes to roses—he spent most days lying on the couch in the family room with a cold cloth over his eyes.

Though Margaret had nagged William to see a doctor, he shrugged off her concerns. A few weeks later, he collapsed on his daily walk around the winding streets of the development, and a concerned neighbor called for an ambulance. When William was admitted to the hospital for symptoms of a stroke, the doctors discovered an aneurysm near his brain. Before Margaret could even get to his side at the hospital, William was whisked into emergency surgery.

"The doctors said it was a miracle that I survived," he said.

Margaret called her oldest son, Alan, and he flew in to help for the weeks that passed before William could come home from the hospital. When it became clear that his father would be in a wheelchair for part of his rehabilitation, Alan headed to a building supply store and bought supplies to install a ramp so his father could navigate the front steps.

Margaret was grateful for her son's efforts, but she was worried. She knew that the homeowners' association was notoriously strict. She called the association and requested a form to allow for special modifications to the front of the home. "I would have walked out to pick it up," she said, explaining that the association office was just down the street. "But I really didn't want to leave William alone. I guess I thought they might just send someone over with the form."

A week later, instead of a form, William and Margaret received a notice that they had been fined $150 for making "unapproved" structural changes to their entry. Their son was furious. He helped Margaret draft a letter explaining why the changes were made and that she had requested the proper forms, but they were never sent. "He told me not to pay the fine," she remembered. "He convinced me that we had the right to do what we had to do to our house. He seemed so certain that it would reverse the fine."

Alan flew back home, and Margaret and William settled into a routine. Between the doctor's appointments and William's medications and physical therapy, Margaret was exhausted, but William was making remarkable progress in his recovery. "I just needed to get back to my home and gardens," he said. After just a few months, he was out of the wheelchair and getting around with a cane. The next time Alan came back to Florida for a visit, he removed the ramp. It seemed that life was finally getting back to normal.

Eight months after William had gone into the hospital, the home-owners' association sent another letter.

"This letter said that we had fallen behind in our association dues," Margaret said. "I thought it was possible, since everything had been so hectic, that I might have missed a payment."

Margaret checked her records and saw that she had indeed missed two monthly payments during William's initial hospitalization. They owed $150 in homeowner's dues. For a couple like Margaret and William, retirees with a fairly tight budget, this was not a small amount. But since they had been making recent payments regularly, Margaret assumed it would be easy to work out a repayment plan.

She called the association office, explained what had happened, and asked if they could repay the dues on an installment plan. "That sounds fine, honey," the woman in the office told her. "But let me dou-ble check with the manager when he comes back from vacation." Two weeks later, when Margaret hadn't heard anything from the manager, she called the office again but was told he was unavailable.

A week after that, Margaret received a letter from a law firm repre-senting the association and requesting immediate payment of all out-standing fines and penalties. The amount had skyrocketed from $150 to $1,500. When Margaret called the association's office, she was told that the amount now included the fees due to the lawyer that the asso-ciation had retained to help collect the debt.

In desperation, Margaret and William sent a check for $400—all they could spare—to the association with a letter explaining the situa-tion once again. After a month, their check had still not been cashed.

Again, Margaret called the association office, finally speaking to the manager and offering to repay the original amount in installments. "I told him we were on a fixed income and it wasn't easy to come up with lump sums of cash."

"They told her that it wasn't their responsibility to make sure that we sent our checks in a timely fashion," William said. "And it wasn't any use calling them anymore, since they'd already turned the debt over for collection."

The next communication they received was from a collection agency. It was a notice that their house had been sold at auction to satisfy an outstanding lien.

When Margaret and William found out the details of the sale, they were horrified. Their $300,000 dream house, which they had owned outright, had been purchased by a real estate speculator for just over $75,000. They were notified that they would receive a check for the selling price, less the amount owed to the association.

Desperate, they contacted the man who had bought their house. "We thought that maybe he might have some compassion for our situation," Margaret said. Instead, the investor offered to sell it back to the couple for $400,000!

William and Margaret were given thirty days to vacate the property. They had no idea where they would go. All their savings had been put into their house. They had been so proud of owning it outright and had counted on booming Florida real estate values to ensure that it would be a good inheritance for their children.

"Sometimes I think we should just stay here, make 'em come and get us out," William said. "My doctors told me to avoid stress. But I'm seventy years old and soon to be homeless with just $75,000 to my name. Brain surgery didn't kill me, but this battle with the homeowners' association might just do the job."

HOW I WOULD HAVE COUNSELED THE BRADLEYS

Certain areas of the law seem so inequitable and unfair that you would think "there ought to be a law against this." This is one of them. Without a doubt, dealing with homeowners' associations is an area of the law that can trip up unsuspecting homeowners and potentially cost them their home, their life savings, and their future. Don't let what happened to the Bradleys happen to you. Know your rights.

Homeowners' associations are organizations that receive monthly dues or assessments in order to provide insurance coverage and maintenance for common areas within a residential development. In the case of condominiums, these associations will maintain the grounds, replace the roof, and repaint the outside of the buildings. In order to function, the association must collect monthly dues.

Most homeowners' associations implement rules and regulations covering all types of matters, including how homeowners may redesign or alter their home, what guests may be permitted to live in the home, and even how cars may be parked in the community. Violating any of these rules can cost the homeowner money in the form of fines. This is what happened to the Bradleys.

You have to pay the monthly homeowner's dues or any fines relating to your violation of any of the community rules. Never ignore these dues or fines. Never means never. Paying these expenses is as important as paying your mortgage. Generally, homeowners' associations collect dues every month, each quarter, or each year, depending on their own particular rules. With regard to fines, you have a certain time period in which to pay the fine or contest the imposition of the fine. If you fail to pay these bills on time, the homeowners' association generally refers the bill to an outside collection agency and lawyer. The extra fees charged by these people almost always significantly exceed the amount of the original bill. I cannot stress this enough: pay your assessments and fines on time.

Each state generally controls the laws relating to rules and regulations governing homeowners' associations. Each state has different laws, so if you run afoul of your neighborhood's homeowners' association, you should promptly consult a lawyer in your state experienced in dealing with these groups. The sad fact is that if the Bradleys had consulted a lawyer regarding the dispute, they would have quickly been able to avoid the late fees, the association's lawyer fees, and the ultimate loss of their home.

In many states, a homeowners' association is given the power to place a lien on your property within the community in order to secure payment of the outstanding assessments or fines. This lien will be paid from the first proceeds from the sale or refinancing of the property. Generally, the homeowners' association must provide you with advance written notice of its intention to place a lien on your property. While the timing of the advance notice varies from state to state, often it is only a short time.

Many states allow a property owner to make payment plans for the payment of any outstanding assessments or fines. If I had been counseling the Bradleys, I would have advised them to communicate with the homeowners' association only in writing and to have promptly filed a complaint regarding the assessment of the fine relating to the wheelchair ramp. This modification to their house might have been covered by applicable federal regulations relating to persons with disabilities.

As the Bradleys found out, homeowners' associations have a very effective tool with which to ensure that you pay all outstanding assessments and fines—the foreclosure of your home. Generally, a homeowners' association may seek the foreclosure of your property for even relatively small amounts of money. In one infamous case, an elderly couple lost their home through a foreclosure sale when the total amount owed in assessments was only $120.

But homeowners now have a tool at their disposal. Most states have a specially appointed ombudsman, an official who will investigate a formal complaint filed by a homeowner against a homeowners' association. The Bradleys should contact their state attorney general's office and find out whether such a resource is available in their state. Even if you are able to use the service of an ombudsman and file a complaint, you should still seek legal counsel because there are so many complaints that it can take months for yours to make its way through the system, and the homeowners' association can still continue to move forward with foreclosure proceedings.

In some states, the normal foreclosure process, which can be very lengthy, is avoided by homeowners' associations in seeking the foreclosure of a lien for unpaid assessments or fines. These types of non-judicial foreclosures can cause you to forfeit many of the protections built into the general foreclosure laws of your state. Don't go it alone—get a lawyer if you're confronted with a foreclosure sale of your property over a minor delinquent assessment or fine.

Chapter 21

MOVING SCAMS

DONNA CAMPANELLO, HER HUSBAND, GARY, AND THEIR TWIN DAUGHTERS had moved into their new apartment almost four months earlier. And while she had expected to be living out of boxes for a while, she hadn't, as she put it, expected to be living "*on* and *in* boxes" for more than a few weeks. But dinner was still being served on an overturned packing box that served as a table, and the whereabouts of the Campanellos' dining room set, as well as several other items from their former home, still remained a mystery.

When Gary accepted a new job in New York City, Donna and their twin eight-year-old daughters were excited about leaving their suburban Chicago neighborhood for the big city. They had talked about how different it would be to live in an apartment, rather than a house, and how they would have to get rid of some of their old larger furniture in favor of apartment-sized pieces. The girls had held a tag sale, clearing out many of their toys in anticipation of the limited storage space in their new apartment.

Gary had gone to New York ahead of his family, living in temporary housing provided by his company and scouting for the perfect apartment. It took him a few weeks of looking, but he finally found a good-sized three-bedroom apartment on the Upper East Side, and he and Donna moved quickly to purchase it. They considered themselves lucky that the closing went off without a problem, and they excitedly began to make plans to move their family east.

Donna admitted to being a real planner. She had Gary fax her scale drawings of all the rooms. She didn't want to move anything they weren't going to use—and she figured she'd avoid paying New York prices by picking up a few new pieces of furniture at the shops she liked near their old home.

Donna measured, planned, purchased new furniture, and got rid of old furniture. Finally she was satisfied that she could get the new apartment in shape quickly. They would move as soon as school ended and be settled in before the new school year started. Donna went online and researched movers. Conscious of the higher living expenses they would encounter in their new city, she was looking for deals. When she found Nation's Easy Movers, she thought she had found the perfect arrangement.

Toward the end of May, Donna called several companies to get quotes for a move from Hyde Park, outside Chicago, to Manhattan. The cheapest all required cash or a cashier's check, but a company called Nation's Easy Movers had the lowest price. Over the phone, the representative asked Donna questions about the amount of household goods she was moving before quoting her a price of $3.50 per cubic foot for 550 cubic feet. The total for the quote was $1,925, plus additional for any packing materials.

"It was a great price," Donna said. She told Nation's Easy Movers to set up the move for the first week in June, and she sent a deposit check for $150 by Federal Express.

On June 10, the movers showed up as promised. The driver of the truck told Donna that he thought she might have more than the 550 cubic feet originally estimated but that he would provide her with an invoice upon arrival in New York.

"Since the quote was well under the amount I had thought the move might cost, I wasn't too worried about the additional charges," Donna said. "Besides, the girls and I were on a tight schedule. We were driving to New York and had to leave that day in order to get there before the moving van."

The movers told Donna that they had a few other houses to pack up, and they expected to arrive in New York within seven days with her furniture. Donna and the girls packed the car with a few suitcases and toys and set off on their drive.

They arrived at their new apartment on June 13. "At first it was fun, sleeping in sleeping bags and getting take-out." Donna said. "It was a great adventure, but I knew I was going to be glad when our furniture arrived on the 17th."

June 17 came and went. Donna called the moving company and was told that the drivers had encountered some trouble on one of their stops but were only a few days behind schedule. She was assured that her belongings would arrive on June 21 at the latest. By June 23, ten days after their arrival in New York, the thrill of sleeping on the floor was wearing thin.

Repeated calls to the company resulted in a litany of excuses: the dispatcher was out sick, the truck had broken down, their furniture was temporarily in storage in North Carolina, there had been a hurricane in North Carolina and the storage facility had sustained some damage but no one was sure whether their belongings had been damaged. The list of excuses went on and on. Donna was persistent, calling the company nearly every day for the rest of June and part of July.

By this point, the family had been forced to invest in some basic comfort items. Although they were still sleeping in their sleeping bags, at least they had mattresses on the floor. They had purchased a new TV and DVD player for some basic entertainment and a few pots and dishes and glasses for the kitchen. Everyone needed new clothing, as they had brought only the basics to last for a week or so.

"I must have spent several thousands of dollars just to get a minimum standard of living," Donna said.

Finally, in mid-August, two months after their belongings had left Chicago, Donna was told that the moving van was en route and would arrive within the week. The woman from Nation's Easy Movers had been very apologetic, and told her that the movers would have an invoice that would reflect a discount for her inconvenience.

At last, on August 27, eleven weeks after the moving van had left Chicago, Donna's apartment buzzer sounded. The truck had arrived. Donna went down to the street, and the mover handed her an invoice, explaining that they would need payment in full before beginning to unload. "All we have from you is a $150 deposit," they reminded her.

Donna opened the invoice and nearly fainted. The total cost of the move: $7,500. Trying to stay calm, she told the movers she had to call the company to confirm the price. "We ain't got all day to stand here, lady," one of the movers told her. "We need the cash or we're not taking your stuff off the truck."

Donna phoned Nation's Easy Movers and asked to speak to Brenda. She was told that Brenda no longer worked for the company. Instead, she spoke to Jay, who confirmed the price. The original quote for $1,925 was for the first 550 cubic feet. Donna's household goods had used an additional 500 cubic feet at $7.75 per cubic foot, for an additional $4,262.50. Moving materials had added another $992.50. There was a storage facility charge from North Carolina for $570. Jay explained that Nation's Easy Movers was crediting back her $150 deposit and a "refund" of $200 because of the late arrival of her items.

"He said this as if it were the most reasonable thing in the world!" Donna said. "I went out and told the drivers that I didn't have that kind of cash available, and they just got into the truck and drove away."

Desperate for her furniture, including family heirlooms and baby photos of the girls—the things that make a home seem like home— Donna called the moving company and agreed to pay the drivers cash if they would return with her furniture.

The drivers came back, Donna handed over a cashier's check for $7,500, and they moved her boxes and furniture into the apartment. "They even had the nerve to tell me that they did accept tips," she fumed.

It would have been bad enough if that had been the end of the story, but in unpacking, Donna discovered that some of the boxes contained items that didn't belong to her and that some of her most treasured possessions were missing. Much of the furniture had been damaged, as well. The furniture she had purchased in Chicago arrived scratched. The new leather armchairs had rips in the upholstery, the antique vanity table that had been passed down to the girls from their great-great-grandmother had arrived with the elegant mirror in shards, and her dining room set was simply missing.

Donna's subsequent calls to Nation's Easy Movers have been unproductive. The company claims that she paid and accepted the delivery and that it has no further responsibility to her. "I thought I was getting a bargain," Donna said. "Now I see that when it comes to movers, the old saying is true: you get what you pay for."

HOW I WOULD HAVE COUNSELED DONNA

Without a doubt, moving is one of the most stressful things we do in life. Besides having to uproot our families, switch jobs, and get used to new surroundings, we have to actually move all our possessions. It's not until you move that you realize how much "stuff" you really have. Unless you have unlimited free time and a lifelong desire to play trucker, you'll probably use a moving company. When you hire a moving company, don't let it box you in with unexpected charges and delays. Doing your research is key. Know what you're getting into before the movers load that first box onto their truck.

When planning your move, it's best to get several written estimates from different moving companies. Estimates given orally are worthless. As a rule, never select the moving company whose estimate comes in well below the other estimates, the way Donna did. This is usually a tip-off that the company is not reputable and will hit you with higher charges and expenses later.

You should insist on having someone from the moving company

come to your home and survey all your belongings before giving you the written estimate. Don't rely on an "estimate" conducted over the phone or the Internet—it will almost always be wrong. Only an experienced estimator from a reputable moving company has the training to properly calculate the total cost of the move.

Moving costs are based on the weight of all your belongings and the distance you are moving them. Additional costs can include packing materials, whether the moving company will be packing your possessions, and incidental items, such as whether the movers will need to haul your possessions up stairs. Make sure you advise the moving company of any special issues relating to your belongings and the move— such as packing and shipping of valuable antiques or irreplaceable items. This will ensure that your written estimate accurately reflects the true cost of the move.

Estimates are either binding or nonbinding. A binding estimate will ensure that the moving company will be able to charge only the estimated amount. Binding estimates usually cost more, since the moving company will have to build into the estimated price any contingencies that may arise or any error in undervaluing the weight of your belongings. A nonbinding estimate will allow the moving company to increase the estimated cost based upon the actual cost of the move. However, any increase is generally limited to a set percentage of the original estimated price.

If you choose a nonbinding estimate, you should carefully check the document to determine under what circumstances, and in what amount, the moving company is entitled to increase the cost of the move. If the written estimate is silent on this issue, request that the moving company provide a written statement reflecting its policy regarding increases in the estimated cost. If the moving company refuses, don't use it.

Donna should have requested that Nation's Easy Movers come to their home and properly estimate the weight of their belongings. By using only a telephone estimate, she ran the risk that the estimate would come in far too low and she would likely be required to pay the extra expense associated with the increased weight. However, depending on the terms of the contract, Nation's Easy Movers might not have been permitted to double the weight estimate and therefore, the moving costs. Donna may have a claim for a refund if the increased charges exceeded the percentage allowed under the moving contract.

You should always insure your belongings for the move. Invariably there will be damage to items during the loading or unloading or in transit. There are generally two types of insurance: one is based on the weight of the item, the other on the replacement cost of the item. Insurance covering the weight of the item, which is generally much cheaper, will compensate you only for the loss of an item based on its weight. Standard insurance by weight is commonly in the amount of 40 to 60 cents per pound. For example, a computer that weighs 10 pounds would be insured for only $6 if the insurance is only 60 cents per pound. You are better off purchasing replacement cost insurance, which would pay for the replacement of the computer as well as the replacement of items that are missing or damaged.

If you have items of great value, not only should you purchase replacement cost insurance, also you will need to specifically list them and their value on your moving documents. Donna should have purchased the replacement cost insurance and specifically itemized her high-value items, such as the antique vanity table. This would enable her to make an insurance claim for the full replacement cost of the damaged items.

If the moving company is late in delivering your belongings, you may be entitled to recover the costs of replacing necessities needed because of the delay. Donna should request a refund of the money she spent on these items.

When the truck arrives at the destination, this is when the real work begins. Before the moving company will unload your property, generally it will require full payment for the move. If possible, use a credit card or a personal or cashier's check. Never give the driver cash. Get a receipt.

While you are also required to sign the moving documents to confirm delivery of your belongings, never sign the receipt until after you have unpacked everything and checked for damaged or missing items. It is your responsibility to notify the moving company of any missing or damaged items BEFORE the driver and crew leave. Take the time to check. If possible, it's a good idea to have friends around to help with this task. Take photographs of any valuable items before they are loaded onto the truck for the move, and take another set of photographs of any damaged items. Don't let the moving company push you into signing the receipt, since if you later find damaged or missing items, the company will use your signature on the receipt in an attempt to discredit your claim.

Chapter 22

TENANTS BANKRUPT LANDLORD

HORROR STORIES FROM TENANTS ABOUND, BUT LANDLORDS WHO OWN investment properties also put themselves at risk each time they sign a lease agreement. Rita and Albert Romero found out the hard way that buying a two-family house and using one apartment for income was not the easy ticket to home ownership they had thought it would be. In fact, renting out an apartment in their home cost them their business and forced them into bankruptcy.

"We had wanted for years to have our own house," Rita said. When she and Albert found a charming two-family town house in an up-and-coming neighborhood in Baltimore, they knew they would be stretching themselves financially to buy it, but they thought the rental income would enable them to afford their dream.

"We never considered that we'd have tenants but no income," Albert said.

They had owned the house for nearly eight years, purchased with savings from Albert's business installing security locks and alarm systems. They had had problems with tenants in the past—late rent, noisy parties, damage to the apartment—but these were minor inconveniences compared to the nightmare that had gone on for the past year.

Their last tenants—college students—had just moved out, and Rita and Albert were planning to repair and repaint when Rita got a call from a local agency that helped people with low incomes find apartments. One of their old tenants worked there and had mentioned that she was leaving a three-bedroom apartment. The agency told them it had a family, with a pregnant mom, that urgently needed an apartment.

"We thought it would be a good thing to do," Albert said. "Help out some people who needed a hand."

"And we thought it would be nice to have a family in the house," Rita said. "We thought they'd be more responsible than college students."

The husband came to look at the apartment, and Rita apologized for the condition it was in, explaining that they would repaint and repair the damage caused by the previous tenants. "No problem," the man said. He repeated several times how grateful they were to have more room, with another baby on the way. Before he left, he told Rita that he'd be happy to do the repainting himself.

The agency gave Rita and Albert a check for $900—two months' rent—and the family moved into the apartment in June. They seemed like ideal tenants. Their two small children were quiet and well behaved, the mother made small talk with Rita when she ran into her outside the building, and the husband began to repaint the apartment. "We noticed that the husband was home most of the time," Albert said. "I began to wonder what he did for a job, but since they had come to us through the agency, we figured they had been approved in some way."

August 1 came and went without a rent check from the tenants. On August 15, Rita stopped by the apartment to ask for the check. The mother met her at the door, holding a newborn. "I didn't even know she'd had the baby," Rita said. "I forgot all about asking for the rent. In fact, I felt bad that I didn't have a baby gift for her." Embarrassed not to have known about the new baby, Rita made an excuse for dropping by and didn't mention the rent. When Albert got home from the shop, she sheepishly asked him to speak to the husband about the late rent.

When Albert talked to the husband, he explained that he was supposed to have started a new job, but on the first day of work he had to take his wife to the hospital. The baby had been born two weeks early; his wife had a difficult time and had been unable to take care of the other two children for a week or two. Because he was unable to show up regularly, he had lost the job he'd been promised.

Albert was sympathetic and agreed to give him until August 30 to pay the August rent. Wanting to be fair, he wrote up an agreement stating that the tenants could pay their rent on the 15th of the month for the next three months, after which it would be due on the first of each month. "I thought that would give them some time to get back on their feet," Albert said. But the rent check Albert and Rita got at the end of August was the first and last full rent check they ever received from their tenants.

On September 15, the tenants handed over a rent check for $100, complaining that there were mice in the apartment. They would withhold the balance, they said, until the situation was taken care of. Rita was shocked. In all of their years in this house, neither she nor Albert had ever seen mice. She offered to get an exterminator, but the tenant said she didn't want poison around the children. So Rita found a pest control service that didn't use poisons and had its service people visit the apartment. The bill for that visit was $175.

In October, the tenants claimed the mice were still a problem and again withheld part of their rent. Rita ordered another round of extermination at $175. At the beginning of November, they claimed the stove was leaking gas, making the apartment unsafe. Although no one had ever complained about the stove before, Rita called the repair service. But when the November rent was due, the tenants said the stove was not working again, and they demanded a new appliance. Rita and Albert bought a new electric stove for $550 and installed it in the kitchen of the apartment.

Rita and Albert suspected that the tenants were making excuses simply to avoid paying the rent. In December, six months after they had allowed the nightmare tenants to move in, Rita and Albert had received only $1,300 of the total $2,700 in rental income that the apartment should have been producing. In addition, they had spent almost $1,000 on repairs to the apartment. They were beginning to feel the financial strain of not receiving rental income. When January brought a fresh set of complaints but no rent check from the tenants, Rita and Albert sent them an eviction notice for nonpayment of rent.

"That's when our troubles really began," Rita said.

In response to the letter of eviction, Rita and Albert received a letter from a "student attorney" at the University of Baltimore Law School. The letter stated that Rita and Albert could not use eviction as retaliation for their tenants' legitimate complaints regarding the safety of the apartment.

Rita and Albert had refinanced the house to help meet some of the expenses. "We were optimistic that we would be able to put these people out and begin collecting rent again," Albert explained. But the higher mortgage payment was taking a serious toll on their finances. When a large company made an offer for Albert's business, he sold it for less than he would have liked. Shortly thereafter he was laid off by the new owners.

After Rita and Albert had received only partial rent checks and a litany of complaints in February and March, it became clear to them that despite repeated statements that they were looking for a new apartment, the tenants were not going to find one. And with their precarious financial situation, Rita and Albert were desperate for the rental income. So, in July, more than a year after the tenants had moved in, Rita and Albert again tried to evict the family.

"That's when they really began to fight dirty," Albert said.

The tenants claimed that the apartment had not been properly deleaded. Rita showed them proof that the apartment had been deleaded when the house had been purchased. The scrape marks removing old paint were still clearly visible on some doorways. But the tenants called the state inspector to examine the apartment, pointing out that the deleading was incomplete because it did not extend to the required five feet. Albert and Rita were shocked when the inspector agreed. When Albert pointed out that the tenants had installed carpeting with a pad (without approval) that raised the base of the floor nearly an inch, and that the deleading had been within the guidelines based on the bare floor, the inspector was sympathetic but insistent—they would have to remove additional lead paint on the trim to ensure that the apartment met standards.

The inspection cost Albert and Rita $500. The fine for having lead in an apartment with children was over $1,000. The lead removal cost another $3,000. To add insult to injury, they were forced to house the family in a hotel while the deleading was taking place. Three nights in a suite at a local chain hotel set Rita and Albert back another $1,200. And because the tenants had been in a dangerous situation, they claimed they did not need to pay full rent until the apartment was deemed safe by a second state inspection.

The nightmare continued. Every month the tenants would pay a small amount of rent and claim that there was a hazardous condition their landlords needed to address.

The combination of withheld rent and apartment-related expenses proved to be too much. Rita and Albert missed several of their own mortgage payments. In October, they received a notice of foreclosure on the home. The news was devastating. "I realized that we could be homeless," Rita said. "I was paralyzed with fear. I couldn't sleep or eat. All I could do was cry." Albert felt equally helpless.

Dipping into their savings, they hired a lawyer, who advised them to file for bankruptcy in a last-ditch effort to save their home. In January, without notice, Rita saw the tenants packing up their belongings in their car. She watched as they drove off. It was the last time she ever saw them again. They left owing her over $5,000 in rental income. Despite attempts to track their former tenants down, Rita and Albert know they will never see that money.

With an empty apartment, a large mortgage, and a bankruptcy ruling, Albert and Rita were trying to decide on their next steps. "I don't ever want to be a landlord again," Rita said. They were considering selling the house but were unsure whether they would ever be stable enough financially to buy another. "It's terrible to contemplate," Albert said. "I'm fifty-five and basically starting over again. Those tenants didn't just 'steal' that apartment. They stole our future."

HOW I WOULD HAVE COUNSELED THE ROMEROS

If you're up late at night watching television, you will see infomercials for the "systems" you can use to buy properties with no or little money down, and then join the ranks of landlords. "Positive cash flow" is the buzzword. It's not always that easy. While most of us pay our bills on time, some people attempt to take advantage of others. This is exactly what the Romeros experienced. While you can try to help others out, don't let them take advantage of you. Know your rights.

As a landlord, you should always perform a credit check on prospective tenants. Your prospective tenants will need to provide you with personal information, including Social Security number, date of birth, and written authorization to allow you to check their credit. Credit reporting agencies such as Equifax can run reports, or you can use an independent company that specializes in credit checks. These companies are listed in the Yellow Pages or online.

No rating or a poor credit rating is a red flag that the person may have a problem paying his or her bills. Don't set yourself up for a problem from the start. While the Romeros wanted to do a nice thing and rent to the low-income tenants, they were taking a huge risk that the tenants would not be able to pay their rent. This is exactly what happened. It is unlikely that the agency that referred the tenants screened their credit before referring them to the Romeros. Don't assume that a prospective tenant is creditworthy—check the person out.

You should always have a written lease agreement that spells out the length and term of the lease, as well as the rental rate and the obligations of both the landlord and the tenant. While there are numerous forms you may obtain online or through legal bookstores, you are generally better off having a lawyer in your area draft a lease agreement in compliance with local and state landlord–tenant laws. Each state's laws are different—sometimes dramatically.

In the case of the Romeros, a written lease agreement could have spelled out when the rental payments were due, including when late charges would commence accruing. The written lease agreement could also require that the tenants promptly notify the Romeros when anything was broken in the apartment. In this case, the tenants simply waited until rent was due each month to make their complaints known to the Romeros. This was a sure sign of fraud on the part of the tenants.

Depending on the laws of your state, it is questionable whether the tenant would be entitled to reduce the rent payment because of the allegations of mice. It appears that there were no mice in the apartment and that this was being merely used to reduce the amount of rent paid to the Romeros. However, given that the Romeros paid for an exterminator, the tenants should have been required to pay the outstanding rent.

When a tenant fails to pay rent, either on time or in the proper amount, the landlord is entitled to seek the eviction of the tenant. These types of matters, generally called unlawful detainer actions, are quick remedies available to the landlord to remove the tenant from the property. Because state requirements vary, it is recommended that you retain a lawyer to handle any unlawful detainer actions, since he or she will know what type of notice must be provided to the tenant and the procedural steps you must take to legally remove the tenant.

While a landlord generally may not evict a tenant in retaliation for reporting legitimate safety violations, a landlord is properly entitled to evict a tenant for nonpayment of rent. The Romeros needed to file an unlawful detainer action to remove the tenants. The Romeros should not have accepted the word of a "student attorney." The Romeros needed to take the tenants to court. It is unlikely that a court would find the tenants' persistent complaints credible.

With regard to the lead issue, the Romeros should not have permitted the carpet to be installed in their property. This should have been spelled out in the written lease agreement. In such a case, the Romeros should simply have removed the carpet and avoided the complaints from the tenants relating to lead. This would have also avoided any issue regarding the Romeros' paying for the tenants to stay at a hotel.

Chapter 23

HOMEOWNER'S LIABILITY FOR INJURY ON PROPERTY

JAKE NELSON'S PARENTS HAD ALWAYS BEEN GRATEFUL THAT THEIR SON enjoyed inviting his friends over to their home. It made them feel that they could always keep an eye on their son's behavior. They felt that they knew his friends, and they worried less about his falling in with the wrong crowd or getting into trouble driving around or hanging out. What they didn't realize was that looking the other way and letting "teens be teens" could endanger the very home that Jake considered such a haven.

"Jake is a good kid, a typical teenager," his parents agreed. While Jake's behavior wasn't always perfect, his mother and father were willing to make allowances. "Kids this age are going to act up, test limits, maybe have a beer or two," his father, Hal, said. "I just always thought it was best if that sort of thing went on at our home, so Jason didn't drive drunk or get picked up by the police for being in the wrong place at the wrong time. Now I realize that we put ourselves in a bad position by being so lenient with him."

It was late spring, nearly the end of his senior year at school, when Jake decided to have a few friends over on a Saturday night. His family's large house, in a quiet neighborhood in Cincinnati, was a great place for a party. The basement was a fully furnished rec room, complete with pool and ping-pong table. His dad had recently installed a huge high-definition wide-screen television in what he now called the media room. Outside, there was a basketball hoop, and because of the unseasonably warm weather, Jake's parents called the service company and had the pool opened early.

Key to guaranteeing a good night, at least in Jake's mind, was the fact that his parents were going to a wedding in Cleveland and would be gone until well after midnight. They had arranged for his younger sister to spend the night at a friend's house, but Jake was on his own. "I know my parents trusted me," Jake said. "And I didn't do anything wrong. Nothing that happened was my fault."

Jake told a couple of his friends from the basketball team to come by on Saturday night to hang out. Three of his buddies, Carl, Taylor, and Nick, showed up around 7:00 p.m. with a case of beer. Two other guys from the team, Ian and Jared, were supposed to come by later, Carl told Jake. Six guys was not a lot to have over. Jake figured they would play some hoops, drink some beer, and just hang out. "We would have done the same if my dad were around," he said.

Jake's father admitted that he knew some parents didn't approve of the fact that he let the kids have a beer or two while they were at the house. He recalled that one girl's mother had called him after a party that past summer to say she was upset that some kids had been drinking. But Hal just told her that he thought that kids would be kids, and he would rather have them drinking where he could keep an eye on them—even take their car keys away if he needed to.

When Jake's friends arrived that evening, they played some basketball for a few hours. They were inside watching a video when the other two guys, Ian and Jared, showed up, along with Travis, a kid from school whom Jake did not know well. "I didn't really know Travis, but Jared said he was cool," Jake said. Jake felt a little uneasy when Travis brought out a bottle of tequila and started doing shots with his beers. He told Travis to take it easy, but Travis didn't stop drinking. "Dude, everyone knows it's cool to party at your house," Travis replied.

As the night went on, Travis became increasingly drunk and obnoxious. "He was really getting on Nick's nerves, in particular," Jake said. "Talking trash about Nick's girlfriend and stuff."

When Travis got up from watching the video and left the room, Nick followed him out. Jake still doesn't really know what happened. The rest of the guys were watching the video when Carl said he was going to go find out where Nick and Travis had gone. A few minutes later, there was screaming from the backyard, and all of the remaining boys ran outside.

When Jake rounded the corner to the backyard, he could see Carl trying to pull Nick out of the swimming pool. "Travis wasn't helping at all. I could see right away that something was really wrong. Travis was just standing there with a big stupid smile on his face," Jake said.

Then Carl yelled that Nick wasn't breathing. Jake called 911 on his cell phone as his friends stood around helplessly. Ian, who had worked as a lifeguard for a few summers, began CPR. Long, tense minutes passed until the paramedics arrived on the scene. In all the commotion, Travis just disappeared.

Jake called Nick's parents and told them there had been an accident. He also called his dad's cell phone and gave him a quick version of the events. When Jake's parents got home, Carl told them what he had seen. He told them he had come out to the yard to see Nick and Travis engaged in a shouting shoving match. Travis had landed a roundhouse punch to Nick's jaw, sending him off balance, and shoved him into the pool. Carl thought he had heard Nick's head hit the side of the pool as he went in. While Travis stood by, Carl had pulled his unconscious friend from the water.

The scenario could have been much, much worse, but thanks to Carl's and Ian's quick actions, and Jake's immediate call for an ambulance, Nick was conscious and responding as the paramedics transported him to the hospital. But Travis's punch had broken his jaw, and he had a concussion from striking his head on the way into the pool.

Months later, Nick still couldn't remember what had happened that night. He suffered from episodes of debilitating headaches and blurred vision. He couldn't play basketball and ended up benched for his whole senior-year basketball season. Nick was disappointed, but his father was furious. This was the year when Nick was supposed to have been scouted by college basketball recruiters.

At the time of the accident, Nick's parents told the Nelsons that they were going to press charges against Travis. "But they ended up coming after us instead," Hal said.

When the police questioned Travis, he had a whole different story about what had happened at the Nelsons' house that night. He claimed that everyone had been drinking and rowdy, and that he had been uncomfortable and left early. On his way out, he claimed that he had seen Nick and Carl "messing around" out by the pool but that they weren't particularly close friends of his, so he just went home. He said he'd only heard about Nick's accident at school.

"Nick's parents said they couldn't get a straight story about what happened that night," Hal said. "But I think that they saw that Travis's family didn't have much money. They weren't going to get any kind of settlement there. The next thing I knew, I was hit with a lawsuit."

Nick's parents claimed that the Nelsons had been negligent in allowing underage drinking on their property, that they condoned such behavior in their absence, and that they were responsible for Nick's injury. They filed a suit looking for damages for nearly a million dollars. They said that Nick needed to have special therapy to treat his memory lapses and that they wanted him evaluated by a neurologist who wasn't covered by their insurance. Additionally, they claimed that the accident would seriously affect Nick's college admission and future earnings. Nick's parents were adamant. Someone had to be held accountable for what had happened. Someone needed to pay.

Hal was worried. His homeowner's insurance had a limit on what it would pay out, but with the kind of money Nick's parents were talking about, he didn't know how they'd be able to settle such a huge judgment. "With Jake at college this year, we don't have any extra money," he said. "I don't know why we should even be in this position. My kid had nothing to do with this. We had nothing to do with this."

HOW I WOULD HAVE COUNSELED THE NELSONS

Whenever we invite someone into our home, we risk potential liability for any injury that occurs. Hal thought he was doing the right thing in allowing Jake and his friends to drink in his home in order to prevent them from getting into trouble "somewhere else." Unfortunately for Hal, the "somewhere else" ended up being his own home. Never let your underage children have parties at your home when you know alcohol will be consumed. Don't let what happened to Hal happen to you. Be careful, and know your rights before something happens.

In many states, a homeowner is liable for injuries resulting from any dangerous conditions that are known to the homeowner. This might include faulty flooring or stairs or even an improperly covered hole in the backyard. If the homeowner has a pool, he can be liable for injuries resulting from others using the pool. In some cases, he may even be liable to trespassers.

Generally, a homeowner can be liable if he or she has reason to know that certain things are occurring on his property, such as underage drinking, criminal activity, or even frequent trespassing. If a homeowner has prior knowledge that underage drinking is occurring on his or her property, then the homeowner may be liable for any injuries or damages that occur as a result. In this case, Hal may be liable for Nick's substantial medical bills and injuries.

Travis is also liable, since Travis actually assaulted Nick. However, Hal is the primary focus of Nick's parents' rage, since Hal has at least some insurance to cover some of the injuries and damages. Hal is also independently responsible, because he allowed underage drinking to occur on his property. Generally, insurance coverage will not cover intentional acts, like Travis attacking Nick; however, insurance will usually cover Nick's parents' claim that Hal was negligent in failing to ensure proper supervision.

If you know that underage drinking is occurring on your property, you have an obligation to ensure that this activity is immediately stopped. Depending on the laws of your state, failure to stop underage drinking may subject you to both civil liability and criminal liability. Hal had an obligation to ensure that no underage drinking was occurring on his property. He should never have left Jake unattended when he suspected that alcohol would be consumed. Everyone knows what happens when you mix alcohol and minors. Don't do it.

Hal's situation highlights an important tool that property owners can use to protect themselves. While homeowner's insurance can cover these types of claims, homeowners should obtain additional insurance coverage in the form of an umbrella policy. The umbrella policy kicks in after the limits of your homeowner's insurance policy have been exhausted. In Hal's case, if he had had an umbrella policy, it would have provided additional insurance to cover Nick's parents' claims. Even if you're renting, you should purchase a renter's insurance policy and an umbrella policy for renters.

Chapter 24

HOMEOWNER VS. CITY HALL

THEY SAY YOU CAN'T FIGHT CITY HALL. FOR RETIRED ELECTRICIAN FRANK DiCarlo, the phrase took on a whole new meaning when his ninety-two-year-old mother, Maria, was fined by the city for running a boarding house in her modest two-family home in a quiet neighborhood in Staten Island, New York.

"They don't fight you so much as outlast you," Frank said. "By the time you wade through all the bureaucracy and jump through all the hoops, you're ready to just give up and walk away." But Frank couldn't walk away. The situation was terrible for his mother and for the whole family. For over two years he had been battling to reverse the fine with no success. His mother had become so upset over the situation that he worried it would literally kill her.

The whole story started with a frantic phone call from his mother. "She was crying and saying that she didn't know what she was going to do, that she was afraid she was going to jail," Frank remembered. He and his wife lived right down the block from his mother's house, so he was able to rush over to check on her.

When Frank got to Maria's house, she handed him a notice from the city's Department of Buildings along with a bill for $15,000. She was being cited for illegally running a boardinghouse in a residentially zoned neighborhood.

To Frank, it was obvious that there had been some kind of mistake. His mother had owned the house she lived in for seventy-five years. It was a two-family home. Maria lived upstairs, and she had tenants who rented the ground floor. But there had never been more than one family in the apartment.

Frank's mother wanted to pay the fine, saying she didn't want any trouble with the city. One of her friends had told her a horror story of another widow, living on a fixed pension, who lost her home when an unpaid fine accrued interest and penalties. She was afraid that the city would take the house if she didn't pay the fine. Frank calmed her down and told her that he'd call the Department of Buildings and straighten out the problem.

It took Frank a solid day of telephone calls to find out the name of the person he needed to speak with and the number of the correct department. By the time he had a name, the offices were closed for the day. "That should have been my first hint about how hard this was going to be," he said. "But I figured that since I was retired, I had plenty of time to spend talking to bureaucrats. I wasn't going to be put off so easily."

Frank continued to call, leaving repeated messages detailing the problem and his mother's address. Finally, one day, while visiting at his mother's home, he answered her phone. It was a clerk at the Buildings Department. She told him that they had a record of an illegal conversion in his mother's home and that she had to attend a hearing or correct the violation.

Frank attempted to explain that there was no violation to correct. "I'm sorry, sir," the woman said. "But the penalties will accumulate daily until we receive the certificate of correction." Since there was nothing for him to correct, Frank told the woman that he'd simply go to the hearing and clear things up.

"Don't bother coming to the hearing unless you have a report from a registered buildings inspector that backs up your claim," the woman told him.

Frank made a few calls and found two separate inspectors who were willing to come out to his mother's house and do an independent evaluation. The inspectors said they could "expedite their service" for an additional fee. That meant they could be out to the house in three weeks or so, rather than their usual six-month waiting time. It cost Frank a couple of hundred bucks apiece for the inspectors' "special service," but as a retired contractor he knew how that went. He had often charged extra for emergency calls when he was working.

Two months after Maria received the fine from the city, she received notice of a scheduled court date. "Every time she got a piece of mail from the city, my mother got so upset," Frank said. Maria wasn't well and was mostly housebound. The thought that she might have to go to court, and the fact that the city suspected her of lying about her tenants, made her so stressed she became even sicker.

Frank was spending most of his time at his mother's house, calming her nerves and wading through required city paperwork. "My wife was understanding at first," he said. "But there's a limit."

He found the original blueprints of the house and gave them to the inspectors when they came to investigate. Both inspectors agreed that no changes had been made to the interior of the house and that the original floor and ceiling moldings showed no signs of having been tampered with to install temporary sheetrock walls, as had been charged.

Frank got signed statements from the tenants: a young couple with a small child who were temporarily allowing the husband's brother to stay with them while he got settled in New York. With all the evidence in hand, he was prepared for a simple hearing and a dismissal of the fine.

Unfortunately, Frank's experience with the system was anything but simple. First, the judge told him that his mother needed to be present. Frank explained that she was elderly and ill. He showed the judge a letter she had written authorizing him to represent her. "I could insist that your mother attend this hearing," the judge told him. "But I'm going to give you a break and let you represent her interests."

The first person to speak was the buildings officer who had issued the violation. He stated that he had written the ticket for the fine several weeks after visiting the home and finding that the downstairs had been illegally converted to several small rooms. Frank was surprised. Maria had never mentioned anyone visiting the house. The tenants had never mentioned anyone coming by. Now Frank was positive there had been a mistake.

When it was Frank's turn to speak, he pointed out that no one had ever visited the house. "Maybe the guy wrote down the wrong address," he suggested. The judge asked for the new inspections, and Frank handed over his paperwork. He was stunned when the judge threw out all his evidence. "The court cannot accept new evidence to show that the violation has been corrected once forty-five days from the date of citation has elapsed," the judge told him. Frank argued that there was no other way he could have obtained the inspection. "First of all, there was nothing to correct," he argued. "And even if there had been, there was no way I could have gotten the inspectors to come out any sooner. I had to pay them 'emergency' fees as it was."

The judge told Frank that he could continue to contest the violation and that a court case would be scheduled. Then he dropped the bombshell. He told Frank that he still had to post the fine immediately, although it could take two to three years for the case to make its way through the courts.

Frank realized that the thought of a $15,000 judgment hanging over his mother's head for three years would be unbearable. He had already gotten into the habit of picking up her mail every day to intercept notices that the fine was due and penalties were accruing. He was afraid that if she got her hands on one of these notices, she would just pay the fine, no matter how large, to get things over with.

He also knew that there was no way the family could afford to have that kind of money tied up for years. And he didn't know what he was going to tell his mother. "She's already a wreck and so very frail," he said. "She's worried all the time about the house, and it's spilling over into the rest of her life, and mine. She's even talking about kicking the tenants out. But that hurts everyone. That family needs a roof over their heads, and my mother needs the rental income to survive."

In desperation, Frank called an old friend who worked for a city newspaper and told him the story. Within a few days of an article about his mother's plight, one of the local news networks picked up the story. Its consumer advocate called the Department of Buildings. Thanks to their pressure, Frank's mother's court date was moved up, and her case was scheduled to be heard within two months instead of two years.

Frank was relieved. The thought of waiting a couple of years for the case to be resolved was unacceptable to him. After all, his mother hadn't broken the law; it was the city that had made the mistake. For Frank, correcting the mistake had become a matter of principle, and he'd been willing to do whatever he had to in order to make sure that his mother's mind was put at ease.

HOW I WOULD HAVE COUNSELED FRANK

Most people don't like to admit they're wrong. Add to that a public forum, such as a courtroom, and most people will dig in their heels and stick to their story. That is what the city buildings inspector was doing. It was clear that Maria hadn't violated any building codes or wasn't running a boardinghouse, but the bureaucratic rules and procedures of the city government were frustrating both Frank's and Maria's good-faith attempts to set the record straight.

Building codes and court procedures are not something the uninformed should lightly undertake. I would strongly recommend immediately retaining a lawyer experienced in building matters to handle this type of situation, especially given the significant amount of money involved. A lawyer would have known that any inspection would have had to be completed within the required time period. Knowing this information, another buildings inspector could have been found, even if at a higher "premium," just to get the inspection completed in a timely manner.

In dealing with any governmental entity, it's best to deal in person and in writing. Memories fade, and people change positions. Also, when dealing with fines, you should not wait for someone to get back to you, because every day you wait costs you money. Go to the applicable office directly, and speak with someone regarding your matter. Even if it takes all day, you're better off getting answers.

Although his efforts were untimely, Frank basically did the right things in responding to the complaint. Retaining the two buildings inspectors was the correct response; however, I would have advised Frank to provide copies of the blueprints of the house, rather than the originals, as these documents can be lost and might be hard to replace, given the age of the home.

Generally, only an attorney may represent someone else in court. Frank was not legally permitted to represent Maria before the court. It's also prudent to have the actual homeowner show up instead of someone else. The court may refuse to hear the matter, and this may result in further fines, delays, or even an adverse ruling by the court.

If you are elderly or ill or need to take special measures to get into the courthouse, you should advise the court in advance of the hearing in order to determine what steps can be taken. If you are physically unable to attend the hearing, you should have your doctor provide a notarized statement confirming your inability to attend court. Once again, notify the court in advance of your hearing in order to determine what to do. The mere desire to not go to court to avoid stress is not a proper excuse.

Frank's situation also highlights an important truism in the law: the law works in mysterious ways. In consumer issues, often the media can assist in getting the wheels of justice to grind a little faster. This is exactly what happened in Frank's case. By highlighting the inequity of the judge's ruling, the media served to speed up the resolution of the case.

Frank will need to ensure that the buildings inspectors who performed the inspections on the house are present in court for the hearing and are able to explain the results of their inspection. In most cases, a party is entitled to compel the appearance of a witness in court. Frank and Maria should also ensure that their tenants are present in court for the hearing to confirm that the house was not subdivided into a boardinghouse. Additionally, these tenants can presumably testify that the buildings inspector never inspected the house the first time.

Chapter 25

YOUR HOME: WHAT YOU NEED TO KNOW

YOUR HOME CAN BE A NEST, OR YOUR NEST EGG; A PRIVATE SANCTUARY, or an investment that others live in. This chapter contains important advice for people who own or rent a home, apartment, or other dwelling—which is pretty much everyone.

HOMEOWNERS' ASSOCIATIONS

Your home is your castle, or so the saying goes. With home ownership comes the freedom of playing your music loudly, changing the look and feel of your residence, and not having to worry about noisy neighbors. But in reality this is not always the case. In today's modern cities, along with the architectural design developments, another trend has developed: homeowners' associations (HOAs). An HOA is an organization run by residents in a particular residential development that is charged with enforcing conditions, covenants, and restrictions (CCRs) relating to the use of every residence in the development.

CCRs are contracts that set out how, and in what manner, you may use, design, and maintain your residence. CCRs "run with the land," which means when you purchase a home within a development covered by CCRs you must conform to the requirements of the CCRs, even if you don't want to. Among other matters, CCRs can—and usually do—limit the manner in which you may modify the exterior of your home, the placement of satellite dishes, and even how many cars and pets you may have.

BIAS ALERT: Before we go any further, I must warn of my own bias against HOAs. HOAs can serve an important purpose of maintaining the integrity of a development and ensuring that the community is free of old furniture in the street and driveways that have the look of used car lots. Unfortunately, in my experience, HOAs tend to overzealously enforce the CCRs and routinely hand out violation notices and fines for matters that would not merit the attention of even the fussiest neighbor. In my opinion, HOAs are the modern equivalent of a hall monitor. But these "hall monitors" have real powers, and failing to conform your behavior to the CCRs or to pay the fines they impose can have serious consequences, including the placement of a lien on your home or even the sale of your house without your consent. Know your rights. And never ignore a notice of violation or fine.

There are special rules that require HOAs to hold public hearings and meetings, as well as regulations governing which fines may be imposed and enforced against homeowners. These rules vary by state, and I would strongly recommend that you promptly consult a lawyer experienced in HOA matters should you find yourself on the wrong end of alleged violations and fines imposed by an HOA. Most state bar associations offer lawyer referral programs. They can be found online or through your local telephone directory. Most states with HOAs have an office or official designated as an ombudsman. This office is charged with the responsibility of resolving disputes involving HOAs and homeowners relating to the enforcement of CCRs. You should check with your state's real estate division for information relating to your ombudsman. Many states now have information online, including a description of the laws applicable to HOAs and the procedures to follow (including online forms) if you have a dispute with your HOA.

I would recommend using this service, as many states require the submission of your dispute through nonbinding mediation or arbitration with the ombudsman before a lawsuit is filed.

Protecting Your Home and Its Contents

Now that you're a homeowner, how do you protect your home and all your possessions from the elements and man-made disasters? Homeowner's insurance. Unless you own your home outright—you have no mortgage—your lender will require that you always have homeowner's insurance covering damage to, or loss of, the home. While you have many options, I would recommend that each homeowner carry the following types of insurance:

➤ **HOMEOWNER'S POLICY:** This is the standard insurance policy that will protect your home from common occurrences such as fire, falling trees, and some types of water damage. If you're in an earthquake-prone area, you should consider getting an additional policy of insurance to cover earthquake damage. Standard homeowner's policies do not cover earthquake damage. Flood insurance is generally not offered in standard homeowner's insurance policies; however, it can be purchased as a separate policy of insurance from the National Flood Insurance Program if your community participates in this federal government program. For more information about obtaining flood insurance, you can go online at www.floodsmart.gov. Most standard homeowner's insurance policies provide for the cost of rebuilding the home in the event of the complete loss of the home. However, these policies are limited to the dollar amount of the coverage and may not include the costs associated with having to bring your home up to any new building code requirements. Estimate the cost of replacement of your home by simply multiplying the square feet of the home by the average cost per square foot in your community to build a similar home. Make sure your insurance coverage provides at least this amount. A standard homeowner's policy will also insure your personal property within your home. The amount of coverage is usually limited to the dollar amount provided in your policy. You should reasonably estimate the replacement cost of all your property and request replacement cost insurance for these items. For items of extraordinary value, such as expensive jewelry, art, and other items, these items must usually be specifically listed in the policy for the coverage to apply. Provide your insurance agent with a separate list of these items.

➤ **PERSONAL LIABILITY:** Most insurance policies also include insurance for personal liability in case someone is injured on your property (or outside of your property) as a result of your negligence.

➤ **UMBRELLA POLICIES:** You can also purchase an umbrella policy, which provides additional coverage to protect you from lawsuits and claims relating to your alleged negligence. An umbrella policy is usually very affordable.

Moving In or Moving Out

You've bought the house and obtained insurance—now you need to move in. Moving can be very stressful, even more so if you're dealing with a dishonest or careless moving company. Do your research before you tape up that first box. The two biggest complaints against movers are that the final price of the move is far greater than originally estimated and that the movers damaged or lost some of your property. Some moving companies are better than most, and some moving companies are far worse than the rest. Know how to spot the bad apples.

Finding the right moving company can make the difference between a successful move and losing a prized family heirloom. Once you have narrowed down your potential choices, call your local Better Business Bureau (BBB) and see whether the moving company you've selected is a member and whether it has any history of complaints. You can find your local BBB online at www.lookup.bbb.org. If the company is not a member or has a history of disgruntled customers, move on—to another moving company. Another resource is the American Moving and Storage Association. Its Web site, www.moving.org, contains helpful links and information regarding moving within the United States.

Initially, make sure that a representative from the moving company actually comes to your home and visually inspects all the items you want moved. This will help ensure that the estimate and the final price are close. You can also request either a binding or a nonbinding estimate. As the name implies, a binding estimate means that the estimate will be the most you will pay for the move, while a nonbinding estimate can be increased according to the actual costs of the move. Nonbinding estimates usually have a cap on any price increase. Make sure you get the moving company's written policy on any increases.

You should always insure your belongings, based on either the weight of the items or their replacement cost. Weight-based insurance is far cheaper than replacement cost insurance, but the amount of coverage, usually 40 cents to 60 cents per pound, will almost never pay to replace the damaged or lost items. I would recommend replacement cost insurance.

Once your property arrives at its destination, make sure you have enough time and people to go through the boxes to ensure that everything is there and that no items have been damaged or lost. Any damaged or lost items should be promptly reported to the moving company and reflected on the documents confirming your receipt of your belongings. You will need to follow up with the moving company or insurance company to obtain reimbursement for your damaged or missing items.

ADVICE FOR LANDLORDS

If you've ever wanted to be a landlord, make sure you know what you're getting into before allowing someone to live in your property. The last thing you need is a tenant not paying rent or damaging the property. Being a landlord is all about creating a relationship—which means learning about the prospective tenant. As a general rule, you should use standard applications for all prospective tenants. These applications should provide information regarding the prospective tenant's prior rental history, employment, and credit. Make sure you contact the previous landlords to inquire about the prospective tenant's history of timely rental payments.

Running a credit check on the prospective tenant is usually a good idea, as people with good credit histories tend to be careful to pay their rent on time and avoid any unpaid claims related to any damage to the rental property. Your tenant application should include a written release signed by the prospective tenant authorizing you to run a credit check. Use a major credit reporting company, such as Equifax, Experian, or TransUnion, to verify credit history. An agency that specializes in screening tenants, such as National Tenant Network (www. ntnnet.com) can provide information on a tenant's rent payment history.

Each state's landlord–tenant laws vary, and it is best to consult a lawyer in your city who has experience with landlord–tenant issues. A lawyer can help you protect yourself when a lease is drawn up and offer advice on dealing with tenant complaints, such as claims for reductions in rent due to alleged problems with the rental unit, or claims related to the collection and return of rental deposits.

Part V

CARS

How to Keep on the Go without Ending Up in Debt, in Jail, or Worse

It's easy to run into trouble when buying, owning, selling, or leasing a car. A car is often the second biggest thing we acquire, after our homes, and buying it is a decision that can be fraught with complication if you're not careful. People go crazy when they shop for cars—I've seen it a thousand times. They let their emotions get the better of them, and when they do, they make mistakes that can come back to haunt them.

America is a car culture. We have more cars per capita than any other country in the world. We drive more than anybody else. We have more roads, more car models to choose from, and more people on the road at any given time than the population of our most populous state. We get into legal trouble pursuing the cars we want, when emotions cloud our judgment. A good car salesman knows just how to push our buttons and play on our emotions. We get talked into cars we can't afford, or deals in which we don't read the fine print until it's too late—all because we can't wait to step on the gas. It's a much better idea to step on the brakes first, and think things through.

Chapter 26

SELLING A CAR

MIRANDA WILSON HARDLY LOOKED LIKE A WOMAN WHO HAD AN OUTSTAND-
ing arrest warrant from the Utah DMV and bill collectors hounding her
day and night. A petite seventy-three-year-old with a fluff of white hair
and bright blue eyes, Miranda had lived in a senior housing community
in Provo since the death of her husband, Lewis, two years earlier.

Miranda's life had changed dramatically since her husband's death.
For fifty-two years she had been proud to call herself a housewife.
Lewis had owned a small appliance store, and she had devoted herself
to maintaining their spacious home and raising their three children.
Even though she had been devoted to her house and family, Miranda
was fiercely independent. When Lewis died, she brushed off offers of
help from her children and took control of her new life. "First I had to
learn all about our finances," she said. "For the fifty-two years we were
married, he took care of everything. It was a real shock to have to manage it all on my own. I had to establish my own credit rating and get my
own checkbook. It was all new to me, but I managed."

It had been an even bigger shock to discover that a businessman
as shrewd as Lewis had died without a life insurance policy. Miranda
needed to figure out how to survive on a small fixed pension and the
limited savings they had put away over the years. She was determined

to do whatever it took to ensure her future and not be a financial burden to her children. Once she found a comfortable studio apartment in a senior community where she felt comfortable, she began to downsize. Her real estate agent told her it would be easier to sell the house if it were empty, so Miranda began by selling the furniture.

Miranda put most of the contents of the house on consignment with an auction company, but she was shocked at the amount of commission it charged. "I thought I would get a lot more for our furniture," she said. "So when it came time to sell the LeBaron, I decided I would just do it myself."

Lewis's 1975 Chrysler LeBaron had been his pride and joy. It was in perfect condition and lovingly maintained. Miranda parked it out in front of the house with a FOR SALE sign on the windshield. After about two weeks, a young couple knocked on the door of the house and asked about the car. "I told them I was asking $3,500 for it," Miranda said. "It seemed like a lot for a car that was more than thirty years old, but Lewis had always been so careful, it was like brand new."

The couple was enthusiastic. The young man chatted with Miranda, telling her that he was a collector. "I thought he seemed awfully young to be collecting cars," Miranda said. "But youngsters these days seem to have so much money to spend." She accepted their offer to pay $2,800 in cash, and they promised to return the next day with the money.

When the young man returned the next day with $2,800 in cash, as promised, Miranda signed the title and handed it to him. She also wrote out a bill of sale, stating that she was selling him the car for the agreed-upon price. Even though she had never sold a car before, she tried to be thorough. She put down the make of the car, the mileage, her name and address, and his name and address. Carl, the man who was purchasing the car, signed the bill of sale and asked Miranda for a copy. Since she didn't have a photocopy machine, she wrote up another copy by hand.

Carl took the license plates off the car and gave them to Miranda. "I won't be needing these," he told her. "I brought the plates from my old car. They'll be fine to use to drive this car home." Miranda watched as Carl attached the new license plates to the LeBaron and drove off.

Miranda canceled the insurance on the car and went about her business of closing up and selling her home and moving into her new apartment. The senior housing community offered a van service that transported the residents to appointments and shopping, and she never thought twice about having sold Lewis's car.

Nearly two years had passed when Miranda received a registered letter from a towing company saying she had an outstanding bill for $900 for towing and storage of her 1975 Chrysler LeBaron. At first the bill seemed like a simple error, and she tried to clear up the problem herself. She called up the towing company and told them she had sold the car two years earlier. The company told her that according to the DMV, the car was registered to her and that it had been abandoned, without license plates, for the past six months. "Ma'am, you owe us $900 for storing your car for you," the manager insisted.

Miranda told the manager that she couldn't pay a $900 bill and that she didn't want the car in any case. "In that case, we'll sell your vehicle at auction sometime within the next six months," the man said. "We'll take the fees you owe us out of the sale price."

"I don't care what you do with the car," Miranda told them. "It doesn't belong to me. I sold it to a young man named Carl."

Just to be sure the towing company had a record of their conversation, Miranda went through her papers and found the bill of sale she had handwritten. She made a copy and sent it to the manager she had spoken with, along with a letter referencing their phone conversation. Months went by, and Miranda didn't hear anything more from the towing company. She figured the company had sold the car or had found the real owner from the information she had written on the bill of sale.

When she received a second registered letter, this one from a collection agency asking for over $1,800, she was upset. "I called the collection agency and told them what I had told the towing company," she said. "But they insisted that I was the registered owner of the car and that I was responsible for all of the fines and fees."

Miranda called the towing company and asked if the car had been sold. She knew she couldn't pay the $1,800 and was hoping that perhaps the money from the sale would be sufficient to cover the bill. She didn't care anymore whether the company believed it was not her car. She simply wanted to pay the bill and have this all be over with.

The man she spoke with at the towing agency wasn't very sympathetic. He told Miranda that the young man she had sold the car to had probably never reregistered the vehicle. He said that the young man had probably driven it around with illegal license plates and then dumped it, explaining that he had seen this happen a million times. Then he told Miranda that they had sold the car but that it had been completely junked. They'd been able to get only $400 for the LeBaron that had been Lewis's pride and joy.

The towing company had turned the balance of its bill over to a collection agency after deducting the auction price of the car. And the company was insistent that nothing further could be done. "The man I was speaking with—he was very rude," Miranda said. "And he told me that I had better pay the bill or my credit would be ruined."

Miranda was very worried. The residence where she lived was very strict, and she thought that if the manager found out she had a collection agency after her, he would worry about her ability to pay her rent and ask her to leave. She worried so much that she couldn't sleep. She felt sick and couldn't eat. She lost weight and didn't want to leave her room. Finally, one of the social workers employed by the residence asked Miranda what was wrong. Relieved to have someone to talk to, Miranda poured out her whole story.

The social worker helped Miranda make calls to the DMV, hoping to get her the proof she needed that she no longer owned the car. The DMV clerk pointed out that Miranda had never turned in her license plates. Copies of the canceled insurance and a handwritten bill of sale were simply not enough proof that she was no longer the owner. There was nothing the DMV could do to help. And then the woman at the DMV told Miranda something truly shocking. "Honey, I'm not supposed to tell you this," the woman said kindly. "But it's a good thing you're not driving that car now, because there's a warrant for your arrest in the system. You've got nearly a year's worth of unpaid parking tickets." She told Miranda that she was going to pretend they never had the conversation but that Miranda had better think about clearing up the problem.

As the calls and letters from the collection agency became more frequent, Miranda grew increasingly distressed. To the towing company and the DMV, it was just an unfortunate mistake. To her, it was a matter of her future security.

HOW I WOULD HAVE COUNSELED MIRANDA

Aside from the haggling over the price, purchasing a new car from a dealership is usually a fairly simple and low-stress experience. In many states, the dealership handles the registration of the car and all the associated paperwork. It's relatively easy to complete the sale and drive off the lot with your newfound pride and joy. However, selling that same car years later to a private party can be a dramatically different experience. Be careful. Don't let what happened to Miranda happen to you.

When you sell your car to a private party, make sure that you, personally, go to the DMV and transfer the legal title to the new owner. Legal title identifies the person the law considers to be the real owner of the vehicle. Even though Miranda thought the car was no longer hers, she was still the legal owner of the car until legal title had been transferred, according to the DMV, the police, and the law. Being the legal owner of a car can make you potentially liable for parking and traffic citations, DMV penalties, traffic accidents, and even criminal fines.

Even when you know the person who is purchasing your car, I would recommend that both parties go to the DMV and transfer legal title to the car as part of the sale. This will ensure that the buyer is now the legal owner and that you are no longer responsible for the car. Better safe than sorry.

While the law of each state may vary, generally placing license plates from your old vehicle on the new vehicle without registering the car first is a bad thing. In fact, it's probably illegal. You've seen all those movies in which the bad guy changes the license plates on the stolen vehicle and then drives away. While it may have been that Carl just innocently never bothered to register Miranda's car in his name, you should still never sell your car to anyone who proposes switching license plates on your vehicle as part of the sale—even if it's just "to drive it home."

Since you are still the owner of the car until legal title is transferred, don't cancel the insurance on the car until legal title has been transferred to the new owner. As the owner of the car you are responsible for maintaining required insurance coverage on the car. If the car is involved in an accident before legal title is transferred to the new owner, you may be responsible under the laws of your state for any damages. By failing to have the required insurance, you could be subject to civil and/or criminal liability and fines. Don't cancel that insurance.

If you've ever had your car towed and stored at a tow or impound lot, you know how much money it can cost. It's a race against the clock as the costs tick up for each hour your car sits on the lot. Miranda, as the legal owner of the car, was responsible for these expenses. When the car was later sold, once again, Miranda was liable for the difference.

If I had been advising Miranda, I would have first advised her to get the car out of the tow lot as soon as possible. Unfortunately for Miranda, she was the owner of the car. Getting the car off the tow lot would stop the additional daily storage charges that mount up so quickly. Most states allow the tow operator to sell the vehicle after a certain amount of time to recover the costs associated with towing the car to the lot and storing the car. If the car sells for less than is owed, guess what happens? The tow operator sends the bill to collections, and the collection agency comes after you.

Miranda needs to retain a lawyer to handle the arrest warrant relating to the parking tickets. You might be surprised, but many states still criminalize parking tickets: if you fail to pay them in a timely manner, an arrest warrant will be issued. A lawyer can seek to have the arrest warrant quashed, or dismissed, and thereby allow Miranda to either seek to contest her liability for the parking tickets or seek a payment plan that is affordable to her limited means.

I would also advise Miranda that if Carl can be located, she should consider filing a claim against him for the towing and storage charges, parking tickets, and fines. Since the total amount is under $5,000, it might be advisable for Miranda to sue Carl in small claims court, wherein she could request that Carl pay for the costs of his failing to register the car. Small claims court is generally a cheap, easy, and quick method of resolving claims. You generally don't even need a lawyer in small claims court, although in some states you are allowed to have a lawyer represent you.

Chapter 27

TWICE A VICTIM: STOLEN AND IMPOUNDED CAR

DARNELL JAMES THOUGHT HE DID EVERYTHING RIGHT WHEN HIS CAR WAS stolen, but following the rules of the system cost him thousands of dollars and hours of time. His business suffered, his credit rating was jeopardized, and his patience was worn thin. "It's become a matter of principle," Darnell said of his quest to recover the money he lost when his car was stolen from his office parking lot.

One night after work, Darnell had gone out with a few other guys from the shop. He knew he was likely to be having a few drinks, so he left his car at work and took a ride with one of his friends. His car was parked out in back of the shop—locked behind a metal gate and out of view from anyone passing by. Darnell figured that his car would be fine for one night, even though the Los Angeles neighborhood where his shop was located was a bit seedy. Still, in the several years he had had his business, he'd never had any trouble, and he personally made sure that the building was locked down tight every night.

The next morning, Darnell rolled into work a little later than usual, but he was still the first to arrive. As the owner of the vending machine rental and repair shop, he spent a big part of his day hustling for new business, making calls, and visiting potential clients. Competition in the area was pretty fierce, and he was hoping to land an account with a building management company to install and service vending machines at several apartment complexes the company owned.

Darnell let himself in the front door and began making calls. He didn't even consider checking on his car until one of his workers came in and told him that the heavy-duty padlock had been cut on the security fence and he'd better come out back. "The guy didn't want to tell me what was wrong," Darnell said. "I guess he figured I'd freak out. He knew how I was about my Escalade."

It didn't take Darnell long to figure out that nothing was missing but his car. He filed a stolen property report with the L.A.P.D. at 10:30 on the morning of Friday, September 12, and figured he'd never see his car again.

Two months later, on November 23, Darnell received a certified letter from the towing company that worked for the city. The letter informed him that his Cadillac Escalade had been in the company's impound yard since September 14. His total bill was over $2,500 and the letter went on to say that daily storage charges would accrue until the posted auction date of January 14. Darnell tried to reach the impound yard to find out what was going on, but it was Thanksgiving weekend, and he wasn't able to reach anyone for a few days.

On November 28, Darnell reached the customer service manager of the towing company and, after making sure the car in the impound lot was indeed his Escalade, asked him why it had taken them two months to contact him. "That's when things really got interesting," he said.

The manager told him that it usually took about two months to track an owner down using the DMV and that the letter had gone out in a timely fashion. "I could never figure out why you just didn't pick up the car after the police told you where they had towed it," the manager told Darnell. Darnell was confused. The letter from the towing lot was the first information he'd received about his car since it was stolen.

Still trying to sort out what had happened, Darnell's next call was to the L.A.P.D. He told the woman who answered the phone that he had filed a stolen car report on September 12 and that apparently his car had been towed to the impound yard on September 14. He wanted to know why he was never notified.

The woman said that he could take a look at the report if he wanted to come down to the police station in person to pick it up. Although it meant closing the shop for the afternoon, Darnell went down to the station house, determined to straighten things out. He figured it would be a simple matter. He'd get a copy of the report, it would show that the car had been reported stolen, it would prove that no one had contacted him to tell him to pick it up at the impound lot, the police and the impound manager would admit there had been a mistake, and Darnell would be able to retrieve his car without paying the storage and towing fees.

Unfortunately, his experience was nowhere near that smooth. According to the report, the officer notes indicated that on September 14 at 4:30 a.m., Officer Blackwell had called Darnell and spoken to him, providing him with full details of the recovery of his car and where he could pick it up. "Unfortunately," Darnell said. "I never received any such call. Not even a voice mail."

Darnell asked to speak to Officer Blackwell, and the clerk gave him the city voice mail number and the officer's badge I.D. Darnell called and left a message asking for more details about the alleged conversation. After a second voice mail went unanswered, Darnell took a Monday morning off from work and went back to the precinct house. He asked to speak to the desk sergeant. The desk sergeant told him he needed to speak to the watch commander. So Darnell waited, losing a whole morning of work, until the commander was available.

The superior officer reviewed the record and said that the report appeared to be in order and that it looked as if the officer had called and informed him about his car. However, the commander agreed that he would discuss it with Officer Blackwell himself and call Darnell personally about the outcome.

Another week passed, and Darnell still hadn't heard anything. He was becoming increasingly frustrated. Each day that passed was another day of money out of his pocket. He thought about letting the towing company just sell the car, but by the time the sale went through, the bill from the impound would be so huge that whatever he got from the auction wouldn't even be enough to pay off the balance of his car loan.

Darnell had a friend who was a police officer down in San Diego. He gave him a call to ask for advice. "File a claim with the City of Los Angeles Risk Management Office," his friend told him. It took Darnell several more days to finish the paperwork involved with the claim. Once he turned the paperwork in, the office told him that it would take up to a week to complete the investigation. Meanwhile, the tow yard still had his car. Darnell was driving a rental. He was spending much of his workday running back and forth to the police station to check reports and talk to people, and his business was beginning to suffer.

When the building management company decided not to give him the account he had been pursuing, because he had been so hard to reach, Darnell decided he had to put an end to the saga of his stolen car. He went down to the tow yard, paid just about $6,000, and took his stripped-down, scratched, and dented Escalade back home.

The next week a man from the Risk Management Office called Darnell back to say that he had talked with the officer and the officer had confirmed that he'd personally spoken to Darnell on the day and at the time noted on the report, so unless he could prove otherwise, there was nothing further they could do. Darnell knew it was his word against the officer's and tried to get some solid proof that he had never received a call about his car.

Darnell called his phone company to try to get a copy of all incoming calls for September 13 and 14, but the representative told him that he couldn't access his phone records without a court order. "I can't believe how much this has cost me," Darnell said. He had spent thousands to get back a car that was virtually worthless, and he'd lost thousands of dollars in business—all because he had been trying to get answers from the people who were supposed to be helping him. And all the best they could tell him was that *he* had to prove someone had made a mistake.

With his personal finances strained by the unexpected expense and his company struggling to make up for the loss of a key account, Darnell wondered how he would recover from the ordeal. "People have told me that I should get a lawyer and sue the city," he says. "But I'm worried that I'll just be throwing more money down the drain. After all, I tried to work with the system the first time—and look where it got me. Why should I expect it to work in my favor now?"

HOW I WOULD HAVE COUNSELED DARNELL

When your car is stolen, a series of events is set into motion. Some you have control over, but for others you're merely a spectator. The car thieves go first: just as in an action movie, they have to make their getaway, hide the car, and then either strip the car for parts or try to sell it. Then it's your turn. And if this case were a movie, I'd say that Darnell forgot some of his lines. Merely filing a police report and waiting for the police to take action was not enough to prevent him from being a victim twice. It's important that you know your rights and know exactly what you need to do if your car is stolen.

You should immediately file a police report once you discover your car was stolen. Provide the police with the vehicle type, make, model, color, and license plate number. Make sure the police have several ways to contact you, including your mailing address, telephone number, and, if applicable, your cell phone number. Make it easy for them to contact you with any questions or to report the status of your case.

After you file your stolen vehicle report, the police will give you a report or file number. Keep this number with you, since this will make it easy for you to reference your case whenever you call the police for an update. Depending upon the size of the community you live in, you're probably just a case number to the police, who are dealing with potentially hundreds, if not thousands, of stolen cars.

Darnell never called the police to follow up on his stolen car. That was his first mistake. Don't expect the police to keep track of your case report and contact you immediately with any developments. Stolen cars are generally not a high priority. You need to keep in regular contact with the police to request regular updates on your stolen car. While Officer Blackwell may or may not have actually called Darnell, if Darnell had simply kept in regular contact with the police, he would have found out quickly that his car had already been recovered, and he could have avoided thousands of dollars in storage charges.

After filing your police report, your next step is to contact your insurance company. You will need to explain how the car was stolen, and you will need to provide the insurer with a copy of the police report. Another advantage to getting your insurance company involved is that insurance companies tend to be very vigilant in keeping track of the status of stolen cars. After all, they're the ones writing the check.

When your car is stolen, insurance companies will usually do one of two things, depending upon whether your car is located within a certain period of time after it was stolen. If, after that certain period of time, your car has not been found, the insurance company will pay you the replacement cost. If your car is found, depending upon the condition of the car—for instance, if it has been damaged or stripped—the insurance company will either get it repaired or "total it out" and pay you the replacement cost.

Storage costs at a tow pound are generally covered under your insurance up to a reasonable amount, based on the circumstances. In some cases, there may be a question whether the car should be repaired or totaled out. In these cases, the insurance company should pay for the storage of the vehicle until this determination had been made.

If I had been counseling Darnell, I would have recommended that he immediately contact his insurance company after he first learned that his car had been recovered, even though it was two months after it had been stolen. He should have advised the insurance company of the status of the car and its location so the company could make a determination about the payout. Never wait to notify your insurance company that your car is in an impound lot, and never keep a vehicle there one day longer than necessary. As Darnell found out, the "nightly rates" for keeping your car usually exceed the nightly rate for an elegant hotel.

Darnell should not have paid the storage fees himself or taken the car from the impound lot. I would have requested that the insurance company pay for these storage charges and asked that the insurance company immediately send an adjuster to look at the car to determine whether the car could be repaired or whether it should be totaled out. Either way, the insurance company should handle getting the vehicle removed from the impound lot. If the insurance company does not act immediately, and there is a chance the car may be sold through impound, you may need to pay and then get reimbursed by your insurance company.

Depending on whether Darnell's car was a company vehicle, and he had applicable business insurance coverage, Darnell could make a claim under his business insurance to cover any business losses he suffered as a result of not being able to work because of the theft.

Chapter 28

CAR DEALERSHIP HORROR STORY

FRESH OUT OF COLLEGE AND NEW TO TOWN, BETHANY CORLISS WAS READY to take on the world. She had moved from a small town in Iowa to the mountains of Albuquerque and was ready to be independent and self-reliant. Bethany's parents had given her a graduation gift of a few thousand dollars, but once she'd made the deposit on her new apartment and paid the first month's rent, she knew she'd have to find work and find it quickly.

When the old Toyota that had hauled Bethany and all her worldly possessions from Iowa to New Mexico finally gave out on the hills of Route 66, she realized that her first priority was to find a new car. She called the restaurant where she was working and let the manager know that she'd have to miss a few shifts because she had no way of getting in. "My boss let me know in no uncertain terms that he wasn't going to hold the job for me for more than a day or two," she said. Her boss at her second job, at a small bookstore, was a little more understanding but encouraged her to get her transportation issues sorted out quickly.

Bethany realized she needed to look for a used car. As much as she would have liked a new car, she was living paycheck to paycheck. She had credit card bills, her rent, and her cell phone—she just didn't see how she could put a new car loan on top of all that.

Bethany spent the first day calling various dealerships. When she explained that she had about $600 for a down payment and was looking for a low monthly rate, everyone turned her down. "There was no way I could meet all their conditions," she said. Each dealership required cosigners or huge down payments. They asked her for local references and copies of her utility bills to prove she had a place to live. Not one was even vaguely interested in taking her beaten-up Toyota on a trade-in.

By day two, exhausted from calling every dealership in the Albuquerque phone book, Bethany called AutoSave Motors and knew she had found her dealership. "They asked me a few questions over the phone," she said. "And then told me I was preapproved for a preowned car."

Bethany went to the dealership with her checkbook in hand. "They were so great," she said. "They offered me a drink, asked about my job and my move to the area. And then a really cute young salesman named Juan took me around the lot." Juan showed Bethany several cars—everything from really nice models to horrible wrecks, worse than her old Toyota. "This is the car for you," Juan told her, pointing out a red Mazda convertible.

Juan told Bethany that the Mazda was a great value. A 1996 model with nearly 90,000 miles on it, the sticker plastered across the windshield read LOW MILEAGE. Given that Bethany's Toyota had rolled past 100,000 miles years earlier, she believed Juan when he told her that the Mazda, compared with her old car, had hardly been on the road. "You'd look great driving this car," Juan told her with a flirtatious smile.

Bethany knew she was supposed to bargain on the price. But when Juan told her they were asking only $9,800 for the car and that he thought he could get her an even better deal if she didn't say anything to his boss, Bethany didn't even try.

Juan took Bethany into the dealership and introduced her to Rick from the financing department. Bethany told them right up front that she didn't have a lot of history to get a loan. "No problem," Rick assured her. He told her that she could go with a lower down payment and extend the term of the loan. Her payments would be about $200 a month. When Rick told Bethany that she needed to put only 5 percent down on the car, she was so thrilled that she didn't pay any attention to the rate.

Bethany started signing the papers that Rick put in front of her and handed over a check for $490 as the down payment. "Rick told me that he just had to go have his boss sign off on the paperwork and they would give me the keys," Bethany said.

When he came back to the office, Bethany thought Rick looked worried. "I'm sorry," he said. "But my boss is really mad that I forgot to offer you the warranty for repairs on the car." Rick apologized again, saying that he was so excited that Bethany was going to be able to buy the car that he had forgotten to look out for her best interests. "For just $50 a month more you can add a service warranty to your sales contract," Rick said. "The way repair bills on these sports cars can add up, it's like buying an insurance policy."

Bethany was so flattered that Rick had her best interests at heart that she immediately signed for the service warranty. Rick left again to get the papers reviewed by his boss. After a few minutes, Juan came into the room. "He told me Rick was too mortified to come back in," Bethany said. He told her that the bank hadn't approved the $200 payment, and Rick was afraid that she couldn't handle the higher payment of $265 that the bank was asking for. Everyone seemed so concerned about Bethany that she ended up feeling as if she needed to reassure the two men that she could handle the payments. And by that time, she really, really wanted that car. "I figured, what was another $65 a month?" Bethany said. "I could make that in tips on a good night."

By the time Bethany left the dealership she had monthly payments of $315, a shiny red convertible, and the feeling that she had made a real deal.

Two days later, the Mazda wouldn't start after Bethany's shift at the restaurant. She called the dealership, which sent out a tow truck, towed the car back to the dealership, and made the repairs. "I remembered thinking how grateful I was that I had bought the extra service warranty," Bethany recalled.

That was the last good feeling she remembers having about the car. That weekend, her boss at the restaurant announced that he had sold the business. The new people coming in were going to close the restaurant and renovate it. He told the staff that they might be hired back, but the renovations were scheduled to last for a few months at least.

Bethany started looking for a new job right away, but business was slow. She asked for extra hours at the bookstore. Even though she just made minimum wage, she figured that any little bit would help. Before long, Bethany was falling seriously behind in her finances. She advertised for a roommate, asked her parents for a loan to help her cover some of her credit card debt, and even considered getting rid of her cell phone. As the months went past, Bethany became even more desperate.

One afternoon, while driving to an interview at a restaurant in Santa Fe, Bethany was in a car accident. "It wasn't my fault at all," she said. "A little old man in a pickup truck pulled out from a stop sign and smashed into the side of my car." While she wasn't badly hurt, Bethany's prized Mazda was not so lucky. The driver's side was totally smashed in.

Bethany contacted the man's insurance company a couple of days after she filed a claim for the accident. When the woman at the company told her that she wouldn't be getting a check for repairs, that the car was totaled, Bethany couldn't believe it. "I'm sure it just needs some bodywork," she told the woman. The woman told her that the estimates they had received for repairing the bent frame, replacing the crushed wheels and shattered windshield, making necessary mechanical repairs, and doing the necessary bodywork would come to about $7,000. "That exceeds the value of your car, so the vehicle is considered totaled," the woman told her. Bethany couldn't understand how a car she had paid $9,800 for could be totaled with only $7,000 worth of damage.

The insurance agent explained that the Blue Book value of the car was about $6,100. She told Bethany that she was afraid that she'd been taken advantage of and asked her if she had gap insurance. Bethany had no idea what the woman meant. Nobody at the dealership had mentioned anything about insurance.

Bethany called the dealership to see if her service warranty could go toward repairs, but a man named Tony, who said he was the boss, told her that the warranty was void if the car had been in an accident—another little detail that no one had bothered to mention when she bought the warranty. Tony finished the call by telling Bethany that she had an outstanding towing and repair bill with the dealership and that if she didn't pay it he was going to send it to collection.

Bethany was frantic. She didn't have a car and couldn't get to work. She had no idea how she was going to be able to pay her rent, yet she was stuck with a car loan for the next five years. The sales and financing team at the dealership had taken advantage of the fact that she'd never bought a car before. They'd counted on the fact that she wouldn't know what to do if something went wrong before, during, or after the sale.

HOW I WOULD HAVE COUNSELED BETHANY

We've all seen them—the constant barrage of television commercials offering $0 down and very low monthly payments for that new or used car. "Just come in and we'll work the numbers right for you!" exclaims the announcer. What they really mean is that they will work the numbers right for them. Unless you know what you're doing, buying a new or used car can be a very costly experience.

Before you step onto a car dealership lot, do your research first. In today's computer age, the price of a new or used car is easily found at several Web sites, where you can also check out the reliability of a car, too. Determine your budget before your eyes catch a glimpse of that shiny red convertible. Once we've found a car we love, we always seem to magically have more money in our pockets for the purchase. Don't stretch your budget.

It's ironic, but people with the least amount of money tend to pay the most for a new or used car. If you have less money and no credit or bad credit, the car dealer is able to push you into financing options that may initially seem affordable but end up costing you a bundle. This was the trap that Bethany fell into. The purchase price of the car is what's important—not the monthly payments. In Bethany's case, the monthly payments alone amounted to almost $16,000 over the five-year loan term. If you're not able to qualify for good credit financing or can be easily swayed by a sales pitch, I would strongly urge you to take a friend with car-buying experience along whenever you buy a car, in the hope that the two of you will be able to spot a rip-off.

While Rick was "embarrassed" for forgetting to advise Bethany of the "extended service warranty," he was more than happy to have her pay $50 a month for the warranty. This alone added an additional $3,000 to the price of the car. While extended warranties may or may not be a good idea, depending on the length of the warranty and the cost, be careful before you sign up. Check to see what is covered and what is not covered. Read the document carefully—don't let the salesman push you into signing. Often only minor or cheap repairs are covered, while you are left to pay for the major and costly repairs. Extended warranties generally will not cover collision damage to a car.

Insurance companies use several major car price guides: the *Kelly Blue Book,* the *Edmunds Guide,* and the *N.A.D.A.* (National Automobile Dealers Association) *Guide*—for determining the replacement cost of a vehicle. These are the same price guides you should use to determine what to pay for the car. Generally, when the cost to repair a car from an accident roughly exceeds 85 percent of its replacement cost, the insurance company will total it out and give you the replacement cost. You or the finance company gets the check, and the insurance company gets your totaled car.

The replacement cost of the car may not equal what you still owe on the car. This was Bethany's problem. In this situation, you would be liable to the car financing company for the difference, which must usually be paid shortly after the car is deemed totaled. The reason for requiring full payment is that since the car is now worthless, the finance company doesn't have any collateral to back up the loan.

Bethany did not have gap insurance. Gap insurance is insurance that will pay the difference between the replacement cost of the car and what is still owed on the car at the time of the accident. Most lease agreements for new cars include gap insurance. You can obtain gap insurance from your insurance company. Gap insurance is very helpful when you make a low down payment on a car's purchase price. Since a car will depreciate in value quickly, and if you do not make a significant down payment on the purchase price, it is very likely that you will owe more to the financing company than the replacement cost of the vehicle if the car is totaled in an accident. This problem is further exacerbated when you pay too much for the car initially.

Bethany should check her extended warranty to see whether it covers the cost of the towing charges for the prior repairs. If towing is covered under the extended warranty, I would advise her to write a certified letter to the dealership demanding that it not charge her for the tow and that the charge is disputed. If the tow charge was not covered under the extended warranty, Bethany is responsible for this expense and should make arrangements for payment of the bill.

Chapter 29

LEASED CAR

LIKE MOST PEOPLE IN LOS ANGELES, GAVIN COOK CONSIDERED HIS CAR A necessity. "I probably spend more time in the car than I do anywhere else," he said. "If I work a ten- or twelve-hour day, at least half of it is spent in the car."

As an independent computer tech, Gavin was a consultant to several businesses in the California sprawl off the network of freeways from San Diego to Los Angeles and up to San Francisco. Without a reliable car, he wouldn't be able to do his job.

Business had been good, and Gavin was looking for a car to reflect his success. He wanted a car he could enjoy driving every day. A friend told him about a luxury import dealership on Sunset that had great lease deals.

Gavin settled on a preowned Saab convertible and quickly negotiated a lease deal that he thought was fair and within his means. The salesman told him the car was valued at $40,000. With $8,000 down, Gavin was looking at monthly payments of just under $500.

Gavin drove off the lot in his new car the picture of L.A. cool—sunglasses on, top down. He felt very pleased with himself. He thought about taking the car for a spin on the freeway, but it was getting late, and he had an early appointment with a client the next morning. He figured he'd have plenty of time to enjoy the car. In fact, he had a dinner date with his girlfriend the next night. He couldn't wait to see her face when he picked her up in the new car.

Gavin's girlfriend loved the car and suggested an after-dinner drive. They turned onto the 405 and headed north. Though it was later in the evening, the freeway was still quite busy. Suddenly the car just started losing power. "I had the gas pedal to the floor, but we just kept going slower and slower," Gavin said. "Cars were whizzing past us and around us, my girlfriend was screaming, drivers were honking and cursing, and we just kept slowing down until the car stalled out."

Gavin managed to get the car over to the side of the road and called AAA. After a ninety-minute wait at the side of the road, Gavin was relieved when the tow truck arrived to take the car to the dealership. Gavin called a cab and got his girlfriend home before finally getting home himself. The next morning, he called his clients and explained that he had had car trouble and would not be making calls that day. He was at the dealership when the doors opened.

The people at the dealership couldn't have been more apologetic. They said they'd look the car over immediately and asked Gavin if he needed a rental car. That night Gavin got a call from the dealership saying the car would be back to him within five days. So for the rest of the week he made his work calls driving the two-door economy rental the company had provided.

Gavin was willing to let the problem go. "After all," he said. "I figured sports cars might be temperamental. At least I got it out of the way immediately."

Unfortunately for Gavin, the unpleasant night on the freeway was just the first of many bad experiences he would have on the highway. His car had been back from the shop for about three weeks when the same thing happened. He was driving on the freeway when the car started idling too fast, then stalled.

Again, the dealership took the car in for repair, and again Gavin was given a cheap rental for the week while his car was in the shop.

When the same thing happened a third time, Gavin had had enough.

He called the dealership and said he wanted his deposit back and he wanted out of the lease. He'd been paying $500 to drive a Saab, and for the past three months he'd spent more days driving a crappy rental than driving the car he'd leased.

This time the dealership wasn't so pleasant. Gavin was told that the car had been repaired and the lease could not be broken. "The guy in the service department had the nerve to imply that I was a difficult customer," Gavin said. "Can you believe that?"

The fourth time the car stalled out, Gavin just pushed it over to the side of the road, waited for a while, restarted it, and drove to his appointment. He was late, and his client was pretty ticked off. For Gavin, his dream car was turning his life into a nightmare. His girlfriend begged him not to drive it. She was worried that he'd get killed when it stalled out on the freeway in the middle of 85-mph traffic.

For the next few months, whenever the car stalled, Gavin did the same thing—pushed it off the road, waited a few minutes, started it up, and drove on with his fingers crossed that it wouldn't happen again. He couldn't afford to miss any more calls to his clients. And every time he brought the car in to the dealership, he lost most of his working day while he waited for a rental and filled out paperwork. "I just couldn't do it," he explained. "In my business, time is money."

Gavin was eight months into the lease when the car stalled out for a fifth and then a sixth time. He was furious. Not only was he putting his life at risk every time he got on one of L.A.'s busy freeways, he was losing days at work, he was paying for a car he couldn't drive, and he was getting no satisfaction from the dealership.

He called a lawyer, who charged him $150 to look at his lease agreement and point out to him that he had signed a clause saying he would go to arbitration rather than sue. "But how was I supposed to discuss this with a dealership that was obviously crooked enough to sell me a nonworking car?" Gavin asked. "I just wanted out of the lease, and I wanted them to make it right by giving back my deposit, at the very least."

The final time he brought the car into the dealership, the people there said they would send it to a Saab dealership for repair. They couldn't tell him how long it would take, though. And they told him that he had exceeded the number of rental car days that he was allowed in his contract with them.

Frustrated, Gavin took the car to a private mechanic who specialized in foreign auto repair. He kept the car for two weeks while Gavin paid for a rental car out of his own pocket, but this mechanic was able to identify and correct the problem.

"I don't want anything to do with this car anymore, though," Gavin said. "I probably drove it only one full month out of eight." The rest of the time he drove whatever rental car the dealership had lying around, or his girlfriend drove him in her car on the weekends because she wouldn't get back into the Saab. In eight months, Gavin had put fewer than five hundred miles on the leased Saab.

Gavin calculated that during the past ten months he had paid $8,000 in cash plus $5,000 in lease payments—not to mention the costs of having the car repaired by a private mechanic and the rental that he drove during those two weeks. "The point is," he said. "I paid that money to drive a Saab convertible. They haven't held up their end of the lease agreement; why do I have to hold up mine?"

HOW I WOULD HAVE COUNSELED GAVIN

As Gavin found out, the supermarket isn't the only place where you can buy a lemon. While today's cars are better built than ever before, that doesn't mean you will not get stuck with a nice-looking car that doesn't work. Just ask Gavin. Fortunately for Gavin and for all of us, many states now have laws on the books to protect you from having to make that monthly purchase or lease payment on a car that seems to enjoy being in the mechanic's garage more than yours.

While there are many examples of unscrupulous dealerships knowingly selling damaged, defective, or unsafe cars, it is not always the case that the dealership knowingly sold you a lemon. In fact, with today's advanced cars, especially from a new car dealership, it is highly unlikely that the dealer would know that the car it sold you was defective until after the car had been operated for some time.

Depending on the state you live in, you may be able to successfully return your vehicle to the dealership for a full refund of the purchase price, including any payments and other expenses associated with the unsuccessful repair and return of the car. This area of the law is generally known as automobile lemon law. These laws generally apply to either the purchase or the lease of a new car, or, as in the case of Gavin, they may also include the purchase or lease of a used car.

While the requirements and your ability to return your defective car to the dealership varies by state, generally all states require that you have taken the car in for service a certain number of times for the same problem and each time the dealership has been unable to correct the problem. Since every car is going to break down, lemon laws are designed only to compensate you for the continued breakdown of your car after repeated attempts to correct the same problem fail.

States with lemon laws generally permit the return of the car only within a certain time period after the purchase or lease of the car. Additionally, you must notify both the dealership and the manufacturer of your intent to declare a lemon. The manufacturer will send a representative to inspect and evaluate the vehicle and will make recommendations to resolve the problem. This process can be time consuming and frustrating, and in the end there is no guarantee of resolution in your favor. If the car is determined to be defective under the terms of the law, the amount you may recover, including the purchase price, prior monthly payments, and any other costs associated with the unsuccessful repair and return of the car, varies by state.

Also, these specific laws generally apply only to the purchase or lease of a car from a dealership. Private party sales are usually not covered. Since the requirements may vary from state to state, I would recommend consulting a lawyer experienced in handling lemon law cases in your state for direction in how to proceed in your particular case.

In all cases, you should keep every record of each service visit and all receipts related to the repairs. Make sure that the dealership clearly puts the exact nature of the problem on the service records, including the number of times the car has been in for service for the problem. You need to prove that you bought a car with a problem.

If Gavin's state's laws did not prevent him from taking his car to a mechanic other than one employed by the dealership where Gavin purchased the car, I would have recommended that he take his car to a mechanic who specialized in repairing his particular car. Today's cars are complex computerized machines that require extensive training and expensive diagnostic equipment to properly repair. In Gavin's case, the mechanic that specialized in his type of car was able to successfully repair the car.

Be careful, in some instances, about taking your car to someone other than the dealership where you purchased the car. That may prevent you from later seeking the return of the vehicle to the dealership. This is another situation in which consulting a lawyer experienced in lemon laws can be crucial to your ability to return the defective car.

If I had been counseling Gavin, and the persistent problem with his car had not been corrected by the dealership that leased it to him, I would have checked to determine whether he qualified under his state's lemon law for the return of his car. Even though there was an arbitration provision in his lease agreement, this would not have prevented Gavin from successfully demanding the return and refund of his deposit and payments if he qualified under his state's laws.

Chapter 30

BORROWED CAR AND INSURANCE SCAM

CHRIS WENNER NEVER THOUGHT HE COULD GET INTO SO MUCH TROUBLE SIMPLY by trying to do the right thing. The recent college graduate found himself in legal hot water when he borrowed, and crashed, a friend's car. The accident was not the problem, however. It was the fact that when he tried to save a few bucks, Chris found himself an unwitting participant in an insurance scam.

Andrew Winston had been a friend of Chris's roommate during his senior year in college, and they had decided to get an apartment together after graduation. Although Chris didn't know Andy all that well, he did know that Andy was considered popular and cool and really generous.

They'd been in their apartment for a few months, and Andy was living up to his reputation. He had a ton of friends, he was completely laid back, and he was generous with all of his stuff. So when Chris's car was in the shop and he needed to get to the restaurant where he tended bar, he wasn't surprised when Andy told him to go ahead and take his Camaro for the night.

Driving home at about 2:00 a.m., Chris was talking to his girlfriend on his cell phone. He admitted that he wasn't paying attention and didn't come to a full stop, and that he had just rolled through a stop sign without really noticing.

He was able to swerve out of the way of the oncoming SUV, but he went up over the curb and scraped along the guardrail. "The car rolled once and then landed back in the road. I know I was lucky that I wasn't hurt. That no one was hurt," Chris said. Andy's car, however, was not so lucky. The Camaro was in bad shape.

The SUV hadn't stopped, and Chris didn't want to stick around to see whether the police showed up. He managed to start the car and drove back to the apartment, trying to think how he would break the news to Andy.

To Chris's great relief, Andy was cool about the car. "Accidents happen, dude," he said. The only thing he was worried about, he told Chris, was putting in a claim to his insurance company, because his insurance didn't cover any other drivers of the vehicle.

"I didn't want to tell my insurance company, either," Chris said. "My payments would have skyrocketed."

Andy told Chris not to worry. He had an idea. He knew some guys who ran a body and repair shop a few towns over, and he told Chris that he thought they would give him a real deal on the work. "The only thing," he said, "is that they need to be paid in cash." Chris told Andy to go ahead and get an estimate, and then he'd see if he could come up with the cash.

Andy came back with an estimate: his friends at the garage would fix the car for $6,000. To Chris it seemed like an unbelievable deal. He worried that maybe the work would be shoddy, but Andy said he was totally comfortable with the guys at the garage and told Chris to just drop off the car and a cashier's check for the $6,000.

Although it just about cleaned out his savings account, Chris was relieved that the problem was handled so smoothly. He figured he could work double or triple shifts until he made up the money. And he considered himself lucky that he had such a laid-back roommate. Andy didn't seem bothered in the least by what had happened. In fact, once the car came back from the body shop, he drove it a few times and then announced he was going to sell it.

Chris was stunned when Andy appeared one day driving a new-model BMW. "Just test driving it," Andy said. "I'm thinking of buying one pretty soon. What do you think?"

Chris didn't want to pry, but he wondered where Andy was going to come up with the money for such a flashy car. As far as Chris knew, his roommate didn't even have a steady job. Sometimes Andy worked as a personal trainer at a health club. The rest of the time he seemed to spend his days hanging around the gym or at the pool at the apartment complex.

The next day, Chris answered the phone at the apartment. The woman who called explained that the cell phone number she had didn't work and that she was trying to reach Andrew Winston. Chris offered to take a message. The woman said to tell him that she was returning his call about the claim on the Camaro and to let him know that the bill from Like New Auto Repairs in the amount of $17,000 had been paid in full. At first Chris was totally confused, and as he began to suspect what Andy might have done, his confusion changed to anger.

When Andy came home that night, Chris confronted him. "I told him that I was trying to help him out when I paid cash for the repairs, and that I didn't appreciate him running behind my back to try to get an insurance payout," he said.

Andy told Chris to calm down. He told Chris that one of the guys at the body shop was an old friend of his and had explained to him how they could turn the accident with his Camaro to their advantage.

"The shop did the work for cash, I put in a claim for a higher estimate, and when the insurance company paid out, we all split the difference," Andy said. "Everybody wins. My car got fixed right away, the boss paid his guys, and we scored a huge discount on the work—like a 100 percent discount." When Chris pointed out to Andy that it had been *his* cash that was being refunded, Andy promised to make it right with him.

Andy told Chris he would get the body shop to send him a check for the original $6,000 he had paid and they'd just all forget what had happened. "I'm selling the car, anyway," he reminded Chris.

When Chris said it sounded as if Andy were trying to rip off the insurance company, his roommate told him to relax.

"That's what an insurance company is for, dude," Andy said. "I pay them thousands of dollars in premiums. I'm just taking a little bit back."

The next week, Chris received a check for $6,000 from Like New Auto Body, and although he felt uncomfortable with the whole deal, he was grateful to have the money back in his bank account and decided he would just put the whole incident behind him.

Chris never mentioned receiving the check to anyone. He was embarrassed that his roommate, a guy he had trusted, had basically tried to steal $6,000 from him.

When the lease ended, Chris left the apartment and found a place on his own. He saw Andy less and less, and gradually he lost track of him entirely. He hadn't thought about the accident in months, when one night while he was working, a man in a suit walked up to the bar, asked him if he was Christopher Wenner, and served him with papers.

Chris was under investigation for insurance fraud. The state attorney general, acting on a tip, had raided Like New Auto Body and confiscated its financial records. Chris's name had turned up on a list of people who had received cash payouts from the company for no apparent reason.

According to the auto shop's records, Chris had never brought them a car to be serviced. Technically this was true. The car had been brought in under Andy's name, because it was his car. But there was no record that Chris was ever billed for repairs and no record of his payment of $6,000. The only thing the company's books showed was a lump sum cash payment to Chris. Chris never meant to do anything illegal. He was dealing with a friend, someone he trusted, and he truly thought that he was following the best course of action to handle a bad situation and save everyone some time and money.

HOW I WOULD HAVE COUNSELED CHRIS

In many states, if you're involved in an accident that results in property damage to the vehicle greater than a certain minimum amount, for example $500, then you are required to report the damage to the police department. These laws are designed, at least in part, to prevent the type of insurance fraud that Chris unwittingly assisted Andy in committing. Don't let yourself get wrapped up in someone else's wrongdoing. Know what to do when you're in an accident.

As a rule, don't drive another person's car unless you know the person and have his or her express permission to use the car. For example, if you are pulled over for a traffic violation while driving another person's car, guess who's going to jail if the police find drugs or other contraband in the car, even if it's not yours? Probably you. You are deemed in control of the car. While you may eventually get out of trouble, it's easier to not put yourself in the situation in the first place.

As for insurance, most insurance policies provide insurance coverage for anyone driving a covered car who has been given permission from the owner to use the car. It is always a good policy to report any accident to your insurance company. But because of the amount of damage to the car, I would have recommended that Chris report the matter to his insurance company. This act alone would have prevented Chris's troubles with the insurance company and the law.

It's never a good idea to pay cash for anything over several hundred dollars. There is potentially no record of the transaction, and the other party may merely deny that you even made the payment. Get a receipt. A canceled check or credit card statement is effective proof that you have paid the bill.

Businesses that insist on cash payments should be avoided. This is often a sign of fraud, and it could mean that the business is not reporting its income to various governmental agencies. Don't unwittingly become a part of their scam. Chris realized that something was amiss because of the low repair estimate—$6,000—to repair the car, and he should have followed up on his instinct. As a safe rule of thumb, if it doesn't sound right, it probably isn't. Walk away.

Chris should not have accepted the "refund" from the auto body shop, as doing so exposed him to potential civil and criminal liability. He had agreed to pay the $6,000, and he should have left it at that. Chris should have gotten a receipt and a release from Andy confirming the payment of the $6,000 and the release of any claim that Andy might have had relating to Chris's damaging the car. This also would have assisted Chris in proving that he was not part of any insurance fraud claim.

Andy's scheme was insurance fraud. Regardless of how much money you spend on insurance, it never entitles you to commit insurance fraud. There are significant civil and criminal penalties for anyone found guilty of insurance fraud. While Andy was certainly entitled to accept the $6,000 from Chris for payment of the damages, Andy was not legally entitled to submit an insurance claim for the same damages at a substantially higher cost.

Unless you have a special relationship or obligation imposed under the law, generally people are not required to report the criminal activity of others to the police or other law enforcement agencies. However, as a good citizen, you should report to the police. But in this case, since Chris became involved in the insurance claim, when he got $6,000 back from the body shop I would have advised him to not take the money and to report the matter to the police.

Now that Chris is in hot water, he needs a lawyer experienced in criminal matters, as he does have potential criminal liability by being an accessory to Andy's insurance fraud because of his acceptance of the $6,000 from the body shop.

Chapter 31

CARS: WHAT YOU NEED TO KNOW

Whether your car is brand new or previously owned, you probably can't imagine life without it. When you decide to get a new car, you first have to work your way through an endless array of choices. Buy or lease? Finance or purchase outright? Trade in your old model? Stay with a manufacturer you trust? Or try a whole new brand? And once you are pretty sure you've made up your mind, you step into the dealership—and the choices start all over again. When you purchase and maintain your car, it pays to be a smart consumer.

BUYING A CAR

Do Your Research

To buy, or not to buy a car? Some people love buying cars. Most of us hate the idea. Here are some simple tips to make walking into that dealership a lot less intimidating:

➤ Know the type and make of car you are interested in before you even start looking for your new or used car at the dealership. This will save you time and money and avoid a large and costly impulse purchase. There are several resources you can research to narrow your search:

Consumer Reports publishes a yearly price and quality guide for most makes and models of new and used cars. The information includes the price of the car, the safety test results, and the reliability of various components of the car. Finding out whether the car you're interested in has significant problems can avoid the hassle and costs associated with "garaging" your car at the dealership's service lot instead of your garage. *Consumer Reports* publishes its information online at www.consumer-reports.org. The Web site is a fee-based service, but the price is affordable.

If you're looking for a used car, www.carfax.com is a great resource for checking a car's ownership history and finding out whether there have been any reported accidents or major damage involving the car. Sometimes car dealers will buy "salvage title" cars, which have been totaled by the insurance company, and then do some repairs and resell them to the unsuspecting public. It's best not to purchase such a vehicle, and if you do, using a service such as www.carfax.com will enable you to purchase with the knowledge that it was formerly a salvage vehicle. This service is also a fee-based Web site, but the price is affordable.

➤ Once you've decided which car you are interested in, make sure you know what to offer the dealership or private party for the car. There are several popular price guides that will provide you with the market price of a car, including new and used cars:

The *Kelly Blue Book* is an automotive industry standard pricing guide for used vehicle prices. Not only will the guide give you the base value of a car, but also it will itemize the options, conditions, and mileage of the car in order to obtain a full estimate of the value of a car. This is the same pricing guide that most dealerships use in purchasing your trade-in and reselling your trade-in to the public. This information is available online at www.kbb.com.

Another resource for determining the price of a vehicle is found at www.nadaguides.com.

➤ You can also search online auction sites and other car-buying Web sites to determine the price of a car.

THE JOYS OF CAR OWNERSHIP

Registering Your Car

You've bought a new car—now it's time to get it registered. Every car on the road must have a valid registration. You know what that means: the dreaded DMV. Fortunately, many states now offer online vehicle registration services. You can find your state's Web site using most Internet search engines or through www.dmv.org. The site, which is privately operated, contains links to each state's DMV Web site and includes explanations and helpful hints on completing the title and registration of your vehicle.

Title to a car is simply a piece of paper that confirms your ownership of the car. A registration is simply a piece of paper that confirms that the car has been properly registered to operate within the state of its registration. You need a valid registration to operate the car and a valid title to sell the car.

If you're buying or selling a car to a private party, make sure both parties go to the local DMV and complete the title transfer for the car. This will relieve the prior owner of any liability for parking tickets and traffic collisions caused by the new owner. Without transferring legal title through the DMV, you're still the legal owner of the car.

Insuring Your Car

If you own a car and will be driving it on the road, or allowing someone else to drive your car, you must have valid automotive liability insurance. In most states, you must carry a minimum of $15,000/$30,000 in liability insurance. This means that if you injure someone with your car, your insurance will pay up to a maximum of $15,000 per injured person and a total of $30,000 for all injured persons in the accident. Failure to have valid automotive insurance can lead to substantial fines and the suspension or revocation of your driver's license.

There are many options for automotive insurance, and you can shop around the Internet or speak with your local insurance broker. If you're in doubt whether a quoted premium is valid or if you suspect fraud, you should first contact your state's insurance commission to inquire about the status of the suspected insurance company. Insurance companies must be registered in each state where they offer insurance and must meet certain minimum requirements to operate. Don't pay your hard-earned money for bogus insurance, and keep proof of insurance with you when you drive.

Insurance companies usually offer discounted rates when you insure more than one car, or when you buy homeowner's insurance with them as well. Shop around and compare prices.

If you purchased a new or expensive used car, and your down payment only scratched the purchase price of the car, make sure that you obtain gap insurance on the car in case the car is totaled before you pay it off. Since cars lose a substantial percentage of their value as soon as they are driven off the lot, being involved in an accident soon afterward can mean that what your insurance company might be willing to pay might not be enough to pay off the car. The aptly named gap insurance is designed to fill the gap between what the insurance company pays you for the car and what is still owed on the car.

WHEN BAD THINGS HAPPEN TO GOOD CAR OWNERS

Uh-Oh—Someone Hit Me: Dealing with Automotive Accidents

Being involved in a car accident can be both painful and costly. Knowing what to do if you are involved in an accident may help make the event less traumatic:

➤ If the accident is just a minor fender-bender, move the vehicles to the side of the road and out of traffic. If it is a serious accident, leave the vehicles in their resting places and make your way to the side of the road and clear of traffic.

➤ Assuming either or both parties are not on their way to the hospital, you should exchange driver's license, vehicle registration, and insurance information, including the name of your insurance company and your policy number, with the other parties. Confirm that the insurance information you are given is current and that the policy has not expired. Someone should also request that the police come to the scene of the accident and take a report.

➤ You should contact your insurance company as soon as possible following the accident, whether or not you are at fault. The company will set up a claim number and begin the process of arranging for the repair or replacement of your vehicle and for a rental car if your policy contains this coverage. If you have medical payments coverage under your policy, the insurance company will pay for any medical expenses, up to your policy's limit.

➤ If the police do not come to the accident scene, generally you should go to the local police station and file a police report yourself. In most states, a driver is required to file a police report if the accident resulted in injuries or if the property damage was $500 or greater.

➤ Take an active role and follow up with your insurance company relating to the repair or replacement of your car. You may be required to give a written or oral statement to your insurance company. Make sure you assist your insurance agent in the handling of the claim, as this is generally a requirement of any insurance policy.

Hey! Where's My Car?

If your car is stolen, you should follow these steps:

1. Immediately contact the police and report the theft. Many times the police will take the report over the phone. Some departments require that you come in and fill out the paperwork. You should have your license plate information and vehicle registration information with you when you report the theft.

2. Once you have filed the police report, you will be given a report number. Keep this number. You should contact your insurance company and report the theft. The insurance company will require the report number and will also assign a claim number to the theft.

3. Make sure you follow up with the police regularly about the status of the theft. Be certain that the police have all of your contact information, including home and work addresses and all telephone numbers (including your cell phone, if you have one) so you can be contacted with any updates.

4. If you have any type of vehicle tracking system installed in your car, make sure you immediately contact the tracking company and notify the police of the activation of the system.

5. Inquire whether your insurance policy provides for a rental car.

6. Your insurance company will likely consider the vehicle unrecoverable after a certain amount of time and then pay you the value of the vehicle. Once the insurance company pays for the vehicle, your right to a rental car will be terminated. If it appears that your car is lost, I would suggest looking around for a

replacement vehicle so that when you get the insurance money, you're ready to purchase your new vehicle.

It's a Lemon

Many states have lemon laws that protect consumers from a defective vehicle. While each state's laws are different, it's best to follow these simple guidelines:

➤ If you car has a recurring problem with a particular part or component, make sure that the problem is written up each time on the service records. Keep these records. If the mechanic or dealership is unable to determine the problem but the car keeps breaking down, make sure this information is also listed on the service records.

➤ Depending on your state, if the vehicle is repeatedly taken in for repairs for the same problem within a preset number of months and a preset number of times after the purchase of the car, the consumer may be entitled to a refund of the purchase price or a replacement vehicle.

➤ Since lemon laws require technical compliance with the statute, which can be confusing, I would recommend consulting a lawyer experienced in this area of the law in order to ensure that you have followed the proper steps to trigger the application of your state's lemon laws to your car.

Part VI

WORK AND BUSINESS RELATIONSHIPS

How to Make a Living without Running into Legal Nightmares

The legal issues that can arise when you decide to go into business with friends, family members, or investors are complex and require careful consideration. Before drafting a business partnership agreement or starting a company on a handshake, you need to pause and take stock of all the potential scenarios that can arise.

Too often, people go into business with each other without preparing the proper paperwork. The start-up phase of any new business is a hopeful time—one full of promise—and too often a partner hesitates to express doubt, the way someone who's getting married can be reluctant to propose a prenuptial agreement. There's often so much to do to get the operation up and running, and no time to think past the next thing you have to do. Yet, the time before you go into business is the time when you want to express your doubts if you have any. It is also just as important to prepare for the successes as it is to prepare for the struggles.

The most common problem I see when people go into business together is a disagreement over how the funds generated by the business should be disbursed. For every commercial enterprise in this country that goes out of business because of market forces, there's another that goes belly-up because of bad management or poorly drafted partnership agreements, often entered into on little more than a handshake. Maybe there are still places where you can do business on a handshake, but there's also an ancient wisdom that advises if you're doing business on a handshake, when you're done, count your fingers. Unless you put everything down in writing before entering into an agreement, I can practically guarantee that there's eventually going to be a disagreement about what you each said or meant.

Business partnerships can become aggravated by tremendous pressures when people's livelihoods—pensions, health benefits, college funds, and all the things we need to provide for our families and feel secure and happy—are at stake. Any time you need to prepare legal documents, whether for partnership agreements or other business arrangements, seeking the counsel of a lawyer is necessary. Otherwise, instead of enjoying the benefits of success, you could end up in court.

Chapter 32

PARTNERSHIPS

RAOUL OCAMPO AND JIMMY ALVES HAD BEEN FRIENDS FOR YEARS WHEN they decided to become partners in a beauty salon/barber shop venture in an old hotel in downtown Cleveland. Raoul had always cut his friends' hair when he was in high school, and when he graduated he went to Europe and trained in the salon of a very famous hairdresser. Jimmy's dad was a barber, and he learned from him how to cut men's hair and give shaves with a straight razor.

The two friends noticed a SPACE FOR RENT sign on the marquee of one of Cleveland's grand old hotels. The hotel had seen better days, but the space was a former barbershop, and both men immediately saw potential for their new business venture. They both borrowed money, asking friends and family for small loans, and cosigned the lease. Without much money to spend, they didn't consult a lawyer. Instead, they asked a friend who was going to law school to write a letter of agreement that laid out some basic terms: it was a 50/50 partnership, they would share equally in all up-front expenses, and they would split the profits. Raoul would concentrate on beauty services for women, and Jimmy would offer men's grooming services.

"I saw this as a stepping-stone to the kind of career I wanted,"

Raoul said. "I always dreamed big—and for years, I thought Jimmy did, too."

For the first few years, R&J Salon ran a bare-bones operation. They didn't invest a lot on the décor of the salon and were very conscientious about having enough income to pay back loans and still be sure there was a little left over to pay both owners at the end of each quarter.

As the years went by, downtown Cleveland underwent a renaissance, and business at the salon grew. Raoul continued to take educational courses; he always wanted to stay on top of the trends. He studied color and cuts, and he even learned about hair extensions and wigs. His goal was to become a big-name hairdresser, and he worked seriously at his craft.

As word of mouth brought in more customers, Raoul lobbied to upgrade the salon. "After five years, we still looked like a barbershop with a changing area for women," he said. He tried to add some inexpensive touches—fresh flowers, a coffee cart, beautiful antique mirrors that he found at an estate sale—but still he felt the salon needed some more expensive improvements such as better lighting and updated fixtures.

But Jimmy was resistant, saying that his customers were satisfied and that spending on improvements to a space they were leasing was a waste of money. The two partners began to argue more frequently, and Raoul often took money out of his own pocket to make small improvements.

After they had been in business for seven years, Raoul couldn't stand it anymore. He strongly felt that the run-down appearance of the salon was a bad reflection on his work. When Jimmy took a two-week summer vacation, Raoul closed the salon, had it repainted, and had new lighting installed.

Jimmy was furious when he came back and found out what Raoul had done. He refused to pay for half of the improvements, arguing that since he had never agreed to them, he shouldn't have to pay for them. Raoul showed Jimmy the books and pointed out that the salon's customer base was made up mostly of women. "I couldn't say it to his face, because we were still friends," Raoul said. "But it was clear that it was *my* clients who were increasing and making the business more profitable."

Raoul slowly realized that he wanted to leave the partnership. He just didn't know how he could break the news to Jimmy. He knew that Jimmy was under a lot of strain. His wife was leaving him after six years of marriage and three children, and he frequently and bitterly complained about how much the divorce would cost him. Then Jimmy's father died, and his mother began to look to him for emotional and financial support.

Jimmy began to tell Raoul how grateful he was for the salon and how much he appreciated the work Raoul had done. Jimmy would say that his father had been a poor barber all of his life, but thanks to their partnership, he was going to do better. Raoul couldn't bear to tell his friend that he was thinking of leaving when obviously the business was so important to him.

Raoul struggled through the next year, trying to concentrate on his clients and maintain the business as Jimmy became increasingly withdrawn and unreliable. "The friendship was certainly strained by this point," Raoul said. "So when an opportunity to have my own salon came along, I knew it would be the best thing I could do for my clients and my career."

The hotel manager approached Raoul to let him know the hotel was planning a renovation project that would add a luxury spa. He asked Raoul if R&J would be interested in becoming the spa's salon. Raoul knew the manager well, and they had a heart-to-heart talk about how Raoul really wanted to go out on his own. The manager agreed that he would give Raoul the lease.

Raoul was in a state of anxiety during the entire time the hotel was being renovated. He was petrified that someone would tell Jimmy what he was planning to do. "I just couldn't face the scene I knew would occur," Raoul said.

Jimmy was so fragile emotionally, and Raoul felt terrible whenever his partner began to rant about how the hotel was screwing R&J Salon by adding a new salon. Raoul considered asking Jimmy to work for him, doing men's hair in the new space, or turning the lease on their old salon over to Jimmy and styling only women's hair in the new space. He had every intent of working something out, but after nearly ten years of sticking with the business for Jimmy's sake, it was time for Raoul to give his own career priority.

Raoul signed a long-term lease for the new space, wiping out his savings and running his credit cards up to the max to do so. The next day, the manager showed up at R&J Salon at closing time. "Hey, Raoul," he called out. "I'm here to renegotiate the lease, so you don't have your name on two leases."

Raoul couldn't believe the manager was so tactless. "I guess it solved my problem of how to tell Jimmy," he said, trying to make a joke.

As Raoul had predicted, Jimmy was utterly devastated. He ranted about friendship and betrayal and money. He vowed revenge and made dramatic threats. Eventually, he calmed down and saw reason—or so Raoul thought. The hotel gave them two months to change over, and both Raoul and Jimmy agreed that they would do everything they could to make those two months the salon's most profitable ever. "I might even take a break from cutting hair," Jimmy told Raoul, "before I come and work for you at your fancy new salon." Raoul felt greatly relieved. He finally believed that everything was going to work out for the best.

Unfortunately for Raoul, despite his outward acceptance of the situation, Jimmy's behavior spiraled downward. Instead of working as promised, he spent the next two months telling lies to all of Raoul's clients. One day, while Raoul was at lunch, Jimmy told one of Raoul's clients that Raoul had quit and wasn't coming back and that he would cut her hair. "I have no idea why she agreed," Raoul said. "But she did, and Jimmy just ruined her hair. She was furious. I haven't seen her since!"

Raoul finally packed up all his equipment one night after closing and called his clients to say he was taking some time off before opening the new salon. When he didn't hear from Jimmy, Raoul was optimistic that the cooling-off period had worked. His new salon opened with a glamorous reception, and his old clients were delighted with the new surroundings. Raoul was ecstatic. His dreams had come true.

A week after his grand opening, he received a registered letter. Jimmy had hired a lawyer and was claiming that a partnership still existed and that he was entitled to 50 percent of all the profits of the new salon for as long as Raoul operated it. The letter said that Raoul could buy him out, but that the buyout would be calculated on the future earnings of the new salon, not on the basis of the old business. The letter named a figure that was in the hundreds of thousands of dollars.

Raoul was panicked. He had no money left—everything he had saved over the years was invested in the new salon. "Jimmy knew I didn't have any money left, that this was a risky venture for me to go out on my own. He had profited more than I had in the old place. Now I was essentially starting all over again, and he was acting as if I had made some huge profit, instead of a huge investment."

With the future of his business and a lifelong dream in the balance, Raoul had no idea what to do next. He was devastated and couldn't believe that a partnership—and a friendship—could come to such an ugly end.

HOW I WOULD HAVE COUNSELED RAOUL

Partnerships are like one of those old wooden rowboats with two oars. Unless both oars are pulled together, you just end up going around in circles. Even though Raoul and Jimmy were friends, that did not stop them from having problems with their business, and ultimately it cost them their friendship. The first and most important rule of going into business, whether with friends or strangers, is to know what you're getting into before you enter into a partnership.

Partners owe certain duties to each other, which the law describes as fiduciary duties. This simply means that each party must not do anything to harm the other in the course of the partnership. If Raoul wanted to end the partnership and start his own business, Raoul needed to advise Jimmy and end the partnership properly. By neglecting to tell Jimmy of his plans to open a new salon, Raoul violated his fiduciary duties to the partnership.

Whenever you go into any business with someone, even friends, you should have a written agreement spelling out each party's rights and responsibilities. While Raoul's and Jimmy's letter of agreement did provide a few essential terms such as profit distribution and cost sharing, it was insufficient to cover other essential items, such as management and dissolution of the partnership. Even though everyone is usually extremely positive at the start of the partnership, you should always plan for the possibility that the partnership will be unsuccessful or that one of the parties no longer wishes to be a partner.

Raoul had an obligation to tell Jimmy about his plans for quitting the partnership and starting a new business himself. Since there wasn't an agreement preventing Raoul from opening a new business, Raoul would have been permitted to open a new business. However, Raoul probably ran afoul of his obligations to Jimmy when he failed to disclose his intentions, opened a new business at the same hotel in direct competition, and then closed down the partnership store without first discussing it with Jimmy.

Although Raoul—individually—obtained a new lease in the same hotel, he and Jimmy are jointly liable under the lease for the R&J Salon. Unless Raoul obtained a release from both the hotel and Jimmy, he will remain individually liable under the joint lease. While the hotel may agree to renegotiate the lease with Jimmy, this will not prevent both of them from being liable for any unpaid rent.

Generally, partners are jointly and severally liable for the debts of the partnership. So even if Raoul and Jimmy no longer operate R&J Salon, unless they fully dissolve their partnership and pay off all their creditors, they are still in business together and are personally and jointly liable for all unsettled debts. This means that any creditor could go after either Raoul or Jimmy, or both, for any outstanding debts.

Generally, as partners, all of Raoul's and Jimmy's assets would be available to any creditor, including any assets from Raoul's new business. This is the primary reason why parties usually decide to incorporate, as the laws of most states provide corporations with protection from creditors for the individual assets of each owner of the corporation.

If Jimmy wants 50 percent of the profits from the new salon, then he must also accept 50 percent of the expenses associated with the new salon. While a court may find that Raoul's new business is an asset of the partnership, and rule that Jimmy owns 50 percent of the new business, Jimmy doesn't merely get to sit back and collect a check every month. Jimmy is also liable for 50 percent of the expenses—including the start-up expenses—or losses of the new salon.

Raoul's situation highlights the need for both a written partnership agreement and a written dissolution of partnership agreement. When the business income of the partnership is derived substantially from the personal efforts and work of each partner, the partnership agreement should have explicit provisions regarding how much work each partner will perform, required income or labor goals for each partner, and other measures of the quality and quantity of work being performed by each partner to the partnership. This will ensure that both oars are pulled together, and it will avoid the type of problems Raoul and Jimmy encountered.

Chapter 33

BUSINESS LOANS

MAGGIE GROSSMAN HAD ALWAYS DREAMED OF RUNNING HER OWN BUSI-
ness. She loved to travel and always managed to pick up items on her
journeys that attracted her friends' attention and envy. Her favorite
story was the one about the time when a woman on the street stopped
her and negotiated to buy the very handbag Maggie was carrying.

Maggie worked hard to earn money to support her travel and
shopping habit. Although she didn't love her job at the telephone
call center where she spent hours talking to customers, the pay was
good and her hours were flexible. Nevertheless, when her company
was downsizing, it felt like just the push she needed. Maggie decided
that the time was right to take the leap and pursue her entrepreneurial dreams.

Maggie was offered a chance to change offices and follow the customer service department to the new location in central Florida, or
take a severance package and stay in New York. She decided to take the
severance and take a chance on starting her own business. "I'm almost
forty and don't want to spend my whole life sitting in a call center," she
said. "It just seemed like a good time to follow my dreams."

With some of the money from her severance, Maggie took a trip to
Hong Kong and researched various manufacturers of costume jewelry

that looked like high-end designer pieces. She negotiated prices with manufacturers and took information on minimum orders for production runs. When she came home she was confident that she could go into business selling costume jewelry and other accessories and expand her choices in merchandise as her business grew.

Maggie drew up a budget for the first year of business. She knew she didn't want to touch her 401K savings, so she kept everything as lean as possible. When she knew how much she could spend on rent, she hit the streets, looking for a location for her new shop. "I checked all the commercial listings myself," she said. "I didn't want to have to pay an agent a commission on a space. Setting up shop had to be done on a shoestring."

After a few months of hunting around, Maggie found a small storefront in a well-trafficked neighborhood. The landlord had run his own small family business from the space for nearly forty years and was sympathetic to Maggie's need to watch her checkbook carefully. "I'll give you a break on the rent," he told her. "Only three months as security on the space, and I'll let you in a month early to paint and clean the place up."

Maggie wrote a check for the three months' security and the first month's rent. She had everything she needed to start her business. Everything—except inventory. Maggie faxed her contacts in Hong Kong and inquired about placing orders. When she received answers from the factories, she was shocked. The cost for the item she had requested had increased significantly. In the months it had taken her to find a space and lay the groundwork for her new business, the manufacturer's prices had risen considerably.

"Frankly, I was stuck," she said. "I couldn't afford to take another trip and source new suppliers."

Maggie went back to her budget and fine-tuned it again and again. But the answer she came up with was always the same. She was out of money. She considered calling her family members and asking for a loan, but her family had not been very supportive of her business venture. And Maggie couldn't stand the thought of having them say "I told you so" if she were to ask them for money before even opening up shop.

Maggie felt that she had gone too far to give up, so she did what she had to do. She withdrew the $10,000 she needed from her retirement savings account and ordered her inventory.

From then on, Maggie expected that everything would go like clockwork. Instead, she encountered the first rule of being in business for yourself: expect the unexpected. Maggie's shipment of jewelry was held up in customs. She needed more money to expedite the order through customs. As she rode the subway home from the custom agent's office, she was in despair.

That night she was channel-surfing, trying to take her mind off the mess her start-up had become. When she saw the ad for a small business line of credit that claimed to specialize in small to medium lines of credit for new business ventures, she immediately picked up the phone and dialed the 900 number.

Maggie spoke to a representative at Small Business Funding (SBF) who assured her that she could apply for a line of credit by filling out the application on the organization's Web site. "We'll have your approval in approximately twenty-four hours," the woman told Maggie. Maggie was relieved. Every moment that the inventory was held up in customs was costing her more.

The next day, Maggie withdrew an additional $5,000 from her retirement account to cover a few outstanding expenses and filled out an online application with SBF. She felt as if a weight had been lifted from her shoulders.

The next day, Maggie got a call from another representative at SBF. She told Maggie that her application was under review, that there was some concern about her business's liquid assets. "It should take about a week to complete our review," the woman told Maggie.

The week passed, and there was no word from SBF. The next week, with rent on both the empty store and her apartment coming due, Maggie called SBF to inquire about her account. This time she spoke with a man who told her that she did not qualify for the SBF line of credit program. "I practically burst into tears," Maggie said.

Then he told her that there was another program that she did qualify for. She would have to make an "advance on interest" deposit of just 1 percent of the total amount she wanted to borrow to secure the full value of the loan. "You simply wire SBF $2,500 and within forty-eight hours SBF will activate a $250,000 line of credit that you can draw upon at any time," the representative said. To make it even easier for her, he continued, SBF could wire advances directly to Maggie's business account. To Maggie it seemed like a reasonable offer, and she really believed it was her last option to save her dream of owning her own business.

With the promise of money only a day away, Maggie withdrew another $25,000 from her retirement fund and paid the rent that was due. She went to customs and paid to have her inventory released. She deposited $5,000 in her business account and wired $2,500 to the account number she had been given at SBF.

Because of the customs troubles and the delays in opening her store, Maggie had spent over $40,000 of her savings—money she had never intended to touch. But her worries seemed to be over. "I remember it was a Friday, when I finalized all the paperwork," Maggie said. "I was so excited to think that by Monday I would be ready to open for business."

On Monday, Maggie arrived at her store to find that the shipment had been released from customs and delivered. Upon opening it, she was dismayed to find damaged and broken pieces. She imagined the nightmare of insurance claims that were in front of her. She picked through the boxes and salvaged what she could. Maggie was ready to give up, thinking she would have to wait for the insurance money before reordering, when she realized that she had a line of credit ready and available to her.

Maggie faxed an order to the manufacturer and instructed her bank to wire the deposit necessary to begin production. Then she phoned

SBF and asked to speak to her account representative. The person who answered the phone said that the representative no longer worked for the company. Maggie thought that it was strange—it had been only a few weeks since she had filled out the application over the phone with him.

When Maggie asked to speak to someone else, she was put on hold, and then disconnected. When she called back, the woman answering the phone said that there was no record of an account matching the numbers Maggie was giving. Maggie asked to speak to a supervisor. Again, she was put on hold and disconnected. Maggie started to feel sick.

For the rest of the week, Maggie tried to contact someone at SBF and request that her line of credit be activated. On Friday, she checked the bank balance in her business account and found that it was down $1,000. The bank told her that a monthly automatic withdrawal to SBF had been set up. "That was when I knew I was really in trouble," Maggie said.

She told the bank to cancel the automatic payment and called the Better Business Bureau. "I'm sorry we can't be of help," the woman at the Better Business Bureau told Maggie. "You've definitely been scammed; you should just be glad that it wasn't for more."

Maggie filed a police report, but after several weeks the police were able to tell her only that her money had been wired to a Canadian bank and that they had no jurisdiction over foreign countries. Maggie even called the FBI but was told that her loss was too small for the FBI to get involved.

Now that she was unable to pay the balance due, the company in Hong Kong refused to honor Maggie's order and told her it did not want her as a customer. "I don't know what to do," Maggie said. "I haven't received any income in months, I've spent most of my savings, I don't have much product to sell, and I have no way to cover next month's business expenses, never mind my own personal living costs. I guess my new career is over before it starts."

Maggie knew that some businesspeople might think that losing

$2,500 wasn't so bad—that she should be grateful that she wasn't scammed for more. But the thought that a line of credit was available had caused her to spend much more of her own savings than she ever should have. Maggie had worked so hard for her financial security and now felt as if she had thrown it all away.

HOW I WOULD HAVE COUNSELED MAGGIE

"I hate my boss!" We've all made this comment and many more colorful expressions unfit to print on these pages. We all want more control over our work lives, more money, better or more flexible hours, and more autonomy. That's not too much to ask—right? Starting your own business is one of the most exciting and frightening things you can ever undertake. No more bosses hounding you each day for a report on this thing or that. You're the boss now! However, with this freedom come unique challenges and obstacles you probably never considered before taking the entrepreneurial plunge. Don't let what happened to Maggie happen to you—watch your step before quitting that steady job and sinking your hard-earned cash into a new business venture.

You should not start a business unless you have done your research and determined, or reliably estimated, the cost to run the business, the potential market for your product or service, and how you will operate your business. Before Maggie signed the lease agreement and began purchasing inventory for her business, she should have determined what the rent and cost of goods would be, including the extra time and expense associated with shipping the goods from abroad.

If Maggie had kept up with the prices of the goods, then she would not have been surprised that the prices had substantially increased—especially if she had not checked on prices for several months.

It does not appear that Maggie got a break on the rent, as three months rent as a security deposit, in many markets, exceeds the routine security deposit charged to new tenants. Maggie would have been better off retaining a real estate broker to find a business location and negotiate a better lease term. This would have also freed up Maggie's time to get her new business started. Maggie should have already made arrangements for the purchase of goods for her business before entering into the lease agreement. Had she done that, she could have adjusted her budget to reflect the increased cost to purchase her inventory.

Maggie was unrealistic about the costs associated with starting her new business. While a little home-based business is generally much cheaper to start, a retail establishment is far more costly. Maggie should have anticipated the need for capital before even signing the lease agreement. She should have also determined where the money would come from instead of having to seek emergency funds at the last minute. This made her susceptible to the sales tactics of scam artists.

Generally, any financial institution will lend money based on collateral pledged, on the borrower's credit rating, or both. In the case of an unsecured loan, the financial institution will usually require a strong personal credit rating. If Maggie did not qualify for the SBF line of credit, it was unlikely that she would qualify for an even greater unsecured line of credit for an advance of only a 1 percent interest. This too-good-to-be-true offer should have tipped Maggie off that the deal was a scam. Additionally, any requirement that you "pay" in advance for the loan is usually a sign of fraud. Be careful.

When dealing with businesses you are unfamiliar with, you should not permit any automatic payments to be made from your bank account, as these funds may be difficult to retrieve if they have been fraudulently obtained. Use a credit card, or pay by check. In either case, you can stop payment or dispute the charges. In addition to stopping the automatic payments, Maggie will need to close the checking account and reopen it under a new account number. This will ensure that SBF does not later attempt to withdraw additional funds from her checking account.

Maggie should also file a claim for the damaged goods. While this may take some additional time, it should help her recover their value. Unless Maggie can come up with the money necessary to complete the purchase of the replacement goods, she will not be able to obtain them quickly. If Maggie had purchased business insurance to cover this type of loss, the insurance might have provided for quicker repayment of the cost of the damaged goods. This would have enabled Maggie to repurchase the goods more quickly.

If Maggie cannot come up with additional funds to operate the business, or if she is unwilling to further borrow from her 401K, she should consider closing the business to avoid any further financial losses. She must comply with any notice periods provided under her commercial lease agreement regarding when she can vacate the premises. If it is possible and permitted under the lease, Maggie could consider subleasing the commercial space to another tenant.

Even if Maggie decides to sublease in order to have help with the rent, she remains liable under all her original obligations to the landlord. If she is certain that she is not going to want the space in the future, she should attempt to find a new tenant and, if the landlord approves, ask the landlord to cancel the underlying lease and relieve her of all obligations.

Chapter 34

SMALL BUSINESS WOES

JONELLE EDGERS THOUGHT SHE HAD HIT UPON THE PERFECT WORK-AT-home solution. With two small children and newly pregnant with her third, Jonelle was exhausted after spending the day on her feet as retail clerk at a superstore on the strip of highway near her residential neighborhood in South Carolina.

One night, while talking to her neighbor, he mentioned that he had started running a computer troubleshooting company out of his home. He was doing really well with it, he told Jonelle. By the time she went home to make dinner for her family, Jonelle was already making plans for starting her own business.

After the girls had gone to bed that night, Jonelle and her husband sat down, and she laid out her plan. She told him she wanted to sign up for an eight-week course in cosmetology. She'd always been good at doing beauty treatments. As the youngest of six girls Jonelle had loved playing "beauty salon" with her sisters. She still played at it, doing her daughters' hair and nails. "Doing what I loved? In my own home?" Jonelle said. "How could I beat that for a job?" The course was expensive, but Jonelle and her husband put the cost of the classes on their credit card. It was an investment in their future.

Jonelle gave her boss two weeks' notice but was relieved when he told her she had to work out only the rest of her schedule for the week. She couldn't wait to start her new career. The next week, Jonelle started her training. She loved her classes, and her instructors often complimented her on her aptitude for hairstyling.

Eight weeks later, she finished the course and received her certificate. Although money was getting tight without the family's second income, Jonelle and her husband turned to their credit cards again, purchasing hundreds of dollars of equipment for the salon. For the next few weeks, after dinner, her husband and a few of his friends worked to install plumbing, sinks, and beauty stations in the spare bedroom of their stucco ranch house.

"I was thrilled with the space," Jonelle said. "And eager to get some customers." She'd racked up nearly $4,000 in credit card debt, and it was scary to think about having to pay it all back.

With the investment of a few hundred dollars more, Jonelle obtained her license from the state to practice cosmetology and filed for her business license with the county. "Somehow, standing in the county assessor's office, filling out that application with the name and address of my new business—Salon Jonelle—made me really feel like an official business," Jonelle said. "I was so excited."

Four months and several thousand dollars after her brainstorm, Jonelle was set to begin working for herself. She spread the word among her girlfriends and the mothers at her daughters' preschool and day care. Within a few months, she found herself fully booked for all the hours she cared to work.

By this time, Jonelle was about seven months pregnant, and being on her feet all day was impossible. She knew she had to do something or she would start to lose business. So she began looking for an assistant to work a few days with her. Unfortunately for Jonelle, it would turn out that having her business grow so quickly was the worst thing that could have happened to her.

Jonelle began asking around to see if there was anyone who would be interested in working a few days at her salon. One of her girlfriends told her about a young stylist at a salon a few neighborhoods away, who had cut her teenaged son's hair. "She's great," the woman said. "And she's not happy at the other place at all. You should snap her up."

Jonelle told her friend to give the woman her number. A few days later, Evie stopped by the salon at the end of the day. Jonelle liked the younger woman from the beginning. "She had a great, outgoing personality," Jonelle said. "She was really hip and already had some of her own clients—plus she had tons of energy; she said she could take care of as many of my clients as I wanted her to."

Jonelle didn't want to complicate her growing business by actually hiring an employee, so she just suggested that they have a trial period during which Evie would get 30 percent of any of Jonelle's customers that she worked on and 60 percent of any of her own whom she brought in to the salon. Evie said she thought the arrangement sounded "cool." And the two women shook on their new partnership.

For the first few weeks, Jonelle thought she had found the answer to her prayers. She would sit at the desk and book appointments and do customers' nails while Evie worked on hair. For the first time since her business opened, Jonelle was able to pick up her daughters after school and make dinner for the whole family while Evie handled the late afternoon appointments. "Things were going so well," Jonelle said. "I figured the salon would start to turn a profit in the next month or so. And just in time, as the baby was due in about six weeks."

When Evie suggested that Jonelle let her keep the salon open a few evenings a week so she could work on her friends who kept later hours, Jonelle and her husband did a quick calculation of the additional income and added a private entrance from the side yard to the salon so that Evie's clients could keep later hours.

However, Evie's late evening clients weren't as discreet as Jonelle's midday regulars. Groups of girls would show up, some with their boyfriends in tow. Pulling up to the house with music blaring, they would park their cars in Jonelle's driveway, in the road, and once, unfortunately, on the neighbor's lawn.

"I began to get calls from people in the neighborhood asking me what was going on at the house, complaining about the noise and such," Jonelle said. "I'd never had any problems with the neighbors, and I didn't want any now."

Only two weeks after telling Evie she could keep later hours, Jonelle had to tell her that it wasn't working out. Evie became very upset. She accused Jonelle of discriminating against her friends. Jonelle tried to explain that it wasn't as if the salon was in the strip mall. She stressed that they worked in a residential neighborhood and needed to respect their neighbors.

But over the next few days, Evie's attitude got worse. She was careless and disrespectful to Jonelle's clients, and when Jonelle looked over the books at the end of the week, she found that Evie had done most of her friends' hair on "credit." When she mentioned she was having problems with her new employee to one of her friends, the friend said she had heard from the other salon owner that Evie was trouble and that she had wondered why Jonelle had hired her. "Why she waited so long to share this information with me, I don't know," Jonelle said. "But I guess it was really my fault for not checking with Evie's former employer."

After a long talk with her husband, Jonelle decided that bad as the timing was, she had to let Evie go. Jonelle gave Evie two weeks' notice, but Evie didn't take the news very well. She stormed out, slamming the door behind her. Jonelle had been sitting alone in the quiet salon for about thirty minutes when someone knocked at the side door. Her first thought was that Evie was coming back to apologize for being so rude. Jonelle opened the door and was shocked to see a county sheriff standing outside.

The sheriff told her that she was in violation of zoning laws by running a hair salon in the neighborhood and that he was closing down her business immediately. Jonelle protested, showing him her county license to practice. But the sheriff was firm. "Ma'am, I don't know how you got that license," he told her. "But we've got complaints from your neighbors, and you are in violation of the law."

Jonelle spent the rest of the afternoon calling customers and canceling appointments. She called Evie and left her a message telling her not to come in at all the next day. "I was hysterical," Jonelle said. "In a month I was going to have a baby. I had no one to help in the salon, and until I could straighten out whatever confusion was going on, I couldn't do any business."

Jonelle spent much of the next day at the county's offices. To her dismay, she found that she was indeed in violation of the zoning laws for her neighborhood. One of her neighbors, upset about the late-night crowds, had complained. Jonelle asked the official how the county could have issued her salon a business license when her neighborhood wasn't zoned for that kind of business. "We're the tax collector's office," the man told her. "We're not responsible for knowing the zoning laws." Jonelle was stunned. "Basically, they admitted that the right hand had no idea of what the left was doing!" she said.

Jonelle headed home to give her husband the bad news. She would have to close the salon. When she got home, she found a certified letter in the mail. Evie had filed a suit in small claims court, alleging that Jonelle had dismissed her without paying her for all her work. "She was the one who cut all her friend's hair on credit," Jonelle said. "How was I supposed to give her 60 percent of nothing?"

That night Jonelle had pains and premature contractions. Her doctor admitted her to the hospital overnight and warned her to avoid stress until her due date. "I'd like to know how I'm supposed to do that," Jonelle said. She and her husband were thousands of dollars in debt, she would be out of work for the next several months at least, and they were about to add another child to their household. None of this—investing all their money, being in this mess with Evie—was her fault. She thought she was running a legal business. It was the county that had issued her an invalid license, and it was now the county that was shutting her business down.

HOW I WOULD HAVE COUNSELED JONELLE

When people dream of running their own business, they usually think about the freedom they will have, all the money they will make, and how much less stressful their lives will be without "the man" breathing down their neck. Some of us do achieve this elusive goal, but many do not. Don't set yourself up for failure. Before you take the plunge and start that new business—or, as in Jonelle's case, make the first snip of the hair scissors—make sure you know what you're getting into in order to ensure that your dream doesn't become a nightmare.

Generally, all businesses are subject to a variety of laws and regulations, including taxes, special licenses, health and safety regulations, building and zoning requirements, and even government oversight and inspection. Depending on the type of business, these requirements and regulations can be minimal or substantial. Before starting any new business, you should first consult your local government business planning or licensing department to learn the applicable regulations and special requirements that pertain to your intended business.

Even a seemingly simple business such as a hair salon is usually highly regulated. Hair stylists must generally be licensed, and the business is usually required to comply with stringent health codes and special zoning requirements. These types of businesses generally cannot simply be started on a dime.

If you're going to take the plunge and risk your hard-earned money on a new business venture, I would suggest consulting a lawyer experienced in business formation and operation. Even a brief and inexpensive one-time consultation can help you avoid costly mistakes. While Jonelle may have believed that her "business license" entitled her to operate her hair salon from her home, an experienced lawyer should have quickly been able to advise her that any such business would be prohibited as a home-based business.

Unfortunately for Jonelle, obtaining a business license was only one step toward ensuring that her business was legally permitted to operate. While many types of businesses may legally be operated out of the house, many more are not permitted to be run out of the house. Generally, businesses that regularly require customers to come to the business location will be prohibited from operating in a home. Traffic congestion, which was Jonelle's problem, is one primary reason for this type of regulation.

Other issues include special health and safety requirements and building code requirements for the business that only a commercial business setting is designed to accommodate. While you may be able to secure a variance to any applicable requirements, and thereby operate a traditional commercial business in a home-based environment, this is never guaranteed and should be sought first.

If you're running a business out of your home that is either unlicensed or not permitted to be operated out of the house, you may be subject to both criminal and civil liability. Depending on your state or local laws, these fines can be substantial. Do your research first, and avoid these problems. I would have recommended that Jonelle determine whether a variance is possible to allow her to operate the salon from her home. If so, she would have to apply for the variance and not operate her business until she receives it. However, Jonelle would probably still be liable for any fines or penalties associated with the initial operation of the business.

Aside from the fact that Jonelle can no longer operate her business out of her home, she must still deal with Evie's small claims lawsuit. If I were counseling Jonelle, I would advise her to contest Evie's claim based on the argument that the agreed profit distribution applied only to income actually received by the business. Since Evie was not actually requiring payment from her friends, Jonelle should not be required to pay Evie until and unless Jonelle receives payment from Evie's customers. However, depending on the laws and regulations of your particular state and locality, the operation of an unlicensed business may prevent the collection of these debts.

Jonelle's situation highlights the need to have a written agreement relating to any partnership relationship. The agreement could have provided, among other matters, the terms and conditions upon which Evie would be paid. By setting out these requirements and obligations in writing, both parties avoid any confusion relating to their respective rights and obligations.

Chapter 35

INTELLECTUAL PROPERTY AND PARTNERSHIPS

IN COLLEGE, TINA AND BRENDAN WERE THE MOST UNLIKELY OF FRIENDS. Tina was an art student with an amazing talent for sketching and a passionate interest in fashion. Brendan was a math genius with a nose-to-the-grindstone work ethic instilled by his very successful parents. After graduation, Brendan went to work on Wall Street for a private investment bank, and Tina took a year off to bum around Europe before attending design school for a year and then finding work as a sportswear designer for a large fashion house.

Although they hadn't stayed in touch, when the two reconnected at their tenth reunion, they began talking about their dreams back when they were in college. "I was telling Brendan how frustrating it was to be designing for someone else," Tina said. "I had to report to several bosses and get their comments on my work. I never felt as if the finished designs were my own."

Brendan said he understood how Tina felt. He had left the investment bank after only five years and had started his own hedge fund. In five years, he'd made literally millions and attributed his success to being willing to take the risk of doing his own thing, rather than do what someone else wanted him to do with his talents.

As they talked over drinks that night, Tina thought Brendan became more impressed with her ambition. He told her he'd love to see some of her sketches. The next day, she sent him an e-mail suggesting they meet for lunch. "I said that maybe he could offer me some career advice, since he'd done so well with his own business," Tina said.

Brendan and Tina met for lunch, and she showed him some of her sketches for evening gowns. "I'm not really into fashion," Brendan said. But he told Tina that he thought her dresses were really beautiful. He was also impressed with Tina's creativity in getting her outfits photographed. She'd gotten some of the fitting models at her workplace to try on her designs and took photos of them wearing her evening gowns instead of the company's sportswear designs.

Tina could tell that Brendan was really into the whole idea of the fashion shows, the parties, the social scene, and models that swirled around them. "He didn't come right out and ask me if I could hook him up with one of the models," Tina said with a laugh. "But I knew he wanted to."

Instead, Brendan told Tina that he thought she shouldn't be designing sportswear, that it was a waste of her time and talent. Tina was impressed with his insight and told him that her dream was to start her own business. She felt confident that if she could just concentrate on designing high-end evening wear, she could break even in a year or less.

Tina told Brendan that she spent about half her workday creating and refining her own designs. She talked about having a show in the big tents during Fashion Week. "I told him I was totally ready to go," Tina said. "I had the sketches for my first collection finished, and I had all the connections to make it happen."

Toward the end of their long lunch, Brendan proposed that he and Tina start a fashion label. Tina was shocked. "You've got great ideas," Brendan said. "And I've got the business background." Tina was skeptical about working with someone with no fashion background, but Brendan assured her that it would be a good match. "You've got the talent and I've got the money," he said.

Tina was persuaded. "He was an old friend, had the money to burn, and was so confident—how could I not go for it?"

Brendan drew up a general partnership agreement. He gave each of them 50 percent ownership of the new company, explaining to Tina that if they were as successful as he thought they would be and wanted to find an even bigger equity investor, or sell the company, they would share equally in the net profits.

Tina signed the agreement, quit her job, and moved downtown to a loft workshop that Brendan had found and leased for the company. Brendan paid for Tina to travel to Europe and Hong Kong to source materials and trims for her designs, he took care of all the bills for the workspace, and he encouraged Tina to take a weekly stipend so she didn't have to live off her limited savings.

"I was working my butt off," Tina said. "So it seemed totally fair that he'd take care of the bills."

Tina's first collection was ready in time for the big fall fashion shows but was turned down for inclusion with the major designers who had booked most of the coveted time slots for the big tents where the celebrities flocked during Fashion Week. Tina was discouraged, and she worried that Brendan would back out, but instead he encouraged her to do her own show.

Tina's show was a modest success. Her collection was well received by specialty stores, and she even managed to call in a few favors and get some press down to cover the event. Several pictures of Tina and Brendan, surrounded by models in Tina's designs, made the glossy pages of a few fashion trade magazines.

Tina was getting ready for her next collection when all hell broke loose.

Tina's former employer had seen the pictures and had found sketches of gowns in some files Tina had carelessly left at her old job. He served her with a lawsuit, saying that since she had been creating designs for evening gowns while in his employ, he owned those designs. "He had some big hotshot lawyer talking about how they were going to take over our company and drive us out of business," Tina said. She was totally freaked out, but Brendan said he would take care of it. He used his own lawyers, and they settled with Tina's old boss for $250,000.

News of the lawsuit traveled through the fashion grapevine, and Tina's company got some buzz. Brendan said it was like buying $250,000 worth of publicity. Their next show was well attended by both buyers and press, and Brendan was thrilled that an up-and-coming star was photographed in a borrowed gown at an awards ceremony.

Tina finally felt that she was seeing the results of hours and hours of hard work. "I'd been doing this basically by myself for the past two years," she said. "Designing, finding fabrics, sewing the samples, finding the manufacturers—I was exhausted." She began to suggest to Brendan that it was time for them to think of bringing in an outside investor, as they had discussed at the very beginning of their partnership.

Brendan seemed to welcome the news. His hedge fund was having a down year, and the constant cash infusions into his and Tina's company were creating a huge strain on his personal income. They decided to begin looking to sell the company.

Tina's reputation as a designer increased. The young actress who wore the gown to the awards ceremony referred several of her friends to Tina, and soon she was known for dressing some of Hollywood's hottest young stars.

The publicity paid off. Brendan told Tina that he had found an investor who would take a majority stake in the company. "That's when everything fell apart," Tina said.

Brendan negotiated the deal, and when Tina was called to the boardroom of his downtown office to sign off on the agreements, she was shocked to discover that, despite the huge cash infusion from their new investor, she was not getting any money. She asked Brendan what was going on. As a 50 percent owner of the company Tina was expecting to receive 50 percent of the sale. She couldn't understand why Brendan was taking a huge cash-out and she wasn't getting anything.

Brendan presented Tina with an itemized accounting of all the money he had put into the company over the past few years, including the stipend he had paid her. "Here's a list of all my investments in this business," he said. "I always expected to recoup them."

"It's not fair," Tina protested. Once Brendan took back his "loans" to the business, there wasn't a cent left in the company for her. In Tina's mind, she was right where she started: working for a boss for a salary. Tina felt that Brendan had taken advantage of her in creating a partnership that was not truly 50/50. Although he had invested cash in the start-up, the business was built on her talent. Now that the company had become successful, all she wanted was her fair share.

HOW I WOULD HAVE COUNSELED TINA

Many of us ignore the instructions or the recipe and jump right into assembling that new device or cooking that new meal. Sometimes we get it right; often we don't. Making a mistake in such situations usually doesn't involve a great cost or expense. However, when you form or operate a new business, failing to "read the directions" first can both be costly and expose you to significant personal liability. Understand what you're getting into before quitting that steady job and signing on that dotted line.

Tina and Brendan's "partnership" is a very common business formula. One side has the know-how, and the other side has the money. However, both sides are contributing money to the partnership, as Tina's efforts actually created the income and customer base for the partnership.

While partnership agreements are generally not required to be in writing, I would recommend that a written agreement always be obtained so that later disagreements regarding income and expenses, control of the business, and profit distribution can be avoided. Partners have a general fiduciary duty to each other, which simply means that they have to act fairly and reasonably with each other in the operation of the partnership. If one partner fails to act in such a manner, that partner may become liable to the other for any associated losses or expenses.

Everyone knows that you're not supposed to conduct your personal business on company time. After all, your employer is paying you to do a job. Unless Tina had an agreement allowing her to design for her own business while supposedly at her desk designing for her employer (which is highly unlikely), her employer would have a strong argument that Tina's designs were his property. This is most likely the real reason why Brendan's lawyers agreed to settle Tina's employer's claim for $250,000. As Tina's partner, Brendan would be equally liable for the costs associated with the settlement, because Tina's liability to her employer occurred because of her efforts that Brendan was aware of on behalf of the partnership.

In partnerships, it's important to remember that the person you are going into business with doesn't just bring assets—he or she also brings liabilities. To put it simply, unless the written partnership agreement or your state's laws provide otherwise, partners are generally equally liable for the debts of the partnership, as well as equally entitled to the profits of the partnership. Unless the partnership agreement provides otherwise, partners generally maintain equal control over the business, subject to their fiduciary obligations to each other to act in a fair and reasonable manner with regard to the operation and management of the partnership business.

Brendan's attempt to personally recover all the costs he had incurred in the partnership was improper, as Tina had similarly incurred costs through her labor and efforts. While Brendan was properly entitled to collect a stipend for his interest in the partnership, he cannot avoid his share of the expenses of the partnership by receiving full reimbursement for his "loans" to the partnership.

If I were advising Tina, I would not recommend that she agree to sell her interest in the partnership to the outside investor unless a full accounting of all monies contributed to the partnership are accounted for, including a determination of the value of Tina's efforts in the operation of the partnership business. Assuming that the partnership agreement or applicable law provides, Tina should receive equal credit for all expenses paid and should be reimbursed through the purchase price of the partnership.

Depending on the percentage of the business the outside investor is seeking to purchase, Tina will still be a part owner of the business. If Brendan is also retaining a portion of his ownership in the business, the partnership agreement must be rewritten to reflect these changes, including how the expenses and profits of the business are to be accounted for. Also, the three will have to agree on who will control the business, how the business will be controlled, and how decisions will be made in the business. Options could include majority rule or rotating who is in charge each year.

Chapter 36

SELLING YOUR BUSINESS

IT WAS THE PERFECT BUSINESS DEAL, STRUCK AMONG GOOD FRIENDS as they enjoyed a leisurely lunch at the golf club in the exclusive Connecticut suburb where one of the couples had a membership.

For ten years, Carol and Ed had owned a specialty shop that had a reputation as the best source in the area for handmade educational children's toys and beautiful classic clothing for children. They had worked long exhausting hours building up their business. Now, having enjoyed several years of success, they were hoping to find a way to scale back their responsibilities as small-business owners.

Their friends Al and Leslie had just returned from their youngest child's college graduation. Al was a successful medical specialist, and Leslie was an avid gardener. As the foursome sat and enjoyed Bloody Marys overlooking the lush greens, Leslie was complaining about how much time she had on her hands, now that their last child had left home. "I miss having the kids in the house," she said. "I'm so bored; I wish I knew what to do with myself until I can become a full-time grandmother," she joked.

Exhausted from a buying trip to Scotland to check out a source of new cashmere baby blankets, Carol laughed and said she'd love to trade places. The discussion turned serious as Ed declared that he, too, had had enough of being self-employed. "I've loved running the store," he said. "But we're not getting any younger, and I'd really like to spend some time in some of the cities we've always whisked through on business. Maybe take a month in Tuscany, or something."

The conversation drifted away from the topic of work and on to the subject of vacations as the foursome lingered over coffee and dessert. Early the next week, Carol was surprised to get a call at the shop from Al. "I've got a business proposition for you," he said, and he invited Carol and Ed to dinner the next night.

At Al and Leslie's lavish home, and after some small talk and a few glasses of wine, Al got down to business. "Leslie and I want to buy the store from you," he said. Leslie jumped in, saying how much she would love to be involved with things for kids and how the travel to do the buying sounded perfect. Al mentioned that he was going to be cutting down on the hours he worked in his practice, and becoming store owners just seemed like a perfect investment of their time and money.

Carol and Ed were caught off guard. Ed told Al and Leslie that they needed to think about it. "They were our friends," Ed said. "And I didn't want to get into some big, complex business deal with them."

But the more Carol and Ed thought about the idea, the more appealing it became. In fact, they rationalized, since they rented the space for the store, and were low on inventory pending another buying trip, there really wasn't that much that needed to change hands. Suddenly the idea of being free of the store was very appealing.

They called Al and Leslie back and accepted their offer. Al said that he wanted to keep the transaction simple: a gentleman's agreement, he called it. And Ed and Carol didn't want to take advantage of their friends or overcharge for their inventory. "We were friends; we wanted to give them a good deal," Ed said.

In order to keep expenses to a minimum for everyone involved, the two couples signed a letter of agreement that said that Al and Leslie would pay $100,000 for the contents of the store and assume the current lease, which would not expire for four more years. The purchase of the store would be made in three equal payments: $10,000 on the signing of the agreement, $25,000 three months after Al and Leslie assumed ownership, and $65,000 after six months from the date of the agreement.

Both couples signed the letter, and the four toasted their friendship and business acumen over glasses of champagne. Carol took a few weeks to show Leslie how the basics of the store ran, giving her lists of vendors, manufacturers, and resources. Ed went over the bookkeeping and accounting procedures with Leslie and gave her all the information on the landlord and utilities for the store.

Feeling free for the first time in more years than they could remember, Ed and Carol cashed the check for $10,000 and rented a house in the Italian countryside for three months.

"It was a splurge," Carol said. "But we were having such a lovely time, and it was so wonderful to be without the daily responsibilities of the store." Leslie sent the occasional card saying how much she was enjoying the business and telling anecdotes about the various customers she was meeting. Ed and Carol really felt they had done the right thing by selling their store to someone who loved it as much as they had.

When the payment due date for the second installment of the purchase price came and went with no word from Al and Leslie, Carol and Ed were not too concerned. Ed called the store and left a message asking Al to wire the payment directly to their account. "I was sure there was a good explanation," Ed said. "Since we were still out of the country, I figured Al had mailed us a check that was being held with all of our personal mail."

A few more weeks passed, and Carol and Ed became more concerned. They hadn't heard anything at all from Leslie or Al, and their bank had no record of having received a wire transfer for $25,000. Still, they rationalized, they would be home in a week or so, and they were sure they could quickly straighten out any confusion.

When Carol and Ed arrived back home, they immediately looked through their mail for a check from Al and Leslie. But there was no communication from them at all. The next morning, Carol drove downtown to the shop and looked through the front window. She was speechless. The merchandise had all been changed. There were no more beautiful hand-smocked dresses and overalls. Instead, there were outfits that looked as if they belonged in an MTV video instead of on a little girl.

Equally distressing was the large CLOSED sign hanging on the front door. Back at home, both Carol and Ed repeatedly and unsuccessfully tried to contact Leslie and Al.

Ed and Carol were concerned, and Ed was beginning to have a bad feeling about the whole deal. He went to Al and Leslie's house and waited by the curb until he saw Al's car pull into the driveway. While he could tell Al was shocked to see him, Ed was cordial. He asked Al how they'd been, and he mentioned that Carol had noticed the shop was closed up.

Al told Ed that things had been stressful in his medical practice. He was facing a lawsuit brought by a patient and was afraid he would be liable for a large monetary settlement. Leslie had gone away to visit her family in California for a few weeks while he handled the lawyers and the depositions. Ed felt awkward, but he still asked Al about the check for $25,000.

Al was instantly apologetic, telling Ed that it had just slipped his mind in the stress of the past few weeks. He invited Ed into the house to wait while he wrote him a check for the full amount.

Ed immediately felt foolish for worrying about the money. He told Al that he hoped things would get better and suggested that they play a foursome of golf when Leslie got back home from her trip.

A few days later, Ed got the news from his bank that the check had bounced. The same day, Carol picked up a message from the store's landlord informing them that no rent had been paid for the past three months and that as the original leaseholders, they were responsible for paying it.

Over the next few days, the news got worse. The store remained closed, and several people came up to Carol in the coffee shop and at the supermarket to tell her how disappointed they were with the quality and selection in what had once been such a nice shop. No one seemed to know that the store had changed hands, and Carol felt as if everyone thought she had suddenly lost her taste and was trying to sell them inferior products. She felt that her reputation was ruined.

Bills from the electric, gas, and phone services—all containing shut-off notices—were forwarded to Carol and Ed's house as well. Leslie had never changed the name on any of them, and Carol and Ed paid the substantial bills plus late charges rather than risk having the accounts turned over to collection.

Through all of this, Al remained unreachable, and Leslie remained out of town. Carol was devastated. She and Ed had lost their business, their reputation, and almost all of the initial deposit that Al and Leslie had given them. Once Ed and Carol had paid the past due rents and utilities, it was as if they had just given Al and Leslie the store for free.

Ed drafted a letter to Al asking him to fulfill the terms of their agreement. He still didn't want to involve lawyers. Al and Leslie were friends, and they were clearly going through a tough time.

In response, Ed received a letter from Al's attorney stating that Ed and Carol had misrepresented the business to Leslie in the sale and that the agreement was void. The letter went on to say that instead of seeking the return of the initial deposit money, Al was "generously" allowing Ed and Carol to keep it because of their prior friendship. Ed was fuming. "The letter made it seem that we were the ones at fault!" he said.

"We made an agreement to sell our business," Carol said. "And we want them to honor that agreement. I don't want the store back—she's ruined my reputation, and I could never bring myself to sell the junk that she's bought for her inventory."

Ed and Carol don't know how things managed to go so bad so quickly. They thought they were making a simple deal with good friends. Instead, they lost a friendship, their good name, and their livelihood. Looking back, Ed said, "We might as well have given away the store!"

HOW I WOULD HAVE COUNSELED CAROL AND ED

When you sell your business, think like a business owner and not like a friend. While Carol and Ed wanted to give their friends a good deal, this was not the best approach in selling a business to which they had devoted a substantial amount of time and money. Make sure that you properly document the entire sales transaction, including what happens if either party fails to live up to their promises. Getting everything in writing not only will help you avoid the problems that Carol and Ed encountered but also will help ensure that friends stay friends.

In my experience, I routinely encounter people like Carol and Ed who find themselves in substantial financial and legal difficulties because of their desire to avoid the tasks required to properly complete the sale or purchase of a business. Instead, they opt to "keep it simple" and avoid these necessary steps to protect themselves from the financial and legal results that often occur when the other party fails to live up to the promises made in their "gentlemen's agreement." The sale or purchase of a business is a complicated transaction, even when the business is a small business like Carol and Ed's. Do your homework and anticipate the problems associated with such an important undertaking.

One of the first issues in the purchase or sale of a business is the physical location of the business, whether the business location is owned by the business or is the space leased from the landowner. If the location is owned and the sale includes the business location, then any agreement transferring the business must also include an agreement transferring ownership in the property. These agreements must be in writing and must conform to the laws of the particular state in which the property is located.

If the business leases the business location, then the lease needs to be assigned to the new owner. Generally, commercial leases will provide for the assignment or transfer of the lease to another party. However, in most cases, the landowner is permitted to either approve or disapprove of the new tenant based on the intended use of the business premises and the financial condition of the new tenant, among other reasons. Read the lease agreement. Get approval.

Importantly, unless the landowner agrees in writing to release the prior owner from its obligations under the lease and only seek payment of any future lease payments from the new owner, the prior owner will remain liable for any lease payments for the remainder of the lease term. This is what happened to Carol and Ed when they learned that no lease payments had been made after the sale of the business.

One way to protect yourself from nonpayment of the lease is to require the purchaser to prepay a certain number of months of the lease into an escrow account in the event that the purchaser fails to pay the lease payments in a timely manner. This would have prevented Carol and Ed from having to make up the three months of lease payments. Separately, it's a good idea to require the purchaser to provide monthly proof of the timely payment of all lease payments for the remainder of any lease term. This will help to ensure that you're not caught by surprise after any failure to make the lease payments.

Regrettably, most new businesses fail—even existing businesses that are purchased by new owners. Knowing there is a strong chance that the new owners of your business might not have your knack for making the business successful, I would strongly urge anyone selling their business to obtain either the full sales price at the time of the transfer of the business or the maximum possible down payment. This will prevent or minimize the seller's losses if the buyer is unable to make the business a go or retain the business's existing customers.

As a condition to the sale of the business, Carol and Ed should have also required that any utilities, vendor agreements, and other agreements were closed in their names and that Al and Leslie entered into new agreements for these services. If you're no longer in business, get your name off everything. This act alone would have saved Carol and Ed substantial amounts of money and prevented them from worrying about their credit rating.

Carol and Ed will have to sue Al and Leslie for breach of the gentlemen's agreement. If they had entered into a more formal sales agreement with Al and Leslie, provisions could have been placed into the agreement providing for either the foreclosure of the business and reversion of the business back to Carol and Ed or the payment of all outstanding amounts owed under the agreement, including any losses incurred by Carol and Ed in enforcing the sales agreement.

Al and Leslie's claim of misrepresentation doesn't hold much water because of the nature of the business and the sales agreement entered into. Generally, a sales agreement should not include any representation that the new owners will be successful in the business.

Chapter 37

WORK AND BUSINESS RELATIONSHIPS: WHAT YOU NEED TO KNOW

AS IN ANY RELATIONSHIP, WHEN THINGS ARE GOING WELL IN A BUSINESS, everything seems easy, satisfying, and profitable. When things are going badly, even the easiest of decisions becomes an epic struggle between the parties in the relationship. You need to plan ahead for when your business has problems, or for when personal and professional differences between the controlling parties erupt into a feud that threatens the viability of the business.

CORPORATIONS AND PARTNERSHIPS

Every state allows someone to incorporate an entity. While states can differ as to the requirements for a corporation, generally there must be articles of incorporation, bylaws, and an initial set of officers and directors of the corporation. A corporation generally limits the personal liability of its owners to the value of their ownership interest in the corporation. There are also tax benefits to conducting a business as a corporation.

Most states regulate and enforce corporations created in their state through the secretary of state's office. Most states have online information relating to the creation and maintenance of corporations incorporated in their state, including online databases where people can search for information relating to each corporation.

A partnership is merely an agreement, either oral or in writing, describing the relationship between two or more persons or entities who plan to conduct some type of business or provide a service. While partnership agreements do not usually have to be in writing, it is best to create a written partnership agreement in order to avoid any problems arising later between the parties. Here are some points to include in a partnership agreement:

➤ The ownership percentage of each partner, including a placement of value on each respective ownership interest

➤ The partners' entitlement to the profits of the partnership, including how and in what manner profits are to be determined and valued

➤ The partners' responsibility for expenses of the partnership, including how and in what manner the expenses are to be determined and valued

➤ How the control and decision making of the partnership will be maintained; for example, which person(s) is able to make decisions affecting the partnership, including how control of the partnership may be changed over time

➤ How the partnership will conduct business with third parties; for instance, whether certain types of purchases or transactions will require submission to, or approval by, all partners before the transaction is entered into

➤ The manner in which a partner may sell or leave the partnership and how the sale of that partner's interest is to be handled; consider setting predetermined price structures for the sale of the partner's interest in the partnership

➤ Whether a former partner may compete with the partnership following his or her withdrawal from the partnership

I would recommend that you consult a lawyer in your state to draft a partnership agreement before starting your business. By laying out the framework for your business, especially what will happen if the business fails, you will enable all parties to operate under a common understanding that will help alleviate any misunderstandings and disagreements later.

BAD BUSINESS PRACTICES

What to Do If You're Scammed

Even the smartest people can fall victim to scams, and small business owners can be especially vulnerable. The desire to keep costs down and profits high can sometimes lead businesspeople to cut corners or deal with questionable entities. If, despite your best efforts, you have fallen victim to a scam, here are some ideas on how to deal with the situation. If you have lost money or received shoddy or nonexistent products or services, contact the following people or agencies:

➤ INSURANCE—your state's insurance commissioner. A helpful link to each state's insurance commissioner is found at the Web site for the National Association of Insurance Commissioners, www.naic.org.

➤ BUILDING CONTRACTOR—your state's contractor's licensing board. A helpful link to each state's contractor's licensing board is found at the Web site for the National Association of State Contractors Licensing Agencies, www.nascla.org.

➤ TELEMARKETING SCAMS—your state's attorney general's office. A helpful link to each state's attorney general's office is found at the Web site for the National Association of Attorney Generals, www.naag.org. You can also go to the Federal Trade

Commission's Web site, www.ftc.gov, for helpful information and links related to telemarketing.

➤ **INVESTMENT SCAMS**—your state's attorney general's office, as well as the National Association of Security Dealers online at www.nasd.com. You may also contact the United States Securities and Exchange Commission online at www.sec.gov.

STARTING A BUSINESS

Most businesses fail. That being said, the easiest way to help your new business get a leg up on the competition is to be fully informed about what you're getting into and what it takes to run a successful business. Here are some ideas:

➤ **KNOW YOUR MARKET.** Research your potential business before investing a lot of time and money into the venture. Learn about the costs of starting your particular business, including any special licensing or other restrictions on your type of business. Most local government business offices have information packets for new business owners, including the steps you must follow to obtain proper licensing, certification, and tax status for your business.

➤ **RUN THE NUMBERS.** Figure out what it will cost to run your business for at least the first year of operation and how much you can reasonably anticipate making, both in gross sales and in profit. Invariably, a new business will lose money for some time after initially opening its doors. A good resource to look into is the United States Small Business Administration's Web site, which includes ideas and advice for the start-up business. That Web site is www.sba.gov/starting_business.

➤ **UNDERSTAND THE LAW.** Is an employee an employee or an independent contractor? The answer can have serious tax and liability questions. You should contact your state's worker's compensation and employment office for detailed information regarding the status of workers you intend to hire and what type of wages, benefits, insurance, and taxes are required to be provided. You can also go to the United States Internal Revenue Service's Web site for more information on employee taxes and withholding at www.irs.gov.

SELLING YOUR BUSINESS

It's to be hoped that you have made your millions in your business, and now you're just looking to sell out and enjoy the fruits of your labor. Or maybe you just want out and are looking for a change of career or scenery. Either way, you need to sell your business or your interest in a business. Here are some steps to make the transition less painful:

➤ Have a written agreement signed by all parties that details what is being sold, how payment will be made, and how any current or future business expenses or liabilities will be handled. In most cases, the seller should attempt to remove himself or herself from any contracts or long-term agreements, especially if they were personally guaranteed by the seller, as part of the written agreement.

➤ As for leases and other agreements between the business and third parties, if the seller has personally guaranteed or cosigned these leases or agreements, he or she should attempt to have his or her name removed. While the third party may not agree to this release, you're better off at least trying to get this concession. If the third party will not agree to this release, make sure your agreement with the buyer provides for the payment of any damages or losses if the third party seeks payment or collection from you instead of from the business. You should also make sure that you receive copies of all lease payments made during any remainder of the lease term, to ensure that the payments are being made on time.

➤ Change any utility accounts, vendor accounts, bank accounts, and corporate documents to reflect the fact that you are no longer affiliated with the business. In the case of vendors that the business has used, make sure those vendors know that you are no longer affiliated with the business and that any personal guaranties are terminated.

➤ Whenever possible, insist on full or nearly full payment of the purchase price of the business up front. Since most businesses fail—even existing businesses under new ownership—it's best to get as much money up front as possible to avoid any losses should the new owner fail to make a go of the business.

Part VII

FINAL AFFAIRS

How to Tie Up Your Affairs While Protecting Your Interests and the Interests of Those You Love

Problems can arise later in life. Retirement can become anything but peaceful without proper care. It is important to protect the legacy you've created and to defend yourself against predators and influences intent on taking advantage of you or your elders.

The need to protect seniors has never been greater. The elderly represent the fastest-growing segment of the population, selling the houses they've lived in all their lives in a booming real estate market and finding themselves suddenly wealthy. They can be sitting ducks for exploitation in a digital world they can't, or won't, adjust to. Their children, baby boomers from coast to coast, are currently facing the question of how best to provide for their parents, as well as how best to prepare for their own retirements—a prospect that no longer feels so distant and remote. They're looking into nursing homes, medical centers, and home-care providers, trying to do right by the people who raised them. But even as we are meeting the physical and emotional needs of aging parents, we also need to remember to look into their legal well-being. Too often, we trust that they'll be all right, because we don't want to admit that they're getting too old to make decisions for themselves anymore, legal or otherwise. That's when they get into trouble, and the heartaches begin.

I've seen it a thousand times: people fail to prepare adequately for their own demise or the settlement of their estate, as if executing a will were a concession to death rather than a sensible way to prepare for it. The common result is that their departure leads only to misery and heartache instead of the creation of a positive legacy.

Most people work hard all their lives in order to create something they can pass on to the next generation. It can be land or property, a house or a business; it can be heirlooms or family treasures; it can be money; or it can be, and usually is, a combination of all of the above. Nine out of ten times, when someone dies and the will is clear, there's amity all around, the estate is properly and equitably divided, and everybody goes home from the funeral sad but at peace. However, when there's a problem with the will or a disagreement among the heirs, or when old rivalries or feuds begin to surface, then the probating of the estate becomes a battleground. Once again, it's a situation in which a brief consultation with a lawyer before the fact can save your loved ones hours and hours of legal fees after the fact. Probate courts spend *most of their time trying to determine what the deceased wanted, when the answer is almost always "Well, he certainly didn't want this to end up in probate court." Most heirs don't want to be there, either, but they are forced to be because somebody, somewhere along the line, failed to anticipate the eventuality.*

Chapter 38

SWINDLED OUT OF MOTHER'S ESTATE

FOR SEVENTY YEARS, TARA HAD NEVER TRULY BEEN ALONE. NOW THAT HER mother was finally in a nursing home, she felt free, but the freedom felt strange and just a bit wrong somehow. She established a new routine, visiting her ninety-one-year-old mother, Lucille, twice a day at the eldercare residence, once in the morning and once at suppertime. The problem was the hours between visits—hours as empty as the house they'd moved into together two years earlier, hoping to spend their autumn years in the Las Vegas sun.

Tara was lonely and a bit frightened. Her mother had always taken care of everything before, run things, and paid the major bills. Tara's paycheck from her schoolteaching position had gone directly into her mother's bank account. To fight the loneliness, she took to frequenting a place called Mr. G's Café, a 24-hour coffee shop at the Fiesta Hotel and Casino. It was a nice place to sit, only a block and a half from the nursing home, and filled with locals, retirees, and the "snowbirds" who came to Las Vegas for the winter. Tara had come to Mr. G's every night during the first week Lucille was in the home when Tara didn't quite know what to do with herself after her evening visits. She'd stay for an hour or so, perhaps eat from the buffet, and then go home and watch television. She was more or less used to feeling invisible, so she was surprised when a good-looking white-haired man, about her age, well dressed with a neatly trimmed mustache, introduced himself and asked if he could join her at her booth.

"My name is Andrew. I've noticed you've been coming here and wondered if you wouldn't mind a bit of company?" he said. "I'm sort of new here myself. How are the slot machines treating you?"

"I just play bingo," Tara said shyly.

She wasn't used to people paying attention to her, particularly not men. She had friends from church, but she'd never met anyone in a coffee shop. Then again, she'd never really been in a coffee shop, at least not by herself. She'd lived with her mother all her life. It was nice to have somebody to talk to, and Andrew was a good listener. He was sympathetic. He seemed kind, someone she could trust. She found herself telling him things—not secret things, but personal things all the same. She was of Ukrainian descent, a devout Catholic, from Detroit, where she'd taught elementary school, first and second grades. Her mother had worked her whole life, putting in long, hard hours on an assembly line, and had still been able to put two kids through college, kids who never wanted for anything.

She told Andrew how her father had died of a heart attack when she was young, and how strong Lucille had always been, raising her and her brother. Lucille and Tara were as close as a mother and daughter could be, in Tara's opinion. Lucille still had good days when she was mentally all there and focused, but on her bad days, it wasn't clear how much she understood of what was going on around her.

"Is it Alzheimer's?" Andrew asked.

Tara shook her head to say she didn't know.

"That's so tough," Andrew said sympathetically. He seemed sweet and compassionate. It was indeed tough. Losing her mother a little bit at a time was harder than losing her all at once. It was nice to think that someone else understood what she was going through.

When she saw Andrew again a few days later, she was glad to see him, and to her surprise he seemed genuinely glad to see her. Once again, the conversation they had was pleasant. Tara had never had a man in her life before, so she'd never really noticed the lack of one and had never felt deprived of anything. She'd been fulfilled by her teaching and by her relationship with her mother, and was the first to admit that she was an "old maid." Now that she had Andrew, she felt happy, but a bit scared, venturing into new territory—but that was just normal, wasn't it?

Over the next fourteen months, Tara and Andrew grew close. He took her places and showed her things, but mostly it was the simple companionship she came to treasure. Early on, she felt comfortable enough to mention something that was causing her great anxiety. She'd been shocked to discover, the first time she used her mother's savings to write a check for the nursing home, that Lucille had managed to put away a considerable amount of money: more than $300,000. There were no mortgage payments among the bills that piled up each month, which meant that Lucille must have paid cash for the condominium where they lived. Tara found the responsibility frightening. She had never been a "money person" and didn't really care much about money. What she cared about was her mother's health, and money couldn't buy that back.

"I really wish I didn't have to deal with this," Tara told Andrew one day. "I'm just not comfortable with it."

"If it would make things easier," he said, "I'd be happy to handle it for you ..."

She appreciated the offer to help. It was generous of him to give her his time. She went to her bank and added Andrew's name to the account of convenience Lucille had set up for Tara to draw from to pay the bills and medical expenses. She informed the credit card and utility companies that Andrew would be signing the checks. He took care of everything, and she felt relieved. She never got so much as a late notice. There were no troublesome bank statements to fret over or decipher. Andrew accompanied her to the nursing home and visited Lucille with her. On several occasions, he even stopped by the nursing home on his own to visit. He didn't have to do that, but it showed the kind of person he was, Tara thought. She trusted Andrew with everything, and he never let her down.

Then one day, Andrew didn't return her calls, and when she went to Mr. G's Café to look for him, he wasn't there. The next day, the same thing was true. There were any number of reasons why he might have been called out of town, but it wasn't like him not to inform her first. Perhaps something sudden had come up. Maybe a relative of his own needed caring for. Her worst fears were that something might have happened to him. He could have had a stroke or a heart attack. She called him several times, but each time the phone rang and rang.

Not until she visited the bank two weeks after she had last heard from Andrew did she realize what had happened. She hadn't seen any bank statements because Andrew had directed the bank to mail them to a post office box. Looking at the bank records, she saw checks written to pay the electric bill and the phone bill, but also checks for large round numbers—$3,000 here, $6,000 there—a slow siphoning of funds that began shortly after Andrew took over the bills and increased just before he disappeared. Even then, she didn't want to believe what she knew in her heart was true. After a few days, the picture was clear. Andrew had absconded with her mother's fortune.

Every cent of it.

The sense of personal betrayal she felt was profound. The shame was overwhelming. She felt like such a fool. She was too humiliated to tell her mom what had happened. After all her years of saving, her mother would be humiliated to be forced to live off the meager monthly stipend that Social Security provided. Worse was the news, when Tara finally contacted a lawyer, that she had no legal recourse, because she'd given Andrew the legal permissions he needed to do what he'd done. The sheriff Tara spoke with said he doubted that Tara was Andrew's first victim. He said he would see what he could do to help her recover the funds, but he didn't seem to have much hope. It was lucky that the condo was paid for, or she might have ended up on the street.

As it was, Tara didn't know what she was going to do. She was an older woman herself, only a few years away from seventy. She wasn't going to be able to find a job. Her mother's care was only going to become more expensive and complicated. Who knew how many years her small teacher's pension would last her? Tara's reluctance to learn how to manage the simplest financial tasks had cost both her and her mother the promise of security and a comfortable lifestyle in their old age.

HOW I WOULD HAVE COUNSELED TARA

What do you think happens to some young criminals? They become older criminals—and what better place to commit crimes than among their peers? Andrew was a con artist, plain and simple. And Tara made herself an easy target; she basically gave him the keys to the vault. For someone predisposed to crime like Andrew, you could hardly blame him for doing what came naturally. The lesson here: don't try to avoid life's responsibilities—you might just end up like Tara.

We can all sympathize with people like Tara. They devote their lives to others, and in return they avoid many of life's routine obligations, like keeping track of their finances. This is not a good idea. You, like everyone else, should maintain control over your finances. When you delegate control to someone else, you run the risk that he or she will take advantage of your goodwill. That is what happened to Tara. Even while she was living with her mother, she should have taken an active interest in their family finances so she could be prepared for the day when she would need to manage the money for both of them.

The first thing I would have told Tara is that she should never have put someone else on her bank and credit accounts unless that person was a spouse or a highly trusted family member. If you're still insistent on giving someone access to your accounts, open up some new accounts with only minimal funds in them. By limiting access to your funds, you will ensure that your "trusted" friend doesn't get away with all of your hard-earned money should that person suddenly experience a lapse of morals.

And while we're on the subject of trust, I'd offer another piece of advice. Do not discuss personal and/or financial matters with strangers or new acquaintances. You're just asking for trouble.

Because Lucille had handled everything for Tara and herself, Lucille should have set up a plan for her financial affairs against the time when she would no longer be able to attend to this important matter. It was unlikely that Tara would be able to assume this important role so late in her life. One option would have been to create a trust for the benefit of Tara should Lucille become incapacitated. Lucille could have designated a responsible person, such as her attorney or personal banker, to handle the financial affairs. This would have kept Tara from seeking assistance at the coffee shop.

Tara could have spotted the theft earlier by continuing to have the monthly bank statements sent to her. There was no reason for the monthly statements to go to Andrew's separate post office box, thus enabling him to hide his theft from Tara. Tara should have reviewed the monthly bank statements, since this would have quickly tipped her off that Andrew was stealing money. A good rule to follow is this: always open all your mail yourself, even if you are only quickly looking at the charges and balances. If Tara had done this one simple thing, it would have prevented the theft.

Tara should not completely despair, however. If Andrew can be found, I would recommend pursuing a claim against him for theft and fraud. Unfortunately, the likelihood of finding an individual like Andrew is very slim. But if Tara could find the means to pursue it by hiring a private detective, for instance, then she could go through with filing a claim against him.

While the lawyer told Tara that she didn't have a case, since she had freely placed Andrew on the accounts, it's not necessarily a given that she would not prevail in court. At issue is the authority Tara gave Andrew in handling her affairs. It seems clear that she didn't authorize him to take all the money.

If Andrew purchased any property—either real estate or personal property, like a car—with the money, Tara could initiate or pursue a lawsuit and place a lien on Andrew's property pending the resolution of the case. This lien would hinder Andrew's ability to sell or transfer the property until the resolution of the lawsuit.

Tara should also withdraw all monies from any joint accounts on which she placed Andrew's name and notify any creditors in writing of the fraud. She should open new accounts in her name only, with new passwords.

Chapter 39

BLENDED FAMILIES AND CHANGED WILLS

WHEN BRENDA AND DUANE ANDERSON FIRST MET, THEY WERE BOTH young and both recently divorced. They worked together on the late shift at a large aircraft factory in Tennessee. Over the course of many discussions on ex-spouses, kids, and making single parenthood work, they both realized they had found their soul mates. Only six months after they met, Duane proposed. Brenda said yes immediately. She was thrilled to be gaining a wonderful husband and equally excited about becoming a mom to Duane's three young sons.

Brenda and her two daughters, and Duane and his three sons, moved into a big new house in an established family neighborhood. Brenda switched to the day shift, and they began their lives together, raising their blended family. "Those early years were hard," Brenda's oldest daughter, Candy, said. Brenda and Duane were clearly in love, but it cost a lot to support a family of seven. Duane moved up the ranks at the factory quickly. Because they lived such a modest lifestyle, Brenda was eventually able to stop working and look after all the children until they were old enough to leave home.

Candy's sister, Diane, remembers that the families blended together seamlessly. She loved having both older and younger brothers. The family joke was that they were like the Brady Bunch—the kids were all so close. That's why what happened when their parents passed away was so shocking.

Although they didn't have a large estate—the house they lived in, Duane's life insurance, generous retirement benefits from their employer, and a few stocks—Brenda and Duane were conscientious about planning for their kids after they were gone. As most people do, they named each other primary beneficiaries on their retirement plans, and Duane made Brenda the primary beneficiary of his life insurance. They owned their home as joint tenants with right of survivorship and were joint owners of all their bank accounts.

Right after they were married, Duane and Brenda had their wills drawn up by a local attorney. It was a simple "mom and pop" will, which left their respective estates to each other and divided them equally between their five children if they both happened to die at the same time.

Brenda and Duane had lived in Tennessee pretty much their whole lives, and they had always worked at the aircraft factory. So when Duane was ready to retire, they made plans to move to Arizona. They were surprised when they sold the house for a huge amount of money—they had no idea what an investment they had been sitting on. They bought a condo in Arizona and planned to take up golf.

It should have been the happiest time in their lives, but right before they left, their youngest son, Corey, dropped a bombshell. He told them he was gay and planned to move to California with his partner.

None of Corey's siblings were shocked, except his older brother, D.J., who was quite conservative like his parents. The other kids tried to talk to their parents, concerned about the way Brenda and Duane had cut Corey off emotionally. They all told Corey to give them some time and that his brother and parents would come around, but he was so hurt that he just stopped talking to everyone in the family.

Sadly, Duane was never able to repair the estrangement with his youngest son. Six months after he and Brenda moved into their dream retirement condo, Duane suffered a massive heart attack and died.

Brenda returned home, insisting that the funeral be held in the town where they had lived most of their lives.

There was a huge turnout for the funeral: friends, neighbors, grandchildren, and, of course, all of their children—except Corey. He was traveling in Europe on business at the time and was still hurting from his parents' treatment. He didn't come home for the funeral. And Brenda found that, more than anything else, unforgivable.

After the funeral, Brenda sold the Arizona condo, saying that she had no happy memories there. She moved in with Candy and her family in their house in Georgia and spent part of the year there, and part of the year with her other daughter, Diane, at her home in South Carolina.

The shock of Duane's sudden death had taken a toll on Brenda's health. After a few years of shuttling between her daughters' homes, it became apparent that she needed to move into an assisted living community. Without discussing it with any of her family members, Brenda prepared a new will, in which each of her daughters was to receive one third of her estate and Duane's older two sons would split the remaining third. Duane's youngest son, Corey, never forgiven for missing his father's funeral, was disinherited.

Within a year after moving to an apartment in an assisted living community, Brenda suffered a stroke and died. When Brenda's will was read, the children were shocked to discover that she had so dramatically changed the disposition of her estate.

"We were surprised by two things," Candy said. "One: that Mom's estate was so large—over $900,000. And two: that she had divided it so unevenly and had completely disinherited Corey."

Duane's other two sons, both successful businessmen, were fine with the changes Brenda had made to the will. "Diane and Candy took care of Mom and let her live in their homes during the last years of her life," D.J. said. And although they felt sorry for Corey, they weren't surprised by the outcome of his long estrangement from the family.

"I have to admit that I was delighted D.J. and Mikey were so generous in their response to the will," Diane said. "Having Mom live with us hadn't been easy and had stressed our family budget. My husband never said anything, but having the money from Mom's estate was clearly going to make things easier for us."

When the will was offered for probate, however, things began to get messy. Corey filed a will contest, claiming that even though their original wills did not have any specific language to that effect, Duane and Brenda had implicitly agreed that neither would change his or her will after the death of the other.

Corey accused his sisters of manipulating his mother, of talking her into changing her will so they would get more of her estate. He contacted his brothers, telling them that they were being robbed of what their father would have wanted them to have.

As Corey continued to make allegations and contest the will, the good relations between all the siblings began to fall apart. Diane was afraid that lawyer fees would eat away at her portion of the estate, and she wanted to find a way to settle. Candy was furious at her youngest brother and wanted to make sure that her mother's wishes were honored. Duane's older sons began to wonder whether their father, who had worked so hard his whole life, was having his contributions fairly valued.

When, after a nonjury trial, the judge ruled that Brenda's will remained valid, Corey instantly filed an appeal. He reminded his siblings that his partner was a hotshot California lawyer and that since he got all his legal advice for free, he could outlast them in a legal fight until the entire estate was gone. And because none of the other family members could agree on what needed to be done, they each hired separate lawyers.

In the end, five different lawyers and all of the siblings were bitterly contesting Brenda's estate. "I honestly don't know what is the right way to divide up Mom's estate," Candy said. "I just know that neither she nor Dad would have wanted us to spend our inheritance on lawyers' fees."

HOW I WOULD HAVE COUNSELED
THE ANDERSONS

Blood may be thicker than water, but money comes in a close second. Even close-knit families can suffer "inheritance envy" after the loss of one or both parents. At a time when we should be thinking fondly of our departed parent, our thoughts may turn to dollars and cents. While there's no guarantee that someone will not be disappointed by his or her inheritance, plan ahead and let yourself truly rest in peace.

Wills are governed by state law. It's a good idea to consult a lawyer in the state where you live to ensure that your will complies with the laws of your state. This is especially the case when you move to another state, as Brenda and Duane did. Each state has particular probate laws regarding the creation and administration of wills.

As a general rule, you must have sufficient mental capacity to prepare and sign your will. This rule requires that you know what your assets are and that you intend to give them away in a certain manner upon your death. It is unknown whether Brenda had sufficient mental capacity to create her new will, since she required assisted living at the time she created it. If your will is declared invalid, the state—not you—will have final say in your children's inheritance.

When Duane and Brenda first drew up their wills, they should have considered how to provide for their respective children from their first marriages. When a survivor spouse inherits an estate, unless individuals are specifically named, the person to whom the estate passes can do whatever he or she likes with a subsequent will—including changing it to favor certain family members.

You are entitled to give your property away to virtually anyone you wish. You may specifically disinherit children or close family members—after all, it's your money. There are basically two schools of thought regarding disinheriting children or close family members: you can either tell them in advance that you've cut them off, or have your lawyer spring it on them after you're gone. If you hate conflict or disappointment, then it's obvious that the second method has advantages—for you. However, by giving advance notice of your intentions, you may prevent the type of will contest that occurred to Brenda's family, and prevent or minimize dissent among your children.

One word to the wise: if you're going to disinherit a family member, especially a wife or a child, make sure that your will specifically mentions that person by name and states that you are specifically disinheriting him or her from your will. Without this acknowledgment, the disinherited family member may be able to successfully argue to a court that you "forgot" to include that person in the will.

Corey claims that his sisters influenced Brenda to change her will in order to disinherit him from his mother's property. Claims of undue influence are routinely argued in will contests. Be careful. Most wills must be witnessed by several disinterested persons. Generally, if you are going to receive something under the will, you should not be one of the persons witnessing the will. If you do, then a claim could be made that you exerted undue influence in the creation of the will, and you may be out of your inheritance. Even though Diane and Candy did not sign Brenda's second will, a will may be held invalid if others exerted undue influence over the person making the will. Once again, it depends on whether you had sufficient mental capacity at the time you created and signed the will.

Provided you have sufficient mental capacity, you can change your will at any time. Corey's argument that Duane and Brenda "implicitly agreed never to change their wills" is generally not going to hold up in court.

If the will is deemed invalid, then, in some cases, a prior will may still be valid. Generally, however, the law of the state in which the probate is pending will control who receives what from a deceased person following the invalidation of the will. If a will has been invalidated, the family members should contact a competent lawyer in the area of probate law to advise them of the legal effects of a will or a trust.

Chapter 40

LIVING TRUSTS

LEANNA WILSON WAS EXHAUSTED. SHE HAD SPENT THE PAST THREE WEEKS at her father's home trying to pull his affairs together after his doctors had agreed that Kenneth was suffering from Alzheimer's. Leanna had been worried when she began to receive rambling phone calls from her widowed father at odd hours. So she had left her apartment in Berkeley, California, to travel to her childhood home: a neat brick colonial near Boston where her parents had always lived. When she arrived, she was dismayed to find the house in disarray and her father wandering in the yard in his pajamas.

In the whirlwind of stressful days that followed, she had taken a leave of absence from her job, coaxed her dad to a variety of doctor's appointments, arranged for twenty-four-hour home care, cleaned the house from top to bottom, and started to research nearby nursing homes and elder care centers.

Her brother, Kevin, who lived and worked in Europe, was arriving the next day, and they had agreed to make some final decisions about their dad's future living arrangements, his home, and his assets. Leanna had been going through her father's papers and files, hoping to find any kind of instruction or clue as to how he would have wanted to handle things. Though she still hadn't found any final paperwork, such as a will, what she had found was deeply distressing.

Leanna had discovered that not too long after her mother's death, her father had transferred most of his savings into a living trust that was administered by a company called Senior Benefit Assistance (SBA), headquartered in a Midwestern state. Even more troubling were the records showing that over several recent months, her father had also transferred most of his assets into the trust.

"I know that living trusts are supposed to make it easier to disburse your estate," Leanna said. "But the document my father signed is not very detailed, and the company that has control over the trust has not invested it wisely."

Leanna's initial research into her father's living trust revealed that he had named SBA as the trustee and had signed a boilerplate document giving the company broad powers in determining how his assets were managed. Despite repeated calls to the company, Leanna hadn't been able to determine much more than the fact that on the basis of her father's rapidly deteriorating condition, SBA was now claiming to be trustees of the assets and refusing to share information with Leanna, claiming she wasn't "authorized" as a trustee.

"I don't know how to make SBA take me seriously," Leanna said. She was certain that SBA had scammed her father. She had called the police, who came out to her father's house, but Kenneth was having a pretty good day and was able to confirm that the signature on the paperwork was his. The police said there was nothing they could do, that it was pretty obvious that Kenneth had entered into a contract of his own free will. By the time the officers left the house, Leanna had been made to feel as if she were the guilty party, trying to take her father's estate out of his control while he was still clearly in the picture.

As Leanna continued to sort through her father's paperwork, his financial status became even grimmer. Statements revealed that SBA had invested the bulk of his money in a thirty-year annuity—one that paid a 10 percent commission back to the company and named her father, Kenneth, as the beneficiary. "My father is eighty-five years old," Leanna said. "What good does a thirty-year annuity do him?"

Leanna wished she had paid more attention to the details when her father had been talking to her a few months earlier. She recalled several phone conversations with her father in which he mentioned that he was talking to financial planners about his estate. He was extolling the virtues of putting his assets and savings into a trust.

Leanna hadn't wanted to talk about it with him. Her mother had passed away only a year earlier, and she'd thought that her dad was healthy. She didn't want to think about what would happen when they were both gone. She thought that perhaps her father was having a reaction to his wife's death. "Don't worry about me and Kevin," she told him.

Leanna remembered that her father had mentioned several times how nice the young financial planner was and how pleasant it was to have company in the house. "In retrospect, I guess I should have been suspicious about how many times the 'planners' came to the house to meet with my father," she said. "He was probably lonely, and I feel like they took advantage of that."

Letters, notes in her father's calendar, and more paperwork from SBA suggested that the SBA "financial planners" had in fact been fairly frequent visitors. Leanna found marketing materials from the company that touted the benefits of establishing a living trust, including reduced estate and income taxes, elimination of the need for a will, and avoidance of messy family controversies in the division of an estate. The agreement was incredibly general and gave SBA very broad power over Kenneth's money. Leanna couldn't believe her father would willingly tie up his money in that way. She wondered whether her father's illness had already dulled his usually sharp financial acumen.

Leanna was even more worried after an early application at a nearby nursing home was rejected. "Your father isn't eligible for Medicaid, according to his paperwork," the director told her. Leanna spent days wading through various automated telephone help lines and waiting on hold, only to find that by being named a beneficiary of his trust, her father had made himself ineligible for Medicaid. He would have to spend down his trust before Medicaid could begin making payments. The problem was that most of his money was tied up for thirty years.

Leanna was at her wit's end. Her father obviously needed care, and she couldn't keep taking months at a time off from work. She'd taken an extended leave the previous year when her mother had died, and she didn't know how much more her boss would allow.

But untangling her father's financial mess was going to be time consuming. The house, the stocks, his share of his wife's estate, his cash—all were tied up in the SBA trust. Leanna was unsure how they would pay for the increasing care Kenneth would need. Perhaps she and her brother could afford it for a while, but not for thirty years. And since Kenneth was the beneficiary of his own trust, and Leanna had not been able to find his will, she was beginning to doubt that she would ever be able to access the money, even if they were able to wait thirty years for the trust to mature.

Kenneth had always looked out for his family. He had provided a beautiful home and was always there to help his kids if they needed it. He had always been in charge. It was natural for Leanna and her brother to have simply assumed that he had planned for his future as well as theirs.

But in trying to assure the simplest way to provide for his family once he was gone, Kenneth had complicated their lives tremendously. "Now, when Dad really needs us to help him, I don't know how we can," Leanna said. "He never would have wanted things to end up this way."

HOW I WOULD HAVE COUNSELED LEANNA

Most of us never plan on becoming seriously ill or even dying. We spend more time picking out that new car and all those options than we do planning for our eventual deaths or the day when we're no longer able to care for ourselves. By planning ahead, not only do you ensure that your final affairs will be handled according to your wishes, but you don't let yourself fall victim to the con artists who prey on us at our weakest moments.

If I were counseling Leanna, I would recommend that she immediately contest the living trust in court, on the basis of Kenneth's mental incapacity. It appears that Kenneth's ongoing Alzheimer's disease made him susceptible to the fraudulent sales techniques of SBA. When creating a will, a trust, or even a living trust, you must have sufficient mental capacity to understand the nature of what you're doing. You need to understand how you are disposing of your property and/or giving up control over it. If it can be shown that Kenneth lacked this mental capacity, then his living trust can be set aside.

As a trustee of Kenneth's living trust, SBA has a fiduciary duty to ensure that Kenneth's money and property are held and/or invested in a manner consistent with Kenneth's intentions and/or any applicable state law. The issue for the court will be to decide whether a thirty-year annuity is an appropriate investment for an eighty-five-year-old man as part of his estate planning—as well as the 10 percent fees that SBA is charging. They're probably not. If SBA is found to have breached its fiduciary duties to Kenneth, then SBA may be personally liable to Kenneth and his estate for any losses or damages.

One issue that reflects on Kenneth's lack of mental capacity is the fact that the salespeople from SBA repeatedly went to Kenneth's home. The exercise of undue influence over the person disposing of property can serve to invalidate the will, trust, or living trust. In many states, there is a rebuttable presumption of undue influence by anyone who assisted in the drafting or signing of a will, trust, or living trust when that same person receives money or property under the will, trust, or living trust. This appears to be the case with regard to Kenneth.

When you create a living trust, generally all your assets, such as your homes, bank accounts, stocks, and bonds should be transferred into the name of the living trust. Any assets that are acquired after the creation of the living trust should always be placed in the name of the trust. A "pour-over" will should always accompany a living trust. This type of will is designed so that any later assets or money you acquire since the creation of your living will get "poured" in with your other assets, according to your desires. Like regular wills, pour-over wills must be probated, so those assets may take longer to disburse than those in the trust.

A living trust must usually have at least one named beneficiary. Many times, the person creating the trust will be a beneficiary during his or her lifetime and then will name successor beneficiaries upon that person's death.

If the court invalidates the living trust, Kenneth can get his property back into his name. Because of his mental state, however, a guardianship will have to be appointed over him and his property. Leanna will have to go to court for this. Once a guardianship is established, Leanna will have full control over Kenneth's assets and property. She will have to regularly advise the court of what she is doing with Kenneth's assets, including stocks or property, to pay for his long-term care.

If Kenneth does not have a will, and the living trust is invalidated by the court, then it is unlikely that Kenneth will be able to create a will, given his declining mental capacity. In this case, upon his death, Kenneth's assets and property would be transferred intestate according to applicable state law. "Intestate" simply means that state law provides who receives money and property from the deceased.

As with the other matters covered in this book, I would recommend that Leanna retain a lawyer experienced in probate and guardianship matters. Probate law and procedure tend to be highly technical and loaded with procedural rules that can be difficult to understand. Don't go it alone.

Chapter 41

WHEN LAWYERS GET ALL THE MONEY

EVERYONE ACKNOWLEDGED THAT JULIAN OSGOOD WAS AN INCREDIBLY shrewd businessman. After all, generations of the family had heard over and over the stories of how young Jules had arrived in the United States with only coins in his pocket and had, over the years, built up an empire of retail shops and real estate holdings that made the Osgoods one of the wealthiest families in the northeastern state where they lived. A big part of Julian's legend was that no one knew, exactly, the secrets of his success. The only certain thing was that in his business, his word was the final word.

He was an intensely private man, with only a few close associates. He and his wife, Elise, lived alone in a large but modest home near his company headquarters. Although they had no children of their own, they were very close to several nieces and nephews who lived nearby and were frequent visitors to their house for vacations and holidays.

As they grew older, Julian established a foundation in his wife's name and funded it with several million dollars. His longtime secretary, Betty Wilson, and a trusted business advisor, Geoffrey James, were trustees of the foundation. Julian had suggested that once he was gone, the foundation would receive a large gift from his estate and would be able to carry out charitable works in his name.

"We always assumed that Uncle Julian would have his estate in perfect order," his nephew Michael said. "He and Aunt Elise were so close, and Geoff and Betty had worked with him forever. We all just figured that the three of them would be able to see his wishes through."

When Julian died and his family gathered for the reading of his will, it quickly became apparent that the methods of secrecy and hands-on management that had served him so well in building a business empire would have just the opposite effect on building a family dynasty that could continue after he was gone.

"I think we were all shocked when the lawyer told us that seven executors had been named to handle the estate," Michael said. "Aunt Elise, Geoff, and Betty, just as we had supposed, but also me, my cousin Angela, one of my uncle's lawyers, Anthony Marks, and one of his oldest friends, Thomas Keller, who happened to be a judge. I guess Uncle was trying to mix family interests with business acumen and a sense of fairness. I know he never would have wanted the chaos that has resulted. He would be furious if he knew what was happening."

Michael explained that the estate had now been in probate for more than seven years. What was initially estimated to be more than $150 million in assets had been diminished to just over $30 million. What was truly remarkable was that no one had officially been awarded any money from the estate yet—except the lawyers, who were regularly submitting their bills to the estate for payment. Even Julian's widow hadn't received any money. Although Julian thought he had found people he could trust to do his wishes after he was gone, it wasn't long before greed and entitlement took over, and more than a few shocking truths came to light.

Julian's wife fell into ill health as the struggle over the estate dragged out. Her niece Angela had recently convinced her to move to Switzerland, ostensibly for treatments for some physical difficulties caused by a recent small stroke. But Michael suspected another motivation. "Angela wants to convince Aunt Elise that she is the only one looking out for her interests; she's trying to have me removed as an executor, because she knows that I want to follow through on Uncle Julian's wishes, while she only wants to get her hands on more of the money," he said. Michael was afraid that with his Aunt Elise in bad health, Angela would try to have her declared incompetent and removed as an executor. Once Angela managed to isolate Michael's aunt in Europe, he didn't know whether he could prevent that from happening.

While Elise and Angela were living in Europe, Angela also used a real estate agent who was a friend of hers to list Julian and Elise's house on the market. Real estate values had skyrocketed since Julian's death, and Michael was sure that the house had sold for a significant amount. However, no one had been able to find the money from the sale. Angela told Michael that she had acted as Elise's agent and had transferred the proceeds from the sale to a Swiss account she had set up for her aunt. "The worst thing is that I don't know whether to believe her or not," Michael said. "If the money from the house is all Aunt Elise has to live on, then who am I to care how much it is, or where it's gone? But it makes just another loose end for the lawyers to have to tie up."

And the disposition of the estate certainly generated a lot of legal business. Since the initial reading of the will, accusations had flown fast and furiously. Betty and Geoff were removed as executors and also removed from the board of trustees of the Osgood Foundation after a long legal battle that resulted in their being found guilty of enriching themselves at the foundation's expense.

Betty and Geoff countered their dismissal by claiming that the real estate owned by the foundation was actually held in real estate trust and that for a while they had worked as paid consultants, along with the lawyers, to determine the ownership of the holdings. According to Michael, Betty and Geoff seemed to have information that no one else could access, and he wanted to know why all the paperwork wasn't simply in one place. Julian had a safe in his office, and Betty had the combination, but she had always claimed that many of the real estate documents were missing. Even Julian's will was quite difficult to locate, initially.

More time passed. Judge Keller, the seventh executor, died of a heart attack. Paper trails went cold; documents that were previously "lost" would suddenly appear; lawyers brought suits and countersuits on behalf of one or another of the remaining four executors. "Every year brought some new discovery," Michael said. "New bank accounts, different corporate entities, a newly discovered real estate holding company. And each new discovery meant hours of court time and meetings with lawyers."

After five years, Michael's lawyer stopped working on the case. Michael could no longer afford to pay him, and the lawyer was unwilling to work on contingency. "I would have to miss four or five days of work each month to go to hearings or meetings. Some depositions would take all day," Michael said. His boss was frustrated, and finally Michael just left his job. Without a lawyer, trying to settle the estate became his full-time job. He still worked for his old company as a consultant, but about half of Michael's time was spent trying to ensure that his Uncle Julian's wishes would be enacted.

In trying to save his widow the burden of managing the entire estate, and by attempting to micromanage his affairs after he was gone, Julian wreaked havoc for his widow, his charities, and his extended family. "My uncle was always the final word in a dispute," Michael said. "But he's not here, now, to put an end to this."

And Michael couldn't even see an end in sight. He didn't know how much longer he could continue to fight for the estate. And he worried that by the time all the legal battles had been settled, there wouldn't be any money left at all. Mostly, though, Michael worried that the only individuals to benefit from his Uncle Julian's lifetime of hard work would be the lawyers involved in settling his estate.

HOW I WOULD HAVE COUNSELED JULIAN

Where there's a will—there's a way. Fights over what we did or didn't receive from the dearly departed are as common as the day is long. Even estates with far less value than Julian's can fall prey to the same infighting and partisan battles reflected in Julian's case. While it's difficult to create a bulletproof will or trust, you can do some things to prevent the lawyers from becoming your most significant "heirs."

Julian did not need to involve the whole family in the administration of his estate. An executor is charged with the responsibility of administering the estate, disposing of the property, and ensuring that any property is properly transferred pursuant to the express wishes of the deceased. An important note: make sure your will expressly provides for the disposition of all your property. An executor is also generally entitled to receive a fee for his or her services in addition to any property or money received under the will. By naming seven executors to his will, Julian ensured that excessive executor fees would be paid and that the administration of his will would be complicated by the competing interests of each executor. Something about too many cooks comes to mind. While the size of Julian's estate, $150 million, might require more than one person to serve as executor, it was unnecessary for seven people to serve.

Julian should have picked one or two trusted individuals to serve as executor. Additionally, Julian could have designated one or two additional executors in case the original executors either declined to serve or had died. Even though you are named as an executor of a will, you are not required to serve as executor. It is a voluntary position. In the case of a will whose named executor refuses to serve as executor or has died, the court may appoint an administrator of the estate. Each state's laws vary regarding this matter.

When you prepare your will, it should clearly set out your assets and to whom you want the assets to be distributed. If you're merely giving property or money to a named beneficiary, then simply and concisely state this intention in the will. If you intend to give it to a charitable group or foundation, make sure you identify the charitable group or foundation by name, and include the exact amount of money or property you intend to give it. It is impossible to be too clear in stating your intentions in the will. Remember, you will not be around to explain them later.

By expressly providing for the disposition of his property, Julian would have avoided the personal interests and squabbles that ensued after his death. For example, if Julian's home had not been held in joint tenancy with his wife, Elise, then the house would have been an asset of the estate and would have required approval of the probate court for its sale. In many states, sales of real property held by the estate must be sold through the probate court by auction conducted at the courthouse. This will ensure the best possible price for the property. After sale, the proceeds must be accounted for through the probate proceedings, which would ensure that any party did not steal the sale proceeds.

An executor owes a fiduciary duty to the estate and cannot act in his or her own self interest. If one or more of Julian's appointed executors had acted in self-interest, then the probate court would properly be entitled to remove any such person as an executor of Julian's estate. Moreover, an executor who breaches his or her fiduciary duties may become personally liable for any losses to the estate.

Because of the size of his holdings, Julian should have maintained the records reflecting his property and assets in a central and safe location. In fact, even with smaller estates, it's best to keep everything together in a safe deposit box. Make sure that you give a trusted individual access to the documents on your death to ensure that your estate can be resolved with the least amount of difficulty and expense.

With regard to the foundation that Julian set up, the assets of the foundation should have been titled only in the name of the foundation or under the sole control of the foundation. By failing to do this, Julian created an issue as to whether he still owned these assets himself upon his death. Once again, make sure that your will expressly provides to whom your assets and money are to be given upon your death. After all, you will not be around to explain, so make sure your will expressly provides for your desires.

Finally, I would tell Michael that he has basically two choices with regard to his uncle's estate: continue to fight, or retreat. In a case like this one, clear communication and an early resolution could have potentially saved the estate millions of dollars. But once special interests and feelings of entitlement have become part of the equation, there is no way to prevent the due process of the system from grinding on and depleting the resources of the estate.

At best, Michael will be able to ensure that some of his uncle's wishes are enacted. And at the very least, I would point out that he has learned an important lesson: if he ever comes into possession of these assets, he must be sure that his own estate is in order so that these problems are not perpetuated for another generation.

Chapter 42

OPEN PROBATE AND UNSETTLED ESTATES

EXCEPT FOR FOUR YEARS WHEN HE WENT TO COLLEGE IN VERMONT, PAUL Wilson had spent practically his whole life in the small coastal New England town he was born in. He had deep ties to the community and was a member of various civic groups. "When he was alive, my dad— Big Paul—was the unofficial mayor of the town," Paul said. "I always wanted to grow up to be like him—someone who knew the history of the place."

This sense of roots, family values, and continuity helped explain why Paul, a tall burly guy with a penchant for checked flannel shirts, who lived in a small apartment above a local store on Main Street, had been paying for more than twenty years to maintain an empty, rambling, Victorian house perched on a cliff over the ocean—a house where he grew up and where his great-grandparents, his grandparents, his father and mother, and then father and stepmother, lived all their lives.

"My mother died when I was at college," Paul explained. "That was the most awful winter. I was away, and I worried about my dad's being lonely in the big house. But the summer after my mom passed away, my father met one of the folks who vacationed up here, and a romance blossomed."

A year later, the summer after Paul graduated, his father remarried. Paul never really warmed up to his stepmother, Kate, and her two daughters, who were about his age. Deep down, he always suspected that Kate thought his father was a rich widower with a big house on prime real estate. Maybe she thought he'd move down to the city with her and her kids, and they'd just come for the summers. Maybe she thought she'd become lady of the manor. Paul didn't know. What he did know was that his stepmother just never seemed to fit in to life in their small town.

After college, Paul returned home and worked as a furniture craftsman. His father let him set up a studio in one of the outbuildings on the family property. In return, Paul helped his elderly and ailing father and stepmother maintain a house that was, by now, much too big for them. Kate wanted to move to a retirement home. She urged Big Paul to sell the house and take out what was sure to be a substantial profit. But Big Paul stood firm. "This house is my heritage, and the only way I'm leaving is out the front door in a pine box," he said.

Kate and Big Paul's relationship grew increasingly hostile over the years. She accused him of being miserly, of hanging on to an investment that, if sold, could make them both comfortable in their old age. Somehow, everything that was wrong with their marriage always came down to the house.

Although Paul knew that there were many arguments over Kate's determination to sell the house, and Big Paul's insistence on keeping the house, what he didn't know was that his father had deeded one half of the house to Kate as tenants in common, giving Kate control over her half of the house.

When Kate died suddenly and unexpectedly, Paul was not really surprised to find that in her will she had left all her personal property and her half of the interest in the house to her two daughters. Paul and his father were completely disinherited. Kate even put something in the letter to her executor saying that it was her wish that he would convince Big Paul to sell all their communal property and give half of the money to her daughters. Of course, there was no way Big Paul was going to do that.

Kate's daughters came up from the city and cleared out most of their mother's belongings and many of the couples' pieces of furniture that Kate had named as hers in the will. Kate's lawyer and daughters even approached Big Paul about selling the house—since it was considered both Kate and Paul's property as tenants in common—and giving half the profits to Kate's daughters. "My dad ran them off with an old shotgun," Paul said, laughing.

Kate's daughters never pressed the issue of the sale of the house. They made no attempt to help maintain it. Paul thought they probably realized that the value of the house would only go up and that they could only benefit from their share in it.

Meanwhile, Paul continued to help his father maintain the house, acting as a general handyman and groundskeeper and arranging for cooks, health care aides, and nurses, right up until the day, two years later, when Big Paul died in his rocking chair looking out over the ocean.

As expected, Big Paul had left his modest estate, including his share of the house—which was the only real thing of value—to his son. "That was about twenty years ago," Paul said.

Since then, he had been in a battle with Kate's estate to close the probate on her will that has been left open since her death. Although Kate's daughters could have closed the probate, they had never bothered to. And until probate was closed, Paul could not have full ownership of the house that he felt was his rightful inheritance.

After the lawyer read Big Paul's will, his son went down to the recorder's office to have the title to the house transferred to his name. But since it was a tenancy-in-common ownership, Paul couldn't have the house until Kate's daughters gave up their interest in it.

So Paul had not lived in the house, but had spent thousands of dollars each year to maintain the building and the grounds because of respect for his father, an emotional attachment to his family home, and the hope, that one day, it would be his home. He paid fuel bills to keep the house heated in the winter and paid all annual property and city taxes. "It's not cheap," Paul said. "The property values have skyrocketed, and so have the taxes."

What really made Paul angry was that Kate's daughters continued to claim that the house was rightfully half theirs, even though they had never done anything to maintain it. "They've never paid a bill, never checked on the place—except maybe once a year when they drive up and make sure that I'm not living in it," Paul said. "But I wouldn't dare to live in the house—not until it's legally mine."

Kate's daughters told Paul that he could buy out their interest in the house, at the market price, but he felt he had already paid more than their share of the value of the house in the costs of maintaining the property over the years.

The strain of maintaining a large empty house took its toll on Paul. He didn't have much put away in savings, and the expenses of his apartment and his studio, plus all the expenses of the house, were beginning to take a serious financial toll.

While some people advised Paul to make an offer to his stepsisters to buy their half of the house, he stood firm on principle. "I really do believe the house is mine," he said. "I'm the one who's been maintaining it while it appreciated in value; I'm the one who replaced the furnace last year; I'm the one who repaired the roof two springs ago. I'm the one who has put hundreds of thousands of dollars into it. All I want is for Kate's daughters to let go of this idea that the house is half theirs and move on. The house doesn't mean anything to them. And it means everything to me. I'm a patient guy. All I want is what I deserve to have."

HOW I WOULD HAVE COUNSELED PAUL

"Over my dead body!" When it comes to settling the affairs of our family members, long-standing disputes, animosity, and jealousy have a way of creeping back into our consciousness. In many cases, it's a free-for-all, and everyone wants everything he or she can get. Everything. In Big Paul's case, if not for the interference of his stepdaughters, his estate was relatively easy to handle and would have enabled his son, Paul, to move on with his life instead of becoming a caretaker to Big Paul's house. Unfortunately, Paul must face the reality that when his father transferred half the house to Kate as tenants in common, he made it possible for her daughters to have a real legal claim on Kate's part of the house after her death. Understand your rights and what you should do if confronted with a similar situation.

It's not unusual for either spouse to disinherit the other spouse and children—it happens all the time. In many cases, couples stay married out of convenience or necessity and never intend to provide their spouse or children with any money or property upon their death. Generally, disinheriting someone other than minor children is perfectly legal, provided that you comply with the particular requirements of your state. At a minimum, you must acknowledge in your will or trust the existence of the disinherited spouse or child and then expressly provide for nothing to be given to that person. Merely leaving the person out of your will or trust can lead to a claim that you intended to provide for him or her and merely "forgot." Make your intentions clearly known—it's the law.

Generally, the law of the state in which a person dies controls how and in what manner the personal property is disposed of, while the laws of the state in which real estate property is located usually controls its disposition. Laws relating to the transfer of assets, either by will or by trust, are highly technical and vary from state to state. In some cases the variations can be dramatic. You should always consult a licensed and experienced lawyer in your state regarding the creation, probate, and administration of a will or trust.

Assuming that they lived in a community property state, since Big Paul used his earnings during the course of his marriage to Kate to pay for the mortgage and upkeep on the house, Kate is most likely entitled to a portion of the value of the house as her community property interest. In states that recognize community property—property that the law considers is owned equally by both spouses, in the absence of an express contrary intention in a will or trust, the deceased spouse's one half of community property becomes the property of the surviving spouse. If the deceased spouse desires to give her one half of community property interest to someone other than her surviving spouse, this intent must be clearly reflected in the will or trust.

Paul should seek a hearing from the probate court to determine the value of Kate's community property interest in the house. Once a determination is made, the house could be sold and the proceeds divided according to each party's respective interests in the house. Alternatively, either party could attempt to buy out the other's interest in the house if one party desires to retain possession of the house.

One way to avoid probate problems with real property is to title the property in joint tenancy with a right of survivorship. Real property held in this manner generally avoids probate and will automatically transfer full ownership interest to the surviving joint tenant upon the death of the other. To avoid the automatic transfer of property held in joint tenancy, a person may opt to retitle the property, during his or her lifetime, as tenants in common. As in Big Paul and Kate's case, two parties who share real property as tenants in common each own an undivided one-half interest in the property. They each may later transfer or sell the property, and upon their respective deaths the property does not automatically transfer to the other tenant in common, absent an express intention in the will or trust.

Given the fact that Paul and his stepsisters have been unable to resolve their differences relating to the house, Paul is not required to solely maintain the house at his expense. If Paul's stepsisters claim an ownership interest in the house, then they should be required to help pay for the costs associated with maintaining the house, pending the resolution of the probate proceedings. Paul should seek reimbursement of these expenses from the probate court, which could be in the form of reimbursement through a reduction in Kate's community property interest in the house.

Chapter 43

FINAL AFFAIRS: WHAT YOU NEED TO KNOW

NO ONE WANTS TO BE MORBID AND SPEND TIME THINKING ABOUT HIS OR her final days. Really, once you're gone it's not your problem. But for the sake of your family and those left behind, you should be sure you know how things will be taken care of when you are no longer able to attend to them yourself.

WHILE YOU ARE STILL AROUND

Help with Your Finances
When it comes to your finances, you're better off taking care of the little things yourself, like keeping track of monthly bank and credit card statements, your purchases, and your expenses. When you delegate important financial decisions to others, you run the risk that they will not have your best interests at heart, either through negligence or simply by an effort on their part to spend your money on themselves. Be careful, and consider the following ideas to ensure that your nest egg doesn't develop a crack:

➤ If you're not married, do not combine your money into a joint account with your significant other or allow that person free access to your accounts. It's amazing how much financial information and even access to our finances we give to our latest love interest.

➤ When you can't see yourself taking care of your own finances, or if you have a problem with spending, you might want to consider a financial planner. Make sure you check out the credentials of any prospective financial planner, and ask for references. Make sure you contact the references and inquire about that planner's experiences. You can also search for a financial planner online at the National Association of Personal Financial Advisors, www.napfa.org. Check with your local Better Business Bureau for information about any potential financial planners, including whether they have any history of consumer complaints. You can find your local BBB online at www.lookup.bbb.org.

➤ Some of us, no matter how much advice we're given, insist on relinquishing our financial freedom to someone else. Unmarried couples routinely share personal expenses and share bank accounts. If you're dead set on this approach, try sharing only a portion of your money in a joint account and leaving the remainder of your income or savings in a separate account that only you have access to. This way, if you find you have trusted the wrong person, you'll still have the bulk of your savings should your "trusted friend" leave you and your hard-earned money behind.

➤ Don't enter into long-term contracts for consumer purchases and automobiles with your significant other unless it is absolutely necessary. Most relationships end before the financial obligation does. If you're the only one with a stable income or savings, it's not hard to guess who the creditor will go after. If your significant other threatens to leave you if you don't cosign a loan or other long-term agreement, walk away.

ONCE YOU ARE GONE

The End Game—Know the Rules

We're all going to die. It happens to even the best of us. Planning for your demise not only is sound financial planning but protects your rightful heirs and lets them receive—or not receive—according to your wishes. Remember, a will or trust is merely a written document that sets forth your wishes regarding the disposition of your property after your death. Each state has its own laws with regard to the validity of a will or trust; however, certain fundamental requirements are found in most states' laws. If you die without a valid will or trust, the state determines how and in what manner your money and assets are divided among your heirs. When you plan for the distribution of your estate, consider the following recommendations:

➤ A will or trust must be in writing. It's hard for you to explain your intentions after you're gone. A person writing a will or trust must generally understand the nature of the estate (property or assets) and the fact that the person is seeking to dispose of his or her property after death. This concept is called possessing a testamentary capacity. Situations arise when a person suffers from a physical or mental condition that prevents that person from having sufficient testamentary capacity. In such a case, the will or trust would be considered invalid.

➤ A will must generally comply with the requirements of your state. It must set forth the nature of the property being disposed of, and to whom the property is to be given upon your death. These documents are generally witnessed by several people who can later come into court to authenticate that the will was actually prepared or signed by the deceased. Without authentication, the will can be declared invalid.

➤ Holographic (handwritten) wills must carry the same information as a witnessed will, except that no one has signed or witnessed the holographic will except for the deceased. Generally, holographic wills tend to be simple documents. For instance, they may only designate that all the property of the deceased goes to, for example, the person's wife. The key to a holographic will is that it must be written in the handwriting of the deceased and signed and dated by the deceased. The requirement for a handwritten document is to ensure that the will can be verified as having been written by the deceased and therefore truly reflects the deceased's intentions. Typing up a simple will and then merely signing and dating the bottom of the document is insufficient for the creation of a holographic will.

➤ If you want to keep a spouse or child from receiving anything under your will, most states require that your will or trust specifically list each such person in the will or trust and then specifically provide that your intention is not to leave him or her any of your property upon your death. Absent a specific acknowledgment of the person and your intent to exclude that person from your property, the law may consider your failure to include such a person in your will as a "mistake" and infer that you simply forgot to include the person in your will. In such a case, the court would provide a portion of your estate to this person pursuant to the laws of the state.

➤ In most cases, a wife is entitled to her share of any community property acquired during the course of the marriage. Even a will specifically excluding your wife would not hold up in most states; she would still be entitled to her community property interests. As for minor children, you generally cannot exclude them from your estate if such an action would result in their not having any basis for their support until they reach the age of majority.

➤ Trusts, including living trusts, generally must comply with the same laws regarding their creation and implementation as wills. One primary benefit of a living trust is that your property is transferred into the trust during your lifetime; therefore, upon your death this property generally passes to your heirs without needing to go through probate proceedings in court. A pour-over will is a type of will found within a living trust that serves to dispose of any property acquired after the creation of the living trust. Property subject to a pour-over will must generally be disposed of through probate. It's best to continually update your trust property throughout your lifetime in order to avoid the necessity that any property will have to be disposed of through the pour-over will. After all, that is why you created a living trust in the first place.

➤ Even without a will or trust, you can avoid probate for certain types of property:

   PROPERTY held in joint tenancy with a right of survivorship automatically becomes the property of the surviving joint tenant. Real property is commonly held in this manner by spouses. In the absence of a will or contrary intention, the deceased spouse's one half of community property becomes the property of the surviving spouse.

   LIFE INSURANCE proceeds generally pass directly to the beneficiary without the necessity of probate.

➤ I would recommend that you consult a lawyer experienced in wills, trusts, and estates to draft a proper will or trust. The cost of these services is very affordable, far less than the potential time and expense of a lengthy court fight should an heir seek to contest the validity of a will or trust you prepared yourself. Most state bar associations offer lawyer referral services.

FINAL THOUGHTS

I hope the stories in this book have served their purpose: that they have made you think and have left you with some valuable lessons and information. Each of the scenarios in this book should serve as a cautionary tale: what happened to these people could happen to any one of us. And I hope the counseling sessions have served their purpose as well, and you have come away from this book with some practical knowledge that will help you avoid situations with the potential to quickly spiral into a legal disaster.

Although all of us are vulnerable to the situations you've just read about, this book is not meant to make you throw up your hands in despair. Yes, the flaws in today's legal system are prevalent and pervasive. But if you can understand how these systemic problems are part of a vicious circle that we all participate in—from the average person on the street to those who make the highest laws in the land—you can become an active participant in making the legal system work the way it was meant to.

The cycle starts when people fail to understand how to use the legal system. They avoid seeking legal advice because it "costs too much," or they turn to the system for the wrong reason: they are angry, they are seeking legal recourse for minor claims, or they want to exact revenge. Inevitably, the system lets them down, costing them money, impeding solutions, and delaying resolutions. And the cycle is perpetuated. People doubt the system's ability to help, avoid seeking out the legal counsel that can protect them, and often find themselves once again in a situation that, ironically, draws them back into the very system they were trying to circumvent. And the vicious circle continues.

As a baby boomer myself, I come from a generation that always sought the higher ideals of peace, love, happiness, and equality for all. And even while we were out practicing civil disobedience and agitating for change, I always took for granted that we were trying to right the wrongs of a system that was fundamentally sound. When I read the language of the Constitution and the Bill of Rights, I am humbled by the lofty notion that our country was founded on: the belief in equal rights and access for all. But when I compare these fundamental principles with the day-to-day battles my clients face, both in and out of the courtroom, I am frustrated by the ways in which personal opinions and systematized beliefs have hijacked our legal system and eroded the rights of so many individuals. And, coming from a generation that has always believed in the inherent rights of the individual and in the power of a social mandate to initiate change, I believe it is our responsibility to hold the legal system to the high standards of its origins.

Despite its flaws, I believe people are right to look to the legal system for resolution of a dispute, and I understand that the cost, the complexity, and the slowness of the system can be intimidating. That is why I have made it my mission to bring to light the ways in which the system does not serve its constituents, and to call for radical change that will return the legal system to a forum that offers equal access and justice for all—not only for those individuals with the means to afford counsel, but also for those without financial means who need impartial advice.

In my office, in the courtroom, and on local and national television and radio, I have tried to educate people on how the system works and how it could work so much better. Just as you would go to a doctor to seek a diagnosis, treatment, and relief from an illness, so should you be able to go to the legal system to gain clarity, options, and resolution of a dispute. But as the stories in this book so clearly show, the average person today is more likely to get screwed by a legal system that has lost touch with the needs of the people. This book should serve as a wake-up call to those who use the legal system and those who serve the public.

I am proud of what I do as a lawyer, and I acknowledge that much good is done each day by those in the legal profession. And I know that many of my colleagues share both my pride in our profession and my frustration with a legal system that has so many pitfalls. I believe with all my heart that if we all increase our awareness of the problems, and are willing to work to be heard, change can—and will—happen. I look to those in positions of power—from judges on the bench, to legislatures, to the bar associations, to us as lawyers—to work to effect changes that will right the wrongs in the system. I believe that we as experts have a responsibility to help those in more disadvantaged positions by fixing what is broken.

But I also encourage you, the end user of this legal system, to become involved. As a lawyer I know that I can best serve a client who has some knowledge of what can reasonably be achieved by the law, a respect for the legal profession, and a trust that the process will fairly resolve the client's conflict. But this type of knowledge, respect, and trust is lacking in many of the clients who come to me for help. For many, the services of a legal professional have become a last resort. Often, by the time I meet with these clients, their legal problems have become far more complicated than they ever needed to be.

So, in the spirit of optimism and with the hope that you will be inspired to accept responsibility to work for change, I offer some suggestions—for individuals who use the system, for the lawyers who serve the law, for the courts that enforce the law, and for the governments that create the law—that I hope will bring clarity to your understanding of how the system can change to become less intimidating, more accessible, and of better service to us all.

It should be noted that when I discuss these proposed reforms, I am talking about changes to the civil process. Criminal cases always need to go to a lawyer and go through the legal system. If you are involved in a criminal case—guilty or not—get a lawyer immediately. While a streamlined legal system and smoothly functioning courts will certainly benefit the disposition of criminal cases, my agenda for change focuses on civil cases, like those illustrated by most of the stories in this book, which make up about 90 percent of the traffic through the legal system today.

As I've already said, changes to the legal system must be made at all levels, from the highest governing offices to the general public as plaintiff or defendant. So what can we as individuals do to begin this groundswell of change? The answer is simple. *We can become more accountable.* The more information we have about protecting our rights, the smarter we can become about avoiding situations that will inevitably require legal resolutions. This book is only a step in the educational process. In any transaction, take the time to do your homework, and be sure you fully understand the consequences of any agreements, partnerships, or arrangements you enter into.

The next level involves lawyers and the courtroom. Again, I offer a simple prescription for change: *day-to-day legal disputes should be resolved outside the courtroom.* There are several practical reasons to recommend this approach:

➤ **SAVINGS IN TIME AND MONEY.** Settling disputes outside the courtroom would act as a safeguard against unnecessary, drawn-out, and expensive litigation.

➤ **QUICK RESOLUTION.** Resolving a dispute in a timely fashion brings emotional closure and allows both parties to move on.

➤ **PROMOTION OF TRUE NEGOTIATION.** To reach a successful resolution, both parties are forced to consider reasonable means to the achievement of results.

➤ **EQUAL ACCESS.** Individuals without the means to hire legal counsel can still make their case before an impartial arbitrator.

➤ **REDUCTION OF TRAFFIC IN COURTS.** Fewer lower-level cases mean that lawyers and judges can focus on higher-level relevant cases. The court calendars will become more streamlined.

This change is not difficult to implement, and there are some states and areas of the law that are moving toward resolving conflicts outside of a courtroom. *Mediation* is a nonbinding process wherein a qualified legal mind makes recommendations to resolve a dispute. What I like about mediation is that it puts the power to resolve the dispute directly in the hands of the individuals involved. The mediator is present to give each party knowledgeable advice about the strengths and weaknesses of the case according to the law.

Mediation is nonbinding. That is, if you disagree with the solutions proposed by the mediator, you are free to refuse to settle and to pursue resolution through the full legal system—with all the costs and time that course may entail.

Mediation is already often used for marital disputes. It has been shown to be a great process, especially as it is designed to give the parties a cathartic experience of presenting their version of events. It is also far less expensive than a full course of legal action.

Mediation sounds like a great solution to resolving many of the issues that were experienced by the individuals whose stories are told in this book, doesn't it? The problem is that unless you have agreed, by contract or stipulation, to mediation as a means of resolving legal issues, either party can refuse to mediate. Right now, it falls to the legal profession to educate clients and to encourage the use of mediation as a means of alternative dispute resolution. And because there will always be disputes between people who can afford to hire lawyers to advise them and those who cannot, there should be a system that triggers the availability of a mediator to resolve a dispute without the expense of a lawyer. I would like to see mediation become the standard for negotiation resolution to certain civil cases. It should be a mandated first resort.

If individuals are aware of mediation as an option to resolve legal conflicts, and lawyers are consistent about informing their clients or potential clients about mediation as a resource, the involvement of the courts can further facilitate the use of mediation as an immediate, inexpensive form of resolution. For instance, in Nevada, where I practice law, civil cases with a value of $50,000 or less are sent to mandatory arbitration. The plaintiff and defendant present their cases to a lawyer or a retired judge, who makes a ruling. This is slightly different from a mediated settlement in that the ruling is a forced settlement, rather than one mutually arrived at by both parties. But unless both parties agree in advance, this ruling is nonbinding. That is, if one party doesn't agree with the ruling, that party is free to invest time and money to pursue a legal appeal in the court system.

If all lawsuits were evaluated by a settlement judge when they were first filed, and the parties were compelled by the system to appear before a settlement judge to attempt to arrive at a resolution, I would guess that about 95 percent of all civil cases could be resolved outside the courtroom. How can I throw out such a large percentage with such assurance? Well, in my thirty-plus years of practicing law, I'd estimate that about 95 percent of all the civil cases I've handled have been settled outside the courtroom as people grew exhausted by the process (and tired of spending thousands and thousands of dollars to move their cases through the system). It's my experience that when people embark on a legal claim they want it to be resolved quickly. They want to stop spending emotion and money and time on an event that was unpleasant for them in the first place. But the way the system is now, cases can drag on for years, in overcrowded courts, in front of overwhelmed judges, presented by exhausted legal counsel.

The courts can do one more thing to make mediation the most effective method for resolving disputes. The court should be allowed to impose financial sanctions if it finds that either party is refusing to settle as an act of bad faith. I have always found that having to face the actual cost of legal actions, whether we are discussing a potential legal penalty or an award, quickly brings clarity to even the most indecisive client. Furthermore, if both parties are honestly trying to find a satisfactory resolution to their problem, they will be forced to set aside whatever emotions they have brought into the case. The penalties that could be imposed by the court will help to remove the element of revenge from lawsuits.

And while we are on the discussion of courts, I'd like to share my thoughts on judges. If a case cannot be solved by mediation, arbitration, or adjudicated settlement, then what can we do to ensure that the courts work smoothly and efficiently with the cases that they must handle? When a judge in the courtroom is the last resort for resolution of a dispute, that individual has accepted a solemn responsibility to serve both the law and the people who appear in front of him or her seeking the interpretation of that law. I would like to see judges become more involved with the cases in front of them. They should remove intimidation by introducing themselves to litigants. They should closely manage a case, setting firm deadlines for specific actions to ensure that the case progresses smoothly and quickly. The judge should work to make the legal system as transparent as possible to those it serves. I'm sure you've all seen television shows in which the judge bangs the gavel and orders the opposing counsels to chambers, where the lawyers and judge hash out the finer points of their legal maneuvers. I'd advocate that the clients be included in these conversations. As a lawyer I want the people I serve to be educated about the law as it applies to their situation. And I want judges to feel the same way. Judges must acknowledge their power and authority as final interpreters of the law, but they must also work to humanize the legal process.

The final participant in my scenario for a reformed legal system is the legislature, particularly at the state level. Right now, lawyers and judges have the most input regarding changes to the system. But it is the people who are served by this system—and the people who must be heard. I propose that an ad hoc committee made up of constituents of each county review the process of the jurisdiction that serves them.

The system is supposed to fairly represent the people. That means taking into account different ethnic, socioeconomic, and educational backgrounds. It means that the court system must be tailored in each jurisdiction to best serve its constituency. Serving on this ad hoc committee would also expose individuals to the daily tasks and time investment of those who work within the system.

The legal system was meant to create equality and a fair venue for the resolution of disputes. But the erosion of access for those without financial means, the cynical and calloused attitudes of some of those who serve the system, and the dehumanizing processes of an overburdened system have contributed to the erosion of our reverence for the law. We are all accountable to act in ways to change today's system.

There are things we all can do to prevent more stories like the ones in this book from happening. Individuals can take responsibility for their own education and understand what they need to do to protect themselves legally. Lawyers can work to clearly educate their clients on how to work within the system and prevent future legal entanglements. Courts can mandate that individuals resolve their differences through mediation, rather than protracted legal battles. Judges can humanize the face of legal authority and use their powers to make the judicial system transparent to those it serves. And legislatures can listen to the voice of the people they serve and respond in ways that are tailored to individual constituencies.

The very basic changes of making the legal system more transparent, removing intimidation, and empowering individuals to solve their disputes with expedience and minimal expense will go a long way toward restoring compassion and fairness to the practice and implementation of the law. We are all in this together. Today can be a new beginning.

ACKNOWLEDGMENTS

Special thanks to my cowriter, Jill Stern, who labored for hours to make this book a reality. Her dedication and belief in me and in this project are so appreciated. I am blessed and grateful to have her listen to my thoughts and assist in putting form to them.

This book would not have been possible without the love and support of those I love the most.

To my wife Lynn: You are more than my rock, you are my foundation. Through all the years, and no matter the circumstance, you have never said "No," and have, without hesitation, encouraged my dreams and passions. With your support, I can overcome any boundary and achieve any dream. There are no words except the three most important ones of all: "I love you," and I am proud to have you by my side.

To my three beautiful children, Dominic, Genna, and Robert: I have always said you are the perfect love affair because you brought form and meaning to my life. I thank you for your love and your belief in me. I will always love you unconditionally and I thank God for you every day of my life.

To my mother and father who have passed: I feel you every day and my dream is a reality because of your unconditional love and belief in me and because of your hard work to provide me with the opportunity to be educated. You always encouraged me to follow my dreams. I love you and miss you.

To my brothers Jim and Al: What can I say? If you were not my brothers you would be my best friends. I'm blessed to have brothers who always believed in me and, without hesitation, wanted me to follow my passion and dream. Thank you and I love you.

To my literary agents Jennifer Gates and Todd Schuster: Thank you for believing in this project and for all of your hard work along the way. I respect and appreciate your talent, integrity, and encouragement.

To my editor Mary Ellen O'Neill: Without your unwavering belief, editorial insight and ongoing support, this book would not have been possible. Thank you for allowing me to make my voice heard.

Thanks also to the dedicated and talented people in editorial, marketing, publicity, and sales at Collins Books who are fundamental to this project, especially Laura Dozier, Jean Marie Kelly, Shelby Meizlik, Teresa Brady, George Bick, and Georgia Morrissey. Your enthusiasm and creativity inspire me.

To my friend Bob Stoldal, news director at KLAS TV, who gave me the opportunity to begin my TV career in 1985. I also want to express my deepest appreciation to Roger Ailes at the Fox News Network for giving me the chance to reach out to a national audience to explain the importance and the impact of the law. And to Mr. Williams and Clare Reis at radio station KDWN, who have given me the opportunity to broadcast for over 20 years. Thank you for believing in me from the beginning.

Finally, my most sincere thanks to the many other people who gave of their talent and time to make this book a reality: To John Clark for his assistance in the research and development of the book, and to Nicole Jaycox for keeping the office running smoothly.

REFERENCES

AMERICAN ARBITRATION ASSOCIATION

General information about the arbitration process can be found at the American Arbitration Association's Web site, www.adr.org.

AMERICAN BAR ASSOCIATION

You can find out information about attorneys and law firms online at www.abanet.org. You can also contact them at the following addresses and phone numbers:

American Bar Association
321 North Clark Street
Chicago, IL 60610
(312) 988–5000

American Bar Association
Service Center
321 North Clark Street
Chicago, IL 60610
(312) 988–5522
(800) 285–2221

American Bar Association
740 15th Street, NW
Washington, DC 20005–1019
(202) 662–1000

AMERICAN MOVING AND STORAGE ASSOCIATION
Check out movers and rates at www.moving.org.

AUTOMOBILE

Used Car Resources
If you're looking for a used car, www.carfax.com is a great resource for checking a car's ownership history and determining whether there have been any reported accidents or major damage involving the car.

Kelly Blue Book is the same pricing guide that most dealerships use in purchasing your trade-in and reselling your trade-in to the public. This information is available online at www.kbb.com.

Another resource for determining the price of a vehicle is found at www.nadaguides.com.

Registering Your Car
State-by-state online registration can be found at www.dmv.org.

Lemon Laws
Look up state-by-state lemon laws at www.autopedia.com/html/HotLinks_Lemon2.html.

BETTER BUSINESS BUREAU
You can find your local BBB online at www.lookup.bbb.org.

CHILD SUPPORT
Child support calculators can be found at www.alllaw.com/calculators/Child support/.

CONSUMER REPORTS

Find information online at www.consumerreports.org.

CREDIT REPORTS

Obtain free annual credit scores from these agencies:

Equifax
P.O. Box 740241
Atlanta, GA 30374–0241
(800) 525–6285
www.equifax.com

Experian
P.O. Box 9532
Allen, TX 75013
(888) 397–3742
www.experian.com

TransUnion
Fraud Victim Assistance Division
P.O. Box 6790
Fullerton, CA 92834–6790
(800) 680–7289
www.transunion.com

Annual Credit Report Company

Find out about credit reports and what they mean at www.annual-creditreport.com or call (877) 322–8228.

Opt Out

To opt out of receiving credit card applications by mail, call (888) 5OPTOUT [(888) 567–8688)].

DEPARTMENT OF STATE

Contact your department of state online by going to www.dos.[insert your state here].gov.

DIVORCE

A good resource for information, including a state-by-state listing of mediators, is www.divorcehq.com.

DO NOT CALL

Prevent calls from telemarketers by going to www.donotcall.gov or by calling (888) 382–1222.

FEDERAL TRADE COMMISSION

Contact the Federal Trade Commission at www.ftc.gov.

INTERNAL REVENUE SERVICE

Get information on personal and business tax laws, or contact information for your local IRS office at www.irs.gov, or call (800) 829–1040 for personal tax information or (800) 829–4933 for business tax information. People with hearing impairments can call (800) 829–4059 (TDD).

LAWYER DIRECTORY

Research lawyers at www.martindale.com.

MORTGAGE COMPANIES

Many Web sites list mortgage companies throughout the United States. For information on mortgage rates, check www.bankrate.com and www.eloan.com.

NATIONAL ASSOCIATION OF ATTORNEYS GENERAL

Find out where to report fraud or investigate companies at www.naag.org.

NATIONAL ASSOCIATION OF PERSONAL FINANCIAL ADVISORS

Find someone to help manage your finances at www.napfa.org.

NATIONAL ASSOCIATION OF SECURITIES DEALERS (NASD)

Research companies and salespeople online at www.nasd.com.

NATIONAL ASSOCIATION OF STATE CONTRACTORS LICENSING AGENCIES

Check to see whether your contractor is licensed at www.nascla.org.

NATIONAL FLOOD INSURANCE PROGRAM

For more information about obtaining flood insurance and to find out whether your community participates in this federal government program, go online at www.floodsmart.gov.

NATIONAL TENANT NETWORK

An agency that specializes in screening tenants and can provide information on rent payment history. Go to www.ntnnet.com to find out more.

PUBLIC INFORMATION PROFILES

Background information from public sources is called a public information profile, or PIP. Some of the companies that sell these reports are www.mypublicinfo.com and www.onlinechoice.com.

SOCIAL SECURITY ADMINISTRATION

Contact the Social Security Administration at www.ssa.gov or by phone.

Social Security has a toll-free number that operates from 7 a.m. to 7 p.m., Monday through Friday: 1–(800) 772–1213. If you have a touch-tone phone, recorded information and services are available 24 hours a day, including weekends and holidays. People who are deaf or hard of hearing may call a toll-free TTY number, (800) 325–0778, between 7 a.m. and 7 p.m., Monday through Friday. Have your Social Security number handy when you call.

Social Security Administration
Office of Public Inquiries
Windsor Park Building
6401 Security Boulevard
Baltimore, MD 21235

UNITED STATES SECURITIES AND EXCHANGE COMMISSION (SEC)

Report securities fraud at www.sec.gov.

UNITED STATES SMALL BUSINESS ADMINISTRATION

Find ideas and advice for the start-up business at www.sba.gov/starting_business.com.

INDEX